THE PRINCESSES ROYAL

The Princesses Royal

GEOFFREY WAKEFORD

ROBERT HALE
LONDON

© *Geoffrey Wakeford 1973*
First published in Great Britain 1973

ISBN 0 7091 3492 4

Robert Hale & Company
63 Old Brompton Road
London S.W.7.

PRINTED IN GREAT BRITAIN BY
BRISTOL TYPESETTING CO. LTD.
BARTON MANOR - ST. PHILIPS
BRISTOL

For Alexander and Henrietta

Contents

Illustrations

ACKNOWLEDGEMENTS

Nos. 10 and 12 reproduced by gracious permission of The Queen;
6, 7, 16: National Portrait Gallery; 8, 9: Mary Evans Picture
Library; 18: Radio Times Hulton Picture Library; 19: by courtesy
of Harewood House; other pictures from the Mansell Collection

Introduction

WHEN PRINCESS ANNE was born five years after the close of the Second World War she became in effect a presumptive Princess Royal, the seventh British princess who would in due time assume a status which is not the less real for its having no constitutional significance. In this book I have tried to convey, chiefly for the general reader, some idea of the lives led by her six predecessors, their trials, tribulations and triumphs, and the events which encompassed and overwhelmed them.

The style of Princess Royal, for it is neither exactly a rank nor really a title, was created by Charles I for his dazzling and imperious eldest daughter Mary, who married William II of Orange and became the mother of the hero of the Boyne. Another Princess Mary, the only daughter of King George V, was the last to use the style, which fell into temporary abeyance with her death on 28th March 1965. At that time her great-niece Princess Anne was 14 and at her public school, and as there is a somewhat forbidding, prim maturity about the term 'Princess Royal' the demise of Princess Mary was not the occasion for Princess Anne's exaltation, or promotion, if such words may be used in this context. Interest in the prospects of the Queen's only daughter revived when her twenty-first birthday approached in 1971, but no date has ever been specified for the transition of a British princess to Princess Royal. The timing is entirely at the Sovereign's pleasure. In practice Princesses Royal are unexceptionally the eldest daughters of the monarch; secondly, they get no extra monetary grant (just as the Prince of Wales is unfinanced by the fortunate Welsh) for any extra services their status may enjoin upon them. The first point disposes of a contemporary myth that on her aunt's death in 1965 the Queen's younger sister, Princess Margaret, Countess of Snowdon, could have become Princess Royal. As Princesses Royal are not known to the British constitution there is no obligation on Parliament to provide them with funds other than their marriage allowances; but most of them contracted wealthy marriages.

Between the first Mary and the last came Princess Anne, the eldest daughter of George II; Charlotte, Queen of Württemberg, whose father was George III; Victoria ('Pussy'), immortal as the Empress Frederick, as talented as one would expect the favourite daughter of Queen Victoria to be and as remarkable in her way as the great Queen herself; and a very different, if not opposite, personality—Princess Louise, Duchess of Fife, whose reserved nature in the reigns of her father Edward VII and her brother George V earned her the somewhat unkind title of Her Royal Shyness. Two of the six married Dutchmen, the second two chose Germans, the fifth a Scot, the last an English earl with Irish connections. The first four lived abroad all their married lives. Only the last closely identified herself with the activities of the Royal Family at home and, especially after her brother's Abdication in 1936, served the monarchy to the limits of her considerable powers.

The reader may wonder why there have been only six Princesses Royal in some 330 years of royal history since Charles I. One explanation is that the monarch's eldest, elder or only daughter is not created Princess Royal if she is likely to succeed to the throne. That could be why neither daughter of James II became Princess Royal: it was the destiny of Mary and Anne to become queens of England instead. Neither had issue, and as their uncle Charles II also had no legitimate offspring there was a gap of forty-eight years between the death of the first Princess Royal and the second, Anne of Hanover (later of Orange). The first King George's only daughter, Sophia Dorothea, would have qualified, but before her father ascended the English throne she had married the Crown Prince of Prussia, afterwards Frederick William II. After she had become a queen that honour was considered sufficient.

Other lacunae in the list of Princesses Royal are explained by the death of Frederick, Prince of Wales before he succeeded George II, so his eldest daughter Augusta was excluded; by the death in childbed of the Prince Regent's daughter Charlotte, who as her father's only legitimate child would have become queen regnant on George IV's demise; and by the death in infancy of William IV's daughter Elizabeth. The withering away of the Hanoverian line left the monarchy without a Princess Royal between the death of Charlotte of Württemberg in 1828 and the birth of the Empress Frederick in 1840. As successor to the throne after Queen Adelaide's heartbreaking failures to procreate, Queen Victoria could not become Princess Royal; in fact her father, the Duke of Kent, died before he would have become King and, as has been mentioned, only monarchs can confer the style of Princess Royal. The present Queen, like Queen Victoria, could never have become Princess Royal, for her uncle the Duke of Windsor was still young enough to produce a family when he was king; and with the Abdication Princess Elizabeth became heiress presumptive.

Notes prepared by the Home Office for George V indicate that Charles I or his advisers devised the status of Princess Royal to distinguish his daughter Mary Stuart from the ' ordinary ' foreign princess who were not necessarily of the blood royal and some of whom were sadly tainted with morganatic blood. Mary became Princess Royal preparatory to her marriage and subsequent departure for Holland. In 1642 the style ' Royal Highness ', introduced on the Continent in 1640, had not become general in England, but by the end of the seventeenth century it had become established. Apart, therefore, from the fact of too-close proximity to the throne, there is the theory that James II and George I may have thought the special style of Princess Royal was unnecessary to distinguish their daughters—royal highnesses—from princesses of lower rank.

The creation of a Princess Royal is one of the remaining royal prerogatives. It is entirely within the Sovereign's discretion to grant the style for life to an eldest daughter whether born before or after the parents' accession. No one has a prescriptive right to the honour, any more than an eldest son automatically becomes Prince of Wales. But by custom and usage dating back to the thirteenth century the first-born son of an English monarch has always inherited the Welsh title if he survived childhood, and since the seventeenth century the senior daughter has become the Princess Royal, either soon after birth, as in the case of the Empress Frederick, or more usually in later life, and with or without formality, a simple ' declaration ' sometimes having been sufficient.

There is no clue to the style of Princess Royal having been formally conferred before 1905, when Edward VII ' promoted ' his 38-year-old daughter Louise and simultaneously granted the style of ' Royal Highness ' to her two daughters. When the last Princess Royal succeeded her aunt Princess Louise at the age of 34 the distinction was conferred by warrant, prepared by Garter King of Arms, passed under the Great Seal, and completed by the addition of the King's Sign Manual. The warrant was registered at the College of Arms, presented to Princess Mary, and her new style headed the New Year Honours List of 1932.

No Act of Parliament has ever been deemed necessary to formalise the Sovereign's pleasure in what has become a happy family tradition.

London, 1972.   G.W.

Mary of Orange

I

WILLIAM TOSSED his dark love-locks and pouted. Really, these Londoners seemed curiously unaware of his presence. When he stepped ashore from a Dutch man-o'-war at Greenwich on a warm spring day in 1641 only a few faint cheers went up and one raucous boatman had shouted, "Zounds! He's only a slip of a lad!" England was a proud power, but this was hardly the way to treat the heir of Orange, son of the Netherlands Stadtholder, and soon to marry King Charles's daughter. After all, he *was* 14, nearly 15.

The mood soon passed. William's hungry adolescent eye devoured the passing scene as, with the Dutch ambassador Henvlieet at his side, the coach and its equestrian escort lumbered through the crowded April streets to St James's. Along the way he saw a chained and muzzled bear ludicrously trying to dance, a party of dwarfs performing acrobatics in the dust of Cheapside, a Puritan with heaven-cast eyes moving thin lips in silent prayer, apprentice lads chivvying passers-by with brittle cockney patter, coaches and carts rattling over the cobbles, pack-horses picking their way through the throng, and over the rumble of traffic and the murmur and shuffling of the crowds rose the shrill voices of street sellers shouting, "Turnips and carrots-ho!" "Sweet China oranges, sweet China!" "New mac'rel, new mac'rel!" and "Two bunches a penny, primroses, two bunches a penny!" On Ludgate Hill the young prince's coach swerved to negotiate a knot of Londoners who were exercising their inalienable right to demonstrate upon the King's highway. A red-haired butcher in a bloodstained shirt was haranguing them from an upturned meat-basket. Further down the hill citizens gathered in argumentative postures. Suddenly a huge man pressed a flushed, beefy face against the coach window and roared, " Dahn wiv 'im, I say— dahn wiv Black Tom Tyrant! "

William was no stranger to mob violence in Amsterdam, but he was to discover that the present anger of the London crowd would be a prelude to events involving his future happiness. " Black Tom Tyrant " was the Earl of Strafford, then waiting in the Tower for the King's intercession and soon to lose both his faith in monarchs and his head. The King's consent to William's mar- riage to the Princess Mary Henriette had come at an inauspicious time. Strafford's fate was more important to the people of England than a Dutch prince's arrival to claim his child bride.

At St. James's, the old manor house where Henry VIII had bedded Anne Boleyn and which since had been expanded into a squat and gloomy palace, William was made welcome after the formal fashion of the Stuarts. The gentle, melancholy King in- clined his head slightly, and in his high-pitched Scottish voice expressed hope that the prince had voyaged comfortably. He spoke with the easy condescension of the confirmed theocrat. Yet the elegant grave manner concealed a tortured mind; the solemn hazel eyes which the King turned upblinkingly on the young man reflected the torment within. Strafford's fate lay in the King's hands, and William had appeared at the Court of St. James's in the midst of the vacillation which was his future father-in-law's besetting sin. Soon angry mobs would be howling for Strafford's gore outside the palace gates. The air of crisis conspired with the overpowering punctilio of the court to depress the prince, but his nervousness increased when Charles presented him ceremoniously to Henrietta Maria. The Queen was one of the shortest women he had ever seen, not much taller than some of the dwarfs whom the King kept about him, but what she lacked in inches the daughter of Henry IV of France made up for in hauteur. She alone of the women of Charles's court was permitted to sit in the King's presence, and from her throne chair she now extended a small white hand and disdainfully suffered the boy to kiss it.

Charles was 40. Henrietta, in her middle twenties, had already borne seven children, with another yet to come. The King and Queen loved each other deeply, drawn together even more closely by shared resistance to the rising democratic forces. Yet although Henrietta had been married at 15 for reasons of state, she vehemently opposed the marriage of the Princess Royal to this boy from the Binnenhof. William was too immature to understand the Catholic Queen's contempt for Protestants in general and for the Protestant 'Orangers' in particular. Her early life had been dominated by French priests. A small hive of them swarmed to England when she married Charles on his accession in 1625. The King was never closer to rage than when Henrietta flatly refused to be crowned by Protestant bishops. In retaliation Charles wrathfully excluded from the coronation the Catholic 'Monsers' who had been " fomenting discontentments " in his wife's bosom. Goaded beyond endurance, Henrietta drove her small white fist through a glass window to relieve her Gallic feelings.

Religion enveloped the fiery little Bourbon Queen as closely as her own skin. Her profound Catholicism had been early anchored and made fast by her advisers after an ungratifying experience with her mother, Marie de' Medici, who flirted with Lutherans, and her Huguenot father, Henry of Navarre, who cynically believed a crown to be worth a Mass. Accordingly, a century after the Reformation Henrietta's confessor was found by way of penance advising the little Queen to walk barefoot from the palace up the wide green slopes of St. James's, where partridge and pheasant still scuttered in the thickets, and across the lush green grass to Tyburn gallows, there to gaze upon the remains of Catholic martyrs rotting in chains. Under the same influences the Queen desperately practised humility, although to little permanent effect, by waiting on her servants at table and eating from wooden platters instead of gold plate, reflecting, as she submitted to the sacerdotal yoke, that the poor settlers of Maryland, named after her, were freer than their Queen.

After William had made his obeisance the Queen relaxed. She had been frowning at the boy—" none but a queen could cast such a scowl "—but now she suddenly smiled and with a graceful movement of the arm indicated a presence in the shadows which William in his preoccupation with court etiquette had not seen.

In his eleventh year the Prince of Wales was almost as sombre as his father, and equally dark. He suffered from the Stuart tendency to knock knees. His first brother, also called Charles, had died while yet the baptismal water lay wet upon his forehead— a curse upon his father, the Puritans decided, for having married

B

a foreign heretic. When the second Charles was born the Puritans tore their garments and went into mourning. One of them produced a tract denouncing the Queen as " an idolatress, a Canaanitess, a daughter of Heth ". He was fined, imprisoned for life and condemned to stand twice in the pillory, each time to have an ear sliced off, a nostril slit, and a cheek branded.

William and Charles warmed to each other. From the age of 8 the Prince of Wales had been a Knight of the Garter with his own male establishment, where he learned from experience rather than books. William, three years his senior, already enjoyed some reputation as a scholar. He was fair and handsome where Charles was dark and wry-mouthed. But where the Stuart prince was taught self-reliance, fortunately for him in view of the trials ahead, his Orange contemporary was inclined to perverseness and, as the only son among four daughters of his parents, he had been grievously petted and pampered. The two princes came to share a predilection for female company, and had he lived longer William might have excelled at that sport in which his brother-in-law acquired renown. For the present he was all eagerness to claim his bride. After the solemnities of his presentation to his future parents-in-law his quick eye darted past Charles to a small girl who had been standing petulantly at her brother's side. William was dumbfounded by her beauty: he had seen a copy of Van Dyck's portrait, but it did her scant justice. The child, only 10 years old, was perfectly self-possessed, mature in the fashion of her day, and she gave him a cold, insolent stare so penetrating in the intensity of the large round eyes, hazel like her father's, that William felt intimidated. No one had ever outgazed him as did this little chit, with her habit of shaking back her auburn curls and pursing her lips and acting as though the homage of mortal men was as much her Divine right as the King's.

Courtiers remembered that stare, almost from the time she had opened her beautiful eyes in her jewelled cradle at St. James's, where she was born on 4th November 1631, seventeen months after the Prince of Wales. In the halcyon 'thirties of seventeenth-century England the sun always seemed to shine on the little princess. The Royal Family were for ever proceeding magnificently from St. James's or Whitehall down river by state barge to Greenwich, or up river to Hampton Court; or to Windsor, Wood-

stock or Oatlands, in a dusty cloud of swaggering, arrogant
coaches. At court the Princess Royal became accustomed to the
graceful but hollow ritual of professional poets, who sombrely extolled her praises orally and in verse; outside it, she expected
the forelock-touching peasantry and the London citizenry alike
to treat her as a little Ariadne: throughout her life she was to
take for granted the servility of the lower orders. But she was her
natural self, all pretty ways and childish charm, when she romped
with the Prince of Wales and her younger brother and sister,
James and Elizabeth, and the Villiers children whom the King
had adopted after their father's murder. Playing at merry games
in their smocks and overalls among the avenues of yews and
cypress where Van Dyck caught the flush of youth on their
merry, smiling faces, they enjoyed the happiest period of their
stormy lives. The Bohemian artist Wenceslaus Hollar taught
Mary and the other children to draw; a company of tutors and
governesses taught her music, needlework, reading and the dancing which became the passion of her young life. From ' Monser '
Massonet she acquired the art of clear writing and from Master
Fawcett the finer points of archery.

But the magical years of childhood were all too brief: by
the age of 11 Mary was not only married but was also living at
a foreign court while the world she had known at home, and
those whom she loved, were collapsing or dying amid the welter
of a bloody civil war.

Marriage had been discussed even before Mary could walk. Her
mother would have sacrificed much to see her married into the
Habsburg dynasty and a future Holy Roman Empress, or allied
with a future King of Spain. The maiden herself was said to have
indicated a wish to be " matched as well in her religion as
affection ". But by 1641 a Catholic marriage might have in-
flamed the people further against Charles I, whose kingdom was
being zealously prised from beneath his small feet by the extor-
tions and the impenetrable stupidity of Laud and Strafford.

The King desperately needed cash. For six months the Long
Parliament had been inexorably whittling away the royal pre-
rogative; the outcome, given the obduracy of Charles, must be
an armed clash, although the court seemed incapable of reading
the signs. In these straits the King turned for money to one

of the wealthiest princely houses in Europe. The financial in-
centive of a union between his pious if imperious daughter and
the House of Orange was paramount; love did not enter into the
contract. The decision had been approved by Parliament when
Protestant William and Henvlieet appeared on the scene at the
head of a magnificent but largely ignored entourage. The Queen
smiled and smiled, but the veneer masked her exasperation at an
alliance which she felt lowered the King's dignity. In business
terms, to put it more bluntly, the King's daughter had been
sold to the highest bidder. This kind of arrangement was a
commonplace in the rough ruling circles of the day, but the
match was to yield little but Dead Sea fruit. Mary was to carry
her Stuart notions of Divine rank to Holland; she never con-
formed to the Dutch way of life and hated her husband's people
and their country almost from the beginning.

No expense was spared, within the limits of the King's depleted
resources, to make the marriage ceremony at St. James's worthy
of Stuart intentions; but as these usually succeeded more in the
promise than in the performance, many of the festivities normally associated with a first marriage in a young Royal Family were
curtailed. The public was not noticeably elated by the event,
being immersed in the Strafford affair. While the wedding preparations were going forward Strafford languished in the Tower.
It seems remarkable that the young Princess Mary and her
brother Charles should have attended the trial in Westminster
Hall, but the King, who was present with the Queen, probably
expected the proceedings to provide a profitable object-lesson
in the justification of authority, being convinced that as Strafford
was guiltless of treason to the Sovereign he would be acquitted
and the Parliament worsted. The little girl cast uncomprehending
eyes around the great damp hall of justice after her father with
his own hands had angrily torn down a curtain which some
officious minion had hung across the front of his box to protect
the royal party from the stares of commoners. Immediately
below them at the southern end of the hall sat the peers in
parliamentary robes, near them the scarlet-hooded judges on
woolsacks, and then rank after rank of seats crowded by the faithful Commons. Most of the time the Queen and her ladies quilled
notes as Pym and Strafford faced each other in the great vault
of justice.

By the time the Prince of Orange had accustomed himself to life at the English court the King's chief minister was about to be sentenced to death and Charles was writing to Strafford: "I cannot rest in honour or conscience without assuring you, in the midst of all your troubles, that upon the word of a king, you shall not suffer in life, honour or fortune . . . none shall hinder me from being your constant and faithful friend."

Between sentence and execution William, on 2nd May, was married to Mary. The King threw off his melancholy and entered as joyously as any Stuart ever could into the general revels which briefly illumined the darkening scene. Strafford relied on Charles's letter to save his life, and Charles indeed exerted himself. On 11th May, the day before the execution, he hurried the Prince of Wales to the Lords with a letter imploring them to confer with the Commons to save Strafford. Nothing availed. "Put not your trust in princes nor in the sons of men, for in them is no salvation," Strafford discovered at the eleventh hour.

At the twelfth his handsome head rolled from his body on Tower Hill.

A fortnight later William kissed his bride farewell and departed for The Hague. He stayed just long enough for Van Dyck to paint the bridal portrait, in which the two innocent children are shown hand in hand gazing uncertainly into a future which would have horrified them had the court astrologers not convinced them that a long era of peace and happiness stretched before them. In the royal manner of those days the wedding had been celebrated but the marriage remained to be consummated. During their brief acquaintance William had fallen in love with the little princess, whose mixture of piety and hauteur challenged his budding romanticism. Before he left he begged her parents to send the Princess Royal to him soon, as much because he had qualms about her safety as because he was her lawful husband. William was intelligent beyond his years, and his perceptive eye had noted how the land lay; he also had a shrewd adviser in Henvlieet. Little more than seven months later Charles and his family were forced to withdraw to Hampton Court and then to Windsor after the King's fatal attempt to avert the impeachment of Henrietta Maria by arresting her chief enemies, the Five Members. Liberty-loving Englishmen had come to the crossroads. Young Charles was said to have wept for five days and to have been terrified by hideous nightmares. When the King asked what was amiss he replied, a little too glibly, " My grandfather left you four kingdoms, and I am afraid your Majesty will leave me never a one." The voice was the prince's, but the words were those of Newcastle, his tutor, who felt it prudent to resign.

War was inevitable, but the King hesitated. Where was he to get money and equipment? Henrietta Maria alternately nagged and cajoled her husband into compliance with a dangerous plan: that she herself should seek supplies in Holland. Her son-in-law's despised country had become attractive in her eyes, but the problem was how to get there. The Royal Family were not yet prisoners, but Parliament spies watched their every movement. Up to this time Charles had no intention of parting with his cherished daughter, but now the married status of the Princess Royal provided a neat pretext. The bridegroom could be kept waiting no longer. Therefore when the Queen proposed to accompany the child-bride to The Hague the Parliament, which had approved the match, could scarcely object. Mother and daughter and their ladies set out with the King for Dover in February 1642. Just before they left Windsor a priest, entering the Queen's chapel to fetch the pyx containing the Blessed Sacrament, found the sacred vessel gone. One of the Queen's chaplains, Father Cyprien de Garnache, declared, " The news like a thunderbolt to us, and caused us to think that God was forsaking this place."

Some Protestant dog had no doubt made off with the pyx and holy water; at any rate, they were never seen again and some Catholics later ascribed the King's disasters to their disappearance. The King's anguish as the royal coach rumbled along the Dover road with the weeping child and the unhappy Queen at his side alarmed the servants. Charles escorted the sad party aboard the frigate. Then, turning away, he ordered the coach to drive along the coast. From the top of the white cliffs he watched the little vessel plunge into the Channel waves, then drove slowly on for twelve leagues keeping it in view, until mist, rain and his own tears blotted it out. He was never to see his daughter again.

Mary's arrival among her husband's people would have been happier had not her mother in the child's hearing so deprecated and vilified Holland before and after her marriage. The Princess Royal inevitably contrasted the green undulating land of her birth with the flat grey landscape of the Stadtholder's realm

and resented what she saw. Furthermore, she was too inbred a
Stuart to mask her dislike, and to William's joyous welcome she
turned an alabaster face. Her mother tried to make amends by
praising the country and Dutchmen at every opportunity. The
Dutch were a phlegmatic but not inhospitable people except
where their political and commercial antagonisms were engaged,
as their kindness to Charles I's exiled sister, Elizabeth the Queen
of Bohemia, had demonstrated. The Queen's sister-in-law—
" th' eclipse and glory of her kind ", wrote Sir Henry Wootton—
had lived in the Netherlands since her husband Frederick, the
Protestant Elector Palatine, had lost his earthly possessions in
an unseemly attempt to relieve the Catholic Habsburgs of their
hereditary passion for ruling the Holy Roman Empire. Elizabeth
proved to be a second mother to the Princess Royal, although her
loyalty to her brother Charles was sorely strained by his wife's
unyielding *amour-propre*. The Queen of England nevertheless
made herself agreeable to her host and hostess, the Stadtholder
Frederick Henry and his German wife Amalia of Solms-Braun-
feldt. The process of ' settling ' her daughter into her adopted
land enabled Henrietta Maria to mingle family duties with business. Charles had promised the Stadtholder a substantial dowry,
to be delivered when the Princess Royal should consummate the
marriage on achieving puberty. The Queen convinced herself that
her 11-year-old daughter was still *virgo intacta* and thus not
liable to be paid for, and this freedom from immediate financial
liability enabled her to pursue her husband's cause unimpeded.
She opened up her fabulous jewel-cases to the inspection of
Dutch merchants. By pawning her treasures, not to say some of
the Crown Jewels which had been whisked from under the noses
of Pym's agents, and borrowing from her daughter's father-in-
law, she built up a fortune of some £2 million, a vast sum for
those days. This contribution proved a fatal contribution to
royalist funds. When the treasure eventually reached England
despite the vigilance of Parliament, the King rejected all peace
overtures and raised his standard at Nottingham—it was blown
down by a high wind the same night, an ominous incident which
preyed on the mind of the Prince of Wales when he saw his
father's arms lying in the mud.

Once the secret of the Queen's true mission was out her life
was imperilled. Parliament ships lay in wait for her in the

narrow waters. Somehow she escaped. On 20th February 1643
she eluded four hostile vessels as far as Burlington Bay on the
Yorkshire coast. A few hours after landing she was alarmed
from sleep by the arrival of her pursuers, who opened a cannon-
ade directed with suspicious accuracy at the house where she and
her ladies and her pet King Charles spaniel were lodging. The
heavy fire forced the Queen to flee " bare foot and bare leg " to
a moat behind the town; yet even there the fire was so intense
that a soldier was killed at her side. In the midst of this danger
the Queen discovered that her dog had been left behind in the
house. With more valour than discretion the little Queen picked
up her skirts and threaded her way back to rescue her pet.
Cannon-balls continued to shower the neighbourhood until the
tide ebbed and the men-o'-war were sucked seawards out of
range. Henrietta Maria eventually raised a mixed force of 3,000
foot and horse and in the autumn rode behind them to Keynton
Vale near the Midlands battlefield of Edgehill. There she was
joyfully reunited with the King and her family and with the
Queen of Bohemia's son, Prince Rupert, who diverted his aunt
with quaint stories of his impetuous exploits, probably more to
reassure her than to provide clues for future historians of military
tactics. Then the Sovereign and his Queen passed on to Oxford,
which proclaimed them with enthusiasm, and the Queen and her
train were lodged at Merton College.

Once again the Queen was *enceinte*. On 3rd April 1644 she
took leave of the King for the last time at Abingdon, although
there was no doubt in their minds that they would soon meet
again in London, for Charles was about to descend upon his
capital, or so he thought. The Queen journeyed on happily
enough to Bath, but meanwhile the winds of adversity had begun
to blow. The King never reached London. Oliver Cromwell won
his spurs at Winceby near Hull, the Scots flung 20,000 war-
winning troops on to the Parliament's side, and Marston Moor
signalled the beginning of the end. The Queen at Exeter gave
birth to her last child and fourth daughter, named after herself
and destined to marry Louis XIV's brother Philip, Duke of
Orléans. (Of her eight children the first Charles, as we have seen,
died after a few hours; his sister Anne did not survive childhood.)

Messengers from the King urged the Queen that as the way to

London was barred by the extension of the war westwards she had better seek refuge abroad. Leaving little Henriette behind with trusted servants, the Queen escaped to France in a Dutch vessel. For the present we may leave her at Fontainebleau, where she flirted and intrigued with Henry Jermyn, her Master of the Horse, who would one day be created Earl of St. Albans—" full of soup and gold "—and quilled scorching epistles to Charles admonishing him not to make peace inconsistent with the Divine will and Stuart omnipotence.

The Queen had left behind her at The Hague a fearful, tear-stained and sullen little girl. Even at this distance of time it is not impossible to recapture the emotions of conflicting hope and terror through which the autocratic Princess Royal fluttered in the early years of her marriage. William was a healthy and amorous teenager, and while the bevy of forty English ladies and courtiers sent with Mary had orders to protect her virginity as far as it lay within their power, William in his father's country and in his own bed could claim to be the better judge of his bride's inclinations. Mary matured early, as had her mother and as behoved the grand-daughter of Henry of Navarre, but probably not rapidly enough for William. Frederick Henry's heir was no rake, but he could hardly be denied his extra-mural pleasures, and it seemed reasonable for him to beguile some of the sleepless hours with the beauties of Holland while he was waiting for the Princess Royal to grow up within the meaning of, and according to the date agreed in, the marriage settlement.

Sex has ever played a useful role in the lives of royal families, who have always had a vested interest in it equal if not superior to that of the lesser orders of society. But in this case there was no need to rush matters, or so it appeared at the time. Frederick Henry, with his soldierly and chivalrous outlook, entertained a lively sense of the honour done to him by the Stuarts in marrying their daughter to his son, and he took a serious view of his responsibility to the Princess Royal. Originally his ambitions had soared no higher than Charles's second daughter Elizabeth; negotiations for her hand had been opened by Ambassador Henvlieet as early as 1640 when the child was scarcely 6 years old. Arrangements were almost concluded when Henvlieet suffered qualms. Elizabeth was a frail creature, and the zealous envoy advised his master that she might not live long, a prophecy destined to prove tragically true although not quite within Henvlieet's meaning. When the Stadtholder transferred his interest to Mary Henriette her penniless father was in no position to haggle, especially as Frederick William made no great commotion when the dowry was not paid, which was just as well, for there was nothing to pay it with. Indeed, the Princess Royal's marriage portion can be said to have been irretrievably lost, with the King and his kingdom, at Naseby in 1645, after which no more was heard of it. Having made his bargain, the Stadtholder cannot altogether be blamed for having tried to keep the Stuarts to their side of it. Largely at his insistence, and because he wielded the money-power, the Princess Royal was delivered to her bride-groom by Henrietta Maria in the manner described. Historians not conspicuous for their gallantry towards Mary and her mother have alleged that during the years after 1631 until Mary came of age Henrietta Maria ceaselessly plotted to abduct her daughter and marry her into the Spanish Royal Family. This design is said to have been thwarted by William's mother Amalia, who encouraged her son to claim his conjugal rights before the appointed night. Whatever the truth of the matter, Amalia became the Princess Royal's bitter enemy. Amalia was a turbulent blonde with a scorching tongue which, however, she knew how to keep under control when diplomatic methods best served her purposes. The daughter of a penurious German aristocrat, as a young woman she had arrived at The Hague to become lady-in-waiting to Mary's aunt Elizabeth, the Queen of Bohemia. Frederick Henry saw her and succumbed to her charms. Amalia was 23 when they married, a few months before he succeeded his half-brother Maurice as Stadtholder in 1625, the year of Charles's accession to the English throne.

The hubris of the Stuarts failed to stir Amalia, and she expressed her mortification in no halting phrases when her husband, in his fatherly compassion for the forlorn Princess Royal, ordered his family and household to accord to her those royal honours which were withheld even from his wife. This and Amalia's contempt for Henrietta Maria deepened the feud which was to damage Mary's relationship with her mother-in-law throughout their frosty association. The behaviour of the gaggle of Cavalier courtiers around Mary also helped to erect a barrier between their mistress and the Dutch people, who held Amalia in high respect for her homely virtues, even if they did not exactly love her, and needlessly increased the company of the Stuarts' enemies.

It is doubtful whether a proud Romanised princess could have been thrust at a worse time for her own fortunes into the maelstrom of Dutch Calvinist politics. The provinces of the Dutch Netherlands were in theory controlled by the Stadtholder, whose position was analagous to that of a president or a constitutional monarch, although the country was not to become a kingdom until after the fall of Napoleon Bonaparte. The provinces or states made their united voice (when it *was* united) known through a parliament or talking-shop known as the States-General, and in practice whenever a dispute arose between the states the Stadtholder had the last word. If he had a strong wife, like Amalia, his wife probably had the last word. In practice the Stadtholder was the head of the House of Orange-Nassau, the line of William the Silent, who sixty years before this time had flung the Spaniards out of Holland and founded the Dutch republic. For this he had paid with his life, but before he was shot by Balthasar Gérard, an assassin in Spanish pay, the Dutch had cause to be grateful to Elizabeth of England, although the expedition mounted by the English to assist the cause of Dutch independence was notable chiefly for the heroism of Sir Philip Sidney and scarcely at all for military expertise. The whole affair, in fact, was painfully botched, but the Dutch had remained thankful for small mercies, and would probably have been kinder to the Princess Royal had not so many personal and political factors worked against a better understanding. These factors and the internal rivalries of the United Provinces darkened the rest of Mary's life.

The early years of the struggling republic were bedevilled by intrigues and jealousies within the states. William the Silent was succeeded by his second son Maurice, who ruled by the sword what had been won by it. His cardinal error was to clap a number of leading deputies of the States-General into the castle of Lovestein, including the Pensionary of the state of Holland, largest and most prosperous of the states. After a mockery of a trial the Pensionary, John Van Olden Barneveldt, was executed. His martyrdom left a lasting smear on the name of Maurice and roused his partisans to fury. They formed the ' Lovestein Party ', whose activities were to threaten the peace and security of the ruling house and involve the Princess Royal in a vicious constitutional struggle for the rights of her son.

The honest and diligent Dutch took their politics and their pleasures with equal seriousness. The convolutions of their political system often puzzled the foreigner, but they were dictated by the urge of a majority to keep the country together under the House of Orange. Friesland always tended to break away, prob- ably because the Stadtholder was usually the head of the related but rival House of Nassau-Dietz. No clear line could be drawn between the Republicans and the Orangists. The former repre- sented merchant princes as well as ordinary folk; the latter embraced representatives of the people as well as the aristocracy and royalist elements. The Calvinist Reformed Church, guardian of the established Protestant religion, was supported by the state and enjoyed the favour of the House of Orange. Independence had released the native energies and the natural genius of the Dutch. Scholars and men of letters, and philosophers such as Descartes, found freedom to work in Holland, which was also producing artists and scientists and those jurists who were to make an international reputation for The Hague: the great Grotius (Hugo De Groot) had laid down his principles of inter- national law when the Princess Royal arrived in Holland, and young Anthony van Leeuwenhoek was about to discover bacteria.

Unfortunately Mary was not allowed to appreciate the worth of her husband's countrymen. The little Stuart colony around her brooded in isolation from the Dutch: it was embittered by the bloody internecine struggle which had now convulsed their native islands, and Mary was not permitted to forget that she was a royal Stuart. The trials of her early life in Holland sprang largely from all-pervading anxieties about her family overseas. For many weeks after her mother's departure she never knew what had happened to her. Mary's dread increased when civil war broke out in August 1642, and from that time forward she enjoyed little peace of mind. Charles and James narrowly escaped capture at Edgehill. The royalist disaster at Marston Moor— " God made them as stubble to our swords ", wrote Cromwell —was followed by the flight of the Queen to France, and the further disaster at Naseby by the flight of the Prince of Wales to Jersey. The King prepared the heir apparent for the worst with a letter advising him to join the Queen in France, where she was to have " absolute full power of your Education in all things except Religion ", and the younger Charles was to accept the situation with a quiet mind and not " gromble ".

All these calamities when they were reported to the sorrowing Princess Royal at The Hague drove red-hot needles of fear into her heart, and she nearly died of terror.

II

EVENTS IN Mary's adopted country deflected her thoughts temporarily from Stuart misfortunes. In March 1647 her father-in-law died. He had befriended not only the Princess Royal but also her unfortunate family. His tolerant bearing towards the Stuarts shines through the pages of Jacobite history, in marked contrast to Amalia's contempt, although she usually kept a bridle on her tongue in Frederick William's presence for the sake of peace. The Stadtholder had made his name as a military leader, from whom Prince Rupert and even the great Turenne had learned the arts of war, but his son William, who had also won some distinction as a soldier, lost his occupation with the signature of the Peace of Westphalia and soon became bored with the desk work expected of him as Stadtholder and Captain-General of the Dutch States.

In the early conduct of William and Mary at the head of affairs in the United Provinces may be detected the causes of political unrest which were to deprive their son of his inheritance during his mother's widowhood and make life difficult for her. When William II succeeded as Stadtholder he was only 20 and the Princess Royal not 16. They had been married for nearly six years. Both had been spoiled by over-indulgent parents. The sycophancy of courtiers had brought out the more unpleasing characteristics of both. Now that they could do as they pleased they spent money like water on great balls, at which they danced the nights away; decked themselves out in clothes of the most fashionable design and expensive cut; laid out vast sums on jewellery; and equipped the Stadtholder's Quarter at the Binnen-hof Palace with luxurious furnishings and works of art. By temperament no two people seemed less suited to each other. William's natural melancholy and Mary's impenetrable hauteur interacted to produce ' scenes ', after which Mary could lapse into a silence more profound than Amyclae's. From such tantrums the young Stadtholder escaped into orgies of hunting and other pleasures. He became an authority on French actresses as well as on the plays in which they performed, and Mary was often left to sob alone while he pursued his gallantries. William's cousin, Count Dohna, scolded the Stadtholder more than once. How could he act so towards a princess " of so great beauty and merit and one who loved him so faithfully "? William was inclined to return the petulant reply, " I know she loves me now as her own soul, and I care for her more than for anyone in the world. But one cannot live in such constraint *all* the time." Amalia might have exerted a steadying influence, but she had been too often offended by the caprices of her daughter-in-law to interfere, even if she admitted to any fault in her only son, and the mettlesome pair might have drifted apart but for Mary's pious adherence to her marriage vows. For long periods business came to a standstill while William absented himself on hunting expeditions. Foreign ambassadors spent more time on horseback or at the theatre or on the tennis courts than they could spare, but they were the only places where the young Stadtholder could be found.

Across the North Sea royalist hopes yet flickered as the sturdy Scots fought on for the King. Cromwell read his Bible, harangued his crop-haired and prick-eared troops, and cursed Charles, whose intrigues with the Scottish loyalists had begun to irk him. The King was a prisoner at Carisbrooke Castle, and in February 1648 Cromwell contemplated deposing him in favour of the Prince of Wales, but the heir apparent was in Paris out of his reach. The dictator's choice then turned to James, who had been seized at Oxford, but with his escape Cromwell planned to crown the youngest brother Henry, Duke of Gloucester. All these schemes aborted. The princes were nothing if not loyal to their father. From Carisbrooke the unhappy monarch snatched at straws and one at least proved tougher than stubble: the escape of James through the agency of the double-dealing Colonel Charles Bampfylde refreshed the King's spirit.

" I look upon James' escape as Charles' preservation, and nothing can content mee more, therefore be carefull what you doe," wrote the King.

The Princess Royal played a secret part in her brother's escape as, dressed in woman's clothing, the young Lord High Admiral was taken by barge to join a Dutch vessel outside the Thames estuary after he had deceived the guard at St. James's Palace by playing hide-and-seek with his brother Henry and his sister Elizabeth. The only time suspicion fell upon the refugee was when on the barge he laid his leg on the table and plucked up his stocking in " an unwomanish manner ". His Dutch brother-in-law and his sister rejoiced at the success of the stratagem. William set off down the River Maes to meet James, and after an affectionate reunion off Maesland Sluys took him to the town of Sluys. There Mary fell into her brother's arms with tears of gladness; " the affectionateness of that meeting I cannot express ", said one of the royalists who had risked his life to save the prince. However, it was an " affectionateness " which was not to be reproduced later in their lives. The escape was the more adventurous in that the Dutch vessel, with Sir Nicholas Armorer and other of the King's men aboard, had slipped through the Parliament fleet under Rainsborough and made landfall at Middleburg without detection.

James had not seen his sister for seven years. All he told her of the Royal Family's treatment by Cromwell stiffened her resolution to work for her father's liberation and restoration. But, as so often in Stuart history, pledges were ground to dust by irresolution, mistakes and faulty judgements of men and affairs. James, in the titular role which suited him better than the one for which he has come to earn the opprobrium of the prejudiced, hurried to Helvoetsluys on hearing that some of Rainsborough's crews had mutinied and joined the royal fleet. The 15-year-old prince was profoundly moved when the mutineers fell on their knees before him, vowing to serve him to the death. The wily Bampfylde, believing one royal bird in the hand to be worth two out of sight, urged the rough tars to declare for James as king, leaving Charles I and the Prince of Wales out of the reckoning. The news infuriated Mary, and it is possible to discern in subsequent intrigues her part in warning her eldest brother, to whom she was even more devoted than he was to her.

By this time Mazarin and the French Court had tired of the

royal refugees and their seedy and impoverished train with their
constant demands for funds. The 10-year-old Louis XIV and the
Queen Regent might be rich, but they had their problems and
they were not universal providers and philanthropists. When
Charles, probably at his sister's prompting, was urged to speed to
Holland if he would save his crown, Mazarin refused him the
financial means. Somehow Jermyn raised the money and by July
the Prince of Wales and most of his followers were at Helvoetsluys, leaving Henrietta Maria alone with her youngest daughter
Henriette, the child born at Exeter, who had escaped to Paris
disguised as a beggar boy. From St. Germains the distraught
Queen addressed pathetic appeals to the Parliament at Westminster imploring permission to join her " dearest lord, the
King " that she might console him as the day of his trial
approached and " be near him in that uttermost extremity." She
did not then suspect what that extremity was to be. Her letter
was left unread; its existence remained a secret for thirty years,
when it was discovered and opened late in the reign of Charles
II. Meanwhile her eldest son found the royalist fleet at Helvoetsluys bubbling with unrest—" full of anger, hatred and disdain "
and ready to mutiny for their unpaid wages. Charles blamed
James for the crisis, deprived him of his command, and ordered
him to make himself scarce at The Hague. James obeyed sullenly.
From that time until the Restoration relations between the two
brothers smoked and smouldered.

Quarrels and " great distractions " broke out among the exiles
in Holland about the use of the fleet—provisioned for three
months out of Orange William's pocket—to restore the King's
fortunes by invasion from Scotland; alternatively to relieve Colchester then under siege by Fairfax; or, thirdly, to rescue the
King from the Isle of Wight. The last course was vehemently
pressed by Rupert and approved by Charles I, but the King's
emissary, Colonel Will Legge, when he arrived in Holland was
" no more listened to or regarded than if a dog had been sent
to them ". So the fleet under the Prince of Wales tacked up and
down the Channel taking prizes. The crews were too factious
and unreliable to attempt an assault on Carisbrooke, and after
hearing of Hamilton's disaster at Preston, where the Scottish
prisoners were sold for two shillings a head to New England
planters, the Prince of Wales returned to Holland. So the

c

' second' Civil War ended as calamitously as the first. Royalist schemes to recover their losses were crumbling in an atmosphere of mutual antagonism and suspicion as Cromwell triumphed on. One of the sharper blows befell the Royal Family when at Kingston-on-the-Thames the 19-year-old Francis Villiers, a " youth of rare beauty and comeliness of person ", had his horse killed under him and fought with his back to an elm tree, surviving nine sabre slashes until he was viciously cut down from behind a hedge and his blood ran away.

His adoptive father the King had now been brought to trial in Westminster Hall. In the midst of the consternation caused by that ' unholy' event the Prince of Wales nearly succumbed to smallpox at The Hague. James still sulked over his dismissal from the fleet and refused to return to it, although largely because his advisers feared a plot to hand him over to the Parliament. The Princess Royal's cup brimmed over with melancholy and perplexity at Teyling, where she and her husband had been ordered to take refuge from the epidemic. Charles had been received with royal honours and granted an allowance of 1,000 guilders a day for ten days when it was thought that his fortunes might prosper in the second Civil War; but now the States' enthusiasm for the Stuarts abated, and in view of the high controversies and military disasters who can blame them, especially as they wished to maintain neutrality now that Cromwell seemed to be master? But Mary opened her heart and her husband's purse to her brothers, and William invited his brother-in-law to winter in Holland.

Soon Charles recovered. It was Christmas, the Stadtholder and his wife returned to the Binnenhof and despite shadows cast by fears for the King the festivities waxed merry and boisterous. The normally staid court rang with the laughter of the Queen of Bohemia and her daughters, Elizabeth, Louise, Henriette and Sophie. All were handsome, as were their brothers Rupert, Maurice and Philip, and as William's four sisters were also of the company the two Stuart princes enjoyed a revel which long stood out among the happier memories of their lives. Charles was attracted to Princess Sophie, but he scared her away by telling her that she was even lovelier than Lucy Walter. She probably feared some design on her virginity, for at 18 the Prince of Wales had had several love affairs in France and at least one natural child. Lucy Walter, who came of a good Welsh royalist family, was "browne, beautiful, bold, but insipid", according to Evelyn. When Charles arrived at The Hague she was living there with Colonel Robert Sidney. The prince took her by storm and nine months later the future Duke of Monmouth was born in Zeeland.

Christmas wassailing came to a shocked end with reports that the King had been condemned of "High Treason and other high crimes". The Prince of Wales, fated during most of his life to pursue the line of least resistance, on this occasion showed unflinching resolution. He sent Cromwell blank sheets of paper —three, lest two should go astray—each containing his signature. Upon the paper Cromwell was to write such conditions to save the King's life as he pleased, including the disinheritance of the Prince of Wales and even his own execution. But Cromwell had no means of telling whether Charles would be allowed to give himself up, and the manly offer was rejected. At the urgent pleading of Mary and her husband the States-General sent an envoy to intercede with the regicides and convey the heir apparent's offer to surrender himself in exchange for the King's life. The Dutch ambassador was "very loud" in his protests, but no one in power would see him until after Charles I had been sentenced to death. The appeals of European monarchs, their condemnation of the "odious design", all were brushed aside. On 30th January 1649 the King's head was severed from his body in Whitehall, where the crowd emitted one dismal "grone" at the horror, the pity and the futility of it.

> He nothing common did, or mean,
> Upon that memorable scene.

The three Stuarts at The Hague reeled beneath the blow. The Princess Royal summoned up the last reserves of spiritual strength and spent hours in prayerful weeping in her chapel. Charles heard the news when his chaplain, Dr. Stephen Goffe, tremulously addressed him as "Your Majesty". The new King burst into grief and hid himself away in his room for the rest of the day, reading and re-reading through his tears the last letter from his father: "You have already tasted of that cup whereof I have liberally drunk, which I look upon as God's physick, having that in healthfulness which it lacks in pleasure."

Among the royalist exiles the blow hardened that determination which, had it been applied with greater and more harmonious unity, might have restored Charles II to his four kingdoms ten years earlier. Montrose fainted. On coming out of his swoon he vowed revenge, a vow which was to cost him his life before his object was achieved. Rupert published a declaration warning the regicides to expect " condign punishment ". Even the States-General and the provincial states publicly recognised Charles as king, and the Dutch clergy preached in all churches against the " impiety and wickedness " of the " horrid murder ".

Yet even all this accumulated sorrow hardly compared with the agony of the little Queen Henrietta Maria in Paris. Civil war —the war of the Fronde, called after a children's game—had broken out; the French court had moved secretly to the country. The Queen, fretting for husband and family, was exhausted by insomnia and a gnawing fear that the civil war in France might engulf Mazarin and monarchy on the pattern of Strafford and monarchy in England. She was also in desperate need, sometimes even hungry. Her French pension had been unpaid for six months. She had pawned most of her remaining jewels for the Stuart cause. She clung desperately to her Catholic faith and to her little daughter Henriette, the only member of her scattered family left to her until James arrived from Holland on the very day the Fronde war broke out—his first meeting with his mother for five years. The future Cardinal de Retz called on the Queen at the Louvre and found her sitting by the child's bedside on a bitter winter's day.

" You see I am keeping Henriette company," she said. " The poor child cannot get up today for want of a fire."

De Retz, staggered to see the grand-daughter of Henry IV in such straits, usefully petitioned the French Parliament on her behalf. News of the King's execution was kept from Henrietta Maria until well into February, but she had a premonition when a messenger sent to St. Germains took a long time returning. Finally Jermyn was forced to disclose the truth. She listened in silence —" without words, without action, without motion, like a statue ". Indeed, she seemed transformed into a frozen effigy while her servants groaned and sobbed around her. The Duchesse de Vendôme, her sister-in-law, restored movement to the Queen by ceaselessly kissing her face and hands until she came out of her trance. After a short spell in a Carmelite convent she recovered her spirit and plunged into the work of restoring her son to his father's heritage.

Charles borrowed a purple mourning suit from his brother-in-law. He proposed to linger in Holland, but a further stay was made impossible when Dr. Dorislaus, the prosecution counsel at the trial of Charles I, was assassinated by royalists at The Hague, whither he had been sent by Cromwell as the Commonwealth's ambassador. So in June, with some prize money from Rupert and a secret loan of £20,000 from the States, now more anxious than ever to speed the parting guest, he set out with the Princess Royal and her husband, the Queen of Bohemia and members of her family on the road to France. At Breda the Prince of Orange gave a grand fête in honour of the 19-year-old King. The friendly Dutch, not for the first time controverting the politics of their government, hailed Charles all the way to Antwerp, where Mary and William took their leave before the King stepped on to Spanish soil.

The French Court had moved to Compiégne, where, for the first time in many a year, all the surviving members of the Stuart Royal Family except Elizabeth and her father gathered under the same roof. Little King Louis asked eagerly about the hunting habits of the Prince of Orange, but Charles was immersed in paper preparations for an expedition to Ireland, and even the charms of his royal cousin ' Mademoiselle ', and the ploys of Jermyn and Henrietta Maria to marry her to him, failed to divert him from business, which consisted largely of attempts to raise the wind, to play the King in exile (even at the expense of wounding his mother's feelings) and to stop his courtiers bickering and duelling. The French aristocracy cold-shouldered the English royalists, and Madame de Motteville exclaimed bitterly, " Why wonder at their solitude! Misfortune was of their company; they had no benefits to confer."

Ormonde's disastrous Irish campaign and Cromwell's ever-remembered expedition ended the King's hopes of securing one of his four kingdoms, and he retired to loyal Jersey, which alone of his dominions had proclaimed him and where he wintered with James in the sports of the island and meditated yet on ways to win Scotland. Mary at The Hague rejoiced in rumours that

Cromwell had died, but such reports were so plentiful and varied that Will Douglas felt moved to write:

> Cromwell is dead, and risen, and dead again,
> And risen the third time after he was slain.

III

FOR THE present the Princess Royal put her family out of her thoughts and concentrated on worries more directly affecting her. After the peace with Spain in 1648 the extent of disarmament caused dissension among the States. By early 1650 Amsterdam, the chief town of the chief province of Holland, pre-empted decisions by the States-General for the country as a whole and disbanded some of its own troops unilaterally. William headed a deputation to Amsterdam in June, hot words passed, and from that moment a gulf of emnity opened between city and Stadtholder. When William caught a severe chill in a swimming pool at Ryswyk his enemies muttered that should he die Holland would refuse to elect a successor. But by August the Stadtholder had recovered and the States-General empowered him to bring Amsterdam to heel. Troops sent to the city found the stolid burghers preparing to open the dykes and flood all Amsterdam to prevent its occupation. Six leading deputies of Holland, including Jacob De Witt, the Pensionary of Dordrecht, were arrested and jailed at Lovestein. There seemed nothing for it but civil war when William had second thoughts and prudently withdrew his forces. His abortive action was to have difficult consequences for his family, for the problem of whether Holland should be first among equal states was not resolved for another twenty years and was to deprive William's famous son of his father's offices.

When the Prince of Orange descended upon Amsterdam the Princess Royal was with child. At the end of October the Stadtholder had been hunting at Dieren when he felt so thoroughly unwell that he returned abruptly to the Binnenhof. By the following night smallpox had been diagnosed. His young wife, frantic with distress, flew to him immediately, but attendants held her back by main force, as she was nearing her time and to have contracted the disease would have imperilled the baby's life as well as her own. The physicians isolated her in her private apartments while members of the staff and the doctors maintained an unbroken vigil around the sick man's bed.

On the evening of 6th November, after a week of diminishing hope and escalating despair, Henvlieet, who had become Mary's steward, met the prince's gentleman on the stair and was told that in a few hours all would be over. In his delirium William muttered the words of a horoscope which an old crone had thrust into his mother's hand some years earlier: it forecast that the prince would have a son by a widow and would die in his twenty-fifth year. The remembered prophecy is said to have sapped his will to live. Henvlieet swallowed a glass of Rhenish wine to get up courage to break the news to his mistress, but at the last minute his nerve failed, for the pregnant young princess gave him such a despairing look when he started to speak, and fell into such paroxysms of weeping, that the words died on his tongue. Many hours passed before anyone dare break the tidings of William's death; then a chaplain came to tell Mary that he had yielded up his spirit peacefully a little after midnight. He was 24, as the clairvoyant had foreseen.

Mary's bed and furniture, even the empty cradle in the nursery awaiting the unborn child, were draped in black crêpe. In an adjoining room the coffin containing the embalmed body of her husband rested on a catafalque. Candles flickered in the shrouded chambers of the ancient palace. The women among Mary, smothered in black silks and satins, hid their faces beneath huge hoods and muttered and whispered together. The windows rattled in the icy winter blast and swept clouds of rain across the Zuyder Zee against the shutters.

" My poore Neece is the most afflicted creature that euer I saw and is changed as she is nothing but skinn and bone," wrote the Queen of Bohemia.

The Stadtholder's untimely death and his widow's confinement brought public business to a standstill. Between consoling Amalia and her prostrate daughter-in-law the lively Queen Elizabeth found her hands full.

" Uithin 15 days she lookes," she noted, " but I beleeve she uill come sooner."

That afternoon, ten days after William's death, the Princess Royal went into labour. Henvlieet recorded: " This evening, between eight and nine of the clock, Her Royal Highness was safely delivered of a healthy young Prince. God be thanked and send him a long life."

He was wrong in two particulars. The child mewling and puking in the black-caparisoned cot was the sickly infant destined to become William III of England and to die a widower at the comparatively early age of 51. As he was being slapped into life a superstitious nurse saw, or thought she saw, three haloes shining around his head after a sudden draught had dowsed the candles. But the Dutch people threw off their mourning temporarily to light bonfires and toast the heir of Orange. The Queen of Bohemia observed: " There is the greatest joye in the people that can be."

The baby's dead father lay coffined without burial until the following March. In the intervening months it became clear that little William was of no more account in the constitution of republican Holland than any other high-born infant. A feud developed between the republican party and the widowed Princess Royal as deadly to the prospects of the Stadtholder's son as the more personal struggle which opened simultaneously between Mary and her mother-in-law. Undoubtedly the show of force against Amsterdam had been a mischievous error. It curdled the last months of William's short life—a spoiled child often becomes the man or woman who can do no wrong—and fostered a powerful anti-royalist party which believed, not altogether without reason, that William was being egged on by his young Stuart wife to assume absolute power. De Witt had ever been a name of distinction within the emergent Netherlands, and the memory of past ill-treatment spurred the republicans to rebellion. In their rage they prevailed upon the States-General to refuse election to the baby prince as Stadtholder and Commander-in-Chief in succession to his father. Apart from Friesland and Groningen, the States arrogated all the Stadtholder's prerogatives, kept the House of Orange at a distance and, convinced that the Stuart cause was irretrievably lost, serenaded the budding Lord Protector of England.

Charles's long face drooped at the loss of his cherished brother-in-law, for whom he felt more than cupboard love—he was " the most considerable man " in the Stuart cause, according to Abraham Cowley. Hyde, the King's present adviser and post-Restoration scapegoat, saw William's death as Heaven's judgement on the Catholic-minded Charles, who had recently deserted the English Church to sign the Covenant in the vain belief that the Scottish Presbyters, usually so right about everything, would rescue him from the poverty of exile and restore his throne. For that purpose he had been in Scotland when the Prince of Orange expired. It was on hearing of her brother's cynical apostasy, so redolent of her French grandfather, that the 15-year-old Princess Elizabeth Stuart, the lonely and half-forgotten sister, died broken-hearted at Carisbrooke Castle. From Scotland the King wrote to his sister's steward, now Baron van Henvlieet, of his " great sorrow and affliction." Henvlieet had married Lady Stanhope, the daughter-in-law of Philip, Earl of Chesterfield; and Charles, who relied much on her judgement and respected her influence on the Princess Royal, wrote to her: " How my sister does for her health, and with what discretion she bears her misfortune; whether my nephew be lusty or strong, whom he is like, and a hundred such questions, I desire an answer of under your hand, because a lesse evidence will not satisfy the curiosity I have for those I am so much concerned in."

The King, harbouring few illusions about the States-General, also asked, perhaps ironically, what they were doing for " our young General " and " how kind and careful " Amalia was of him, and what provision was being made for his sister. The deceased prince had left instructions with Count Dohna that Mary was to be Regent of Orange during her son's minority. His will, opened before his son's birth, indicated surprising confidence in the 19-year-old widow. Dohna had mustered the chief supporters of Orange and they had all sworn fealty to the unborn child, whatever its sex. The Stadtholder's will also bequeathed to Mary an allowance increased to £15,000 a year, with legacies to all his servants. But the Queen of Bohemia firmly believed that his doctor, either out of ignorance or malice, had failed to warn William of his imminent death and so he had not signed the document. The same doctor, Verstrate, had " treat him verie strangelie, and gaue him so manie cooling things that it killed him ". (It was not the last time that prejudiced witnesses would attribute the death of a Princess Royal's husband to his doctors.)

Yet it was Henrietta Maria who felt William's loss most keenly. This is perhaps not so strange as some historians have represented, for she had lost husband, son (the first-born Charles), two daughters (Anne and Elizabeth), and now her son-in-law— the " last blow ". In the midst of these griefs the King was reported assassinated; falsely, but before the truth was discovered many royalists had proclaimed James. The King's second brother at 16 was " full of spirit and courage ", but he hated the French court, where in his youthful conceit he asserted that his mother loved Jermyn " more than all her children ". In October 1650 he had fled to Brussels, declaring bitterly that he would rather throw himself on the hospitality of Germany, Japan or the West Indies than return to his mother. His intention was to push on to The Hague, but on the insistence of her mother the Princess Royal sent the Marquis de Vieuville to stop him at Dort. Once again the warm-hearted but feckless Queen of Bohemia came to the rescue, and James was lodged in her house at Rhenen. There he spent that miserable Christmas, overshadowed for the second year in succession by a Stuart disaster. From there he had written to Mary expressing sorrow for " this great losse that is happened to us all ". Charles commanded James to return to Paris, but as civil war had resumed the Duke of York was permitted to visit The Hague. He arrived there some days after his elder brother had been crowned at Scone with " a parcel-gilt crown ", having under duress condemned Charles I's marriage to an " idolatress " and the " apostasy " both of his father and his grandfather James I.

Scarcely had the Duke of York reached the Dutch capital than the smouldering feud between the Princess Royal and Amalia burst into flames over the baby's christening. Negotiations were conducted venomously on both sides. Mary, who saw in the son a memorial to her father, wished him to be named Charles. The baby had been conceived at about the time she had learned of her father's execution. But Amalia, although a German, was strongly disposed to her late husband's house. Hers was the more reasonable claim: the baby should be named after his great-grandfather William the Silent, founder of the Dutch Republic, and also Henry after his grandfather Frederick Henry, who had

ushered in Holland's ' golden age '. Vehement was the quarrel.
Mary, almost devoured by grief and the effort to bring her child
into the world alive, was left exhausted and defeated. Impotent
rage seized her. She refused to attend the christening. She also
forbade James to carry the child to church. Her pretext was that
he might " let him fall ", but as it was Amalia's idea any excuse
sufficed to damn it. James, never destined to be the luckiest
prince in Christendom, had arrived at The Hague while this
brouhaha was raging and was thankful to be relieved of the
duty.

On 21st January 1651 the pale little prince, fated to grow up
to be a homosexual as well as King of England, was borne through
the snow to the Groote Kerk. What could be seen through the
starched linen and lace furbelows of the shrunken tiny face, buried
deep in sable velvet and ermine, resembled the pathetic trans-
lucence of a bulge-eyed fledgling. Seen from the high windows
of the Binnenhof, the coaches like squat black beetles and the
black-clad attendants like black ants, crawled at funeral pace
through the flying snowflakes. The cathedral was a vault of freezing air and the sermon was far too long, even for a Calvinist
preacher. The royalists stamped their feet and chattered so
loudly that he had to admonish them. Tiny William Henry,
weak and wailing, at length was returned to his nursery, where
he alternated between one form of infantile sickness and another,
with almost fatal convulsions on one occasion, until in the
following May his mother was at last able to exchange the morbid
atmosphere of the Binnenhof for the palace at Breda, where
she and her son benefited from the purer country air and their
freedom from conniving republicans.

Motherhood and its joys could not restore the Princess Royal's
lost love and she grieved and prayed much. James had been
chief mourner as his sister's representative at the Stadtholder's
state funeral in March, but even this brotherly service was soured
by protocol. The princes of Portugal stood on their dignity as
kinsmen of Orange, took umbrage when Mary denied them precedence over James, and refused to attend the funeral. Mary's
mental ferment was further increased when the English pleni-
potentiaries, Oliver St. John and Walter Strickland, arrived to
negotiate an alliance between the Commonwealth and the United
Provinces. Much as a majority of the States-General desired this

treaty, most Dutch people were predominantly Orangist in outlook. The presence of James at The Hague fanned their loyalties
and Cromwell's envoys were molested in the streets and stoned
in their lodgings.

" We dare hardly peep out of doors in an evening," complained
one of their attendants after several attacks by the Bohemian
Queen's servants shouting " Regicides! " and " King-killers! "
Little wonder that the Parliament besought the States-General
to send James packing. Hyde found him at Breda " in all confusion
imaginable, in present want of everything, and not knowing what
was to be done next ". Money was opportunely provided by the
French Crown and James left the land of canals, ducks and clogs
with measured elegance.

His departure removed one immediate complication. The
Stadtholder had left explicit instructions that Mary was to be
Regent, and Dohna and other trusted counsellors had sworn
allegiance to William Henry even before his birth. Amalia bitterly
contested her son's will in the courts of law, adding " vexation
and trouble to the many sad afflictions of the virtuous Princess
Royal ". In the battle to control her grandson's affairs Amalia
disputed Mary's competence as tutrix because she was a minor.
She further contended that Mary's royal birth and her strong
attachment to her brothers would damage the infant's best
interests. But for the nonce James's withdrawal from Holland
disposed of any suggestion that Stuart pressure was being applied
to the States-General in his sister's behalf. The courts con-
ceded Mary's claim to be sole tutrix of William Henry, but her
mother-in-law fought on, convinced of her own righteousness.
Eventually Dohna came over to her side; he found it repugnant
to take orders from Mary, who treated him like dirt. The House
of Orange also championed Amalia, for the prince was first a
princely Dutchman and only secondly a royal Stuart: he should
be brought up in the traditions of his native land, which even then
was challenging England's command of the seas. His financial
future also needed safeguarding. Mary and her husband had spent
recklessly and lent generously to the Stuarts, and when William
died his estates were encumbered with debt.

Substantial provision had to be made for the two widowed
princesses as well as for the prince's education. Amalia's appeal
dragged on through the courts but at length succeeded to the

extent that she and her brother, the Elector of Brandenburg, were made co-inspectors of William Henry's property. It was in a sense a judgement of Solomon, in the highest range of Dutch judicial wisdom, for Mary was given two votes when any decision affecting her child's future was disputed, so her voice was equal to that of Amalia and her brother. Another advantage conferred by the court was that the Prince would live under his mother's roof and in her care. During the rest of her life, although occasionally she sought her pleasures away from him for longer intervals than seemed judicially acceptable or constitutionally agreeable, this arrangement endured. But the two women were irreconcilable. In public they preserved the graces. In private they quarrelled repeatedly. Probably not a year passed when, for a period at least, they were on speaking terms. Harmony was restored usually by mutual concern for William Henry's health. And once Amalia and her brother joined Mary to resist a common foe.

Cromwell had demanded that the States-General should exclude the prince and his descendants permanently from the office of Stadtholder. No nephew of the Stuarts should preside in Holland; and even the prescient Oliver could not foresee that same nephew's reigning in England. The Dutch republicans had no intention of fighting a war to thwart the Protector's will, and John De Witt as Grand Pensionary avenged himself for his recent incarceration at Lovestein by persuading the state of Holland to pass an Act of Exclusion effectively outlawing the House of Orange from any share in that state's government. The humiliation of this supine surrender threw the House of Orange into hot confusion. Mary wept for three hours and emerged from the crisis with red and swollen eyes. The Dutch people were on her side. They reacted angrily to this unwarrantable servility to a foreign power. Mobs attacked De Witt's mansion with fire and stone.

For the next ten years Mary was to campaign vainly for her son's rights, but another decade would pass after that before the House of Orange recovered its prestige and its fortunes.

The return of James to Paris split the royalist exiles between the supporters of Henrietta Maria and her lover Jermyn, and James and his partisans. Then Charles was reported missing after

Worcester—"the enemy is scattered, and run several ways", gloried Cromwell. Unhappy Mary, now tossed dementedly from one family crisis to another, was secretly visited by Buckingham and regaled with a pitiful story of that day's work among the oak-apples, a day which had seen the death of Hamilton and was followed by the summary execution of Derby and the imprisonment in the Tower of Lauderdale and other Stuart loyalists. Buckingham also spread a tale that Charles had escaped "on this side the sea", and some supposed he was at Teyling with his sister; but these stories were designed to throw pursuers off the scent, and after those incredible adventures which have passed into English history and legend, the disguised fugitive shipped from Shoreham to Fécamp and reached Paris in rags. The faint-hearted deserted the threadbare King and hurried home to make their peace with Cromwell. Ormonde wrote to Secretary Nicholas of the King's Council: "All imaginable trials for the recovery of the royal interest have been made and failed."

IV

SIX YEARS of degrading poverty followed. The expatriates were everywhere shadowed by Parliament spies. Attempts by Charles to enlist the support of the German Emperor through the Princess Royal perished because German memories of the Thirty Years' War lingered on; and the King's hopes of mediating between his sister and her mother-in-law with a view to uniting the States-General on his side melted like cheese in a Dutch oven. Even the outbreak of war between the Commonwealth and Holland in the spring of 1652 helped Charles little, for he had no money. Hostilities, however, brought Mary a mixed blessing in that the Orange Party recovered its *esprit* and fiercely resisted a proposal from Cromwell that the Commonwealth and the United Provinces should weld themselves into one republic. That would have meant the death of hard-won Dutch independence. The Orangists rose up in their wrath. The republicans retreated. In a demonstration promoted largely by teenagers—the so-called ' Children's Riot ' —the mansions of republicans suffered attack and once again Grand Pensionary De Witt found himself on the run while his house was smashed up.

Mary now reluctantly entered the arena of international politics as a figure of no little consequence. De Witt in the sacred cause of trade prepared to bargain with Cromwell, but he spoke only for the State of Holland. The other provinces desperately opposed the appeasement of the English dictator. Zeeland and the Northern Provinces promptly elected William Henry as their Stadtholder, and Guelderland committed itself to restore the House of Orange to supremacy, fight the war to a finish, espouse the Stuart cause, and seek a French alliance. Thus encouraged, Mazarin and King

Frederick of Denmark offered funds for the war if all the States would help Charles. A friendly smile touched the thin lips of the States-General, and with its wan warmth to cheer him, the King wrote to his sister at the end of 1653 exhorting her to throw all her influence into a fresh attempt at reconciliation with Amalia and Count William Frederick of Nassau, who sympathised with Charles but was a potential rival of the related House of Orange. Charles was not sanguine enough to expect a full reconciliation, but he urged his sister: " Let no man be able justly to say that it is declined on your part, but show at least an inclination to it, and preserve civilities to them, that I may perform all ceremonies to them that are necessary to my condition."

But Mary was as unskilled in the diplomatic arts as an obdurate and unaccommodating nature could make her, and the opportunity was missed. By the spring of 1654 the war was over. Cromwell, his navy no longer dependable, lowered his terms. The Dutch snatched at them. The treaty, however, contained clauses clearly inimical to Stuart interests. Both countries bound themselves to expel the enemies of each other and to prevent the House of Orange from sheltering any " rebell or declared enemy of the republique of England " in any " castles, towns, havens, or other privileged or unprivileged places appertaining to any persons, of what dignity or State they may be, within the dominion or jurisdiction of the United Provinces." Once again Cromwell insisted that the Prince of Orange should be barred permanently from the Stadtholdership.

" It has struck us dead!" exclaimed Hyde when the terms were known and one European country after another touched the diplomatic forelock to the English Protectorate. By the middle of 1654 the King had no allies among the powers. France no longer recognised him as reigning monarch, but Louis for family reasons still made him an allowance. Spain loftily ignored him. Christina of Sweden, who had hinted marriage to him, had passed him over in order to embrace the Latin faith. The son of Charles I literally found nowhere to lay his head. No court which had signed on Cromwell's dotted lines dare entertain him for long.

Even his little Dutch nephew's own town of Breda was sealed to the wandering Sovereign. So in July of this year, which marked the nadir of his fortunes, Charles travelled on sufferance

D

to Spa in Flanders. This proved to be one of the more joyous of his expeditions in exile, for it brought him again the company of the Princess Royal. She was not allowed to receive her brother in Holland. Now, in sore need of relaxation, she placed the baby under strict guard and prepared to disport herself on the Continent. Her visit to Spa enabled certain misconceptions to be cleared away. Of all Charles I's wretched family none had been more steadfast and open-coffered in the Stuart cause than the little Princess Royal. Despite her political difficulties she had given unsparingly of her fortune. During the Anglo-Dutch war her eldest brother, although he was " very unwilling to speake in any matter of money ", had written twice for aid in his Scottish campaigns. On the second occasion Mary, who had to avoid upsetting the States-General, acted with great stealth when General Middleton arrived at The Hague "in distresse ", and she gave him 5,000 guilders on condition that he maintained absolute secrecy about the transaction. The King's Scottish envoy kept too quiet. Consequently the King's friends concluded that Mary had sent him away empty-handed. They severely criticised her parsimony, saying she had refused Middleton even the " small sum " of £1,000 without which he could hardly get himself to Scotland.

The Princess Royal disdained to answer them. At last Middleton broke his promise and nailed the injustice.

The proud but penurious brother was aware of all this when one fine summer's day Mary fell into his arms at Spa. Among others she was accompanied by Jane Lane, who with her brother John had helped the King escape after Worcester; to avoid capture she had settled at The Hague as Mary's lady-in-waiting. At 24 Charles had acquired that lean and dissipated bearing and sad mocking air which was to change little during the rest of his life. Apart from political worries, he had quarrelled with his mother and with James and had exchanged angry words with Rupert, who had departed in a huff to Germany after telling him to find another Master of the Horse.

" The King," wrote Hyde, " is now as low as to human understanding he can be."

Thurloe, Cromwell's Secretary of State, scanned intelligence reports from his Charles-watchers at Spa, where the King had plunged into all manner of festivities, and concluded that for all his gaiety the monarch had a heavy heart. The spy John Adams wrote to Cromwell from the watering-place:

All yt comes here are not patients, nor infirme, for I believe the most part meet for the great and good company which is here to passe away the summer merrily. . . . There is not a daye or night but there are balls and dansinge. I think the ayre makes them indefatigable, for they danse the whole afternoone, then goe to suppoer and after they goe into the meadowes and danse there. None so much commended as our King, who indeede is grown a lustie and proper person; gaines the affection of all by his affable and free carriage amongst them. So doth the Princess Royal who is a gallant lady, 'tis admirable in Princes to see how loving they are.

Again he wrote that he had heard " Royal Charles," or R. C., " discoursinge, sportinge, and drinkinge the waters upon a mountain near this town. His sister was with him. . . . They danse, singe, and drinke every night in a green hard by this town. R. C. is given much to dansinge. . . . The traine of R. C. heere is not verie great, he has not above thirtie, but they live well and are verie merrie, all of them." He might have added that the donor of the feast was the Princess Royal, counselled by the " shy and wary " Henvlieet. At this time Mary was giving half her income to her brother without the knowledge of the States-General.

Brother and sister had been unmet four years, royalists recalled, and the Queen of Bohemia wrote to Secretary Nicholas: " I am glad that you found the King and my neece so well in health and so kinde one to the other, which has ever been so since I have known them. I believe indeed the separation will be hard, but when there is no remedy one must be content."

Charles gave a graphic description of the merriment in a letter to his aunt, which he began in his sister's chamber " where there is such noise that I never hope to end it, and much less to write sense. . . . I shall only tell your Majesty that we are now thinking how to pass our time, and in the first place of dancing. . . ."

Foreign royalties descended upon Spa, and Mary danced her shoes almost into holes, but the gaiety ended abruptly when smallpox killed one of Mary's ladies, Kate Killigrew, and the court beat a speedy retreat to Aachen, where the citizens, although overwhelmed by the size and magnificence of Charles's entourage, fired cannon and heaped presents of poultry on the unexpected guests. Mary and the King kept themselves to themselves during the first few days in the town's two grandest hotels, but Charles's swollen company of more than eighty " gallant men " were soon brawling and bickering between gay visits to ' Caesar's Bath '. Adams reported: " All the Cavaliers here doe bathe themselves daylie, but R. C. himself since his coming hither appeares not abroade at all. The reason I do not know, but matter of State, as with Princes."

As it happened, Charles was planning further moves to secure his lost throne, swearing that he would rather die honourably than live in " such contemptible calamityes " as Middleton's disaster in Scotland. But Charles could not remain depressed for long, and in September he made his first public appearance with Mary at vespers in the cathedral, where the Princess Royal devoutly brushed the skull and hand of Charles the Great with her lips and Charles reverently saluted Charlemagne's sword. Cromwell's watchdogs dutifully reported back that the King's inclinations to the Church of Rome could not be doubted. A month later, after sipping the waters at Caesar's Bath daily, and hunting with Count William of Nassau, with whom she was now on cordial terms as her brother had hoped, Mary set out for home. Charles escorted her as far as Cologne, whose friendly citizens greeted the royal travellers with a salute of thirty cannon and a blaze of guns and muskets. Later a party of 200 musketeers presented themselves outside Mary's " very fair and curious house, full of decent rooms and pleasant gardens " and fired three volleys to express their satisfaction. At a Jesuit college seven boys knelt before them chanting psalms of welcome. A Sunday visit to the Reformed Church at Mulmein countered previous suggestions that they had ' turned ' to Rome, but Cromwell appears not to have heard of it and he went on thinking the worst. On Monday the authorities of Cologne cathedral in a rare gesture of hospitality opened up the tomb of the Three Kings. The spies were thrown into utter doubt again when the Papal Nuncio received the visitors at a series of Benedictine, Franciscan and Carmelite convents.

All this hospitality raised Charles's hope that the German princes would endow his cause, but when money was mentioned

they recoiled. Only one, the 30-year-old Count Palatine of Neuburg, showed any kindness, and that was on condition that he
and his wife Elizabeth Amalia of Hesse-Darmstadt should be
addressed as ' Altesse ' and that he should be allowed to kiss the
Princess Royal. No two Stuarts jointly had ever brushed aside a
trivial quirk of court etiquette with greater alacrity, and so they
sailed by barge to the count's sumptuous castle beyond Dussel-
dorf, where the noble pair awaited their guests with a " great
equipage " of a dozen coaches. Feasting that night lasted many
hours, and the visit ended with protestations of mutual affection.
The King was so reluctant to part from his sister that he accompanied her across the border into Holland, and at Xanten slept
in a house whose owner was so sensible of the honour that he
hung Charles's portrait in the chamber where he slept. On the
following day, the anniversary of the Gunpowder Plot, the King
sadly took his leave as it might have been unsafe to proceed
further along the road to The Hague. Mary dissolved into tears
and returned with a heavy heart to the detested country of her
adoption, leaving Charles to journey back to Rome. Recalling
their grief in parting, she wrote to him there: " I do not wish
that sadness to continue," and assured him that until they
met again she would " not receive any real joy."

It reminded her of another dismal parting. In April the previous
year Cromwell had at last released her youngest brother Henry,
Duke of Gloucester, from captivity at Carisbrooke Castle, where
everything had been done to remove all marks of royalty: he was
known only as ' Master Harry Stuart ' and there had been a
plan, afterwards discarded, to apprentice him to some useful
trade. Now he was free, and he set out for The Hague with a
joyful heart. He was a handsome, bright and eager-eyed boy of
13 and the only surviving member of his family to have lightened
the late King's captivity. Little Henry had solemnly assured his
father that he would rather be " torn to pieces " than desert
the English Church or wear the Crown of England during the
lifetime of his elder brothers. So it was as a properly instructed
young man " right affected to the Episcopal Church " that he
set foot on Dutch soil and rushed to greet his sister, for to have
gone to his mother in France might have subjected his religious
scruples to some strain. Mary was so delighted with the brother
who had been born in the year of her departure for Holland that

she asked the King's permission to keep him. Charles agreed, but Henrietta Maria flew into a fury and the King—who was then in Paris—felt bound to command Henry to join him there. Mary, not without reason, feared he would fall under the influence of Papists and parted from him " with great passion of sorrow ".

By that time the exiled Queen Mother felt the Stuart cause to be lost. Her only consolation was to convert Henry to the Old Faith. For various reasons he would have to stay in Paris with her, and if his material future were insecure at least she could protect his soul. That was her thought, but when Henry wrote to his sister explaining this the Princess Royal, who had loyally abided by the Protestant faith in her adopted land, felt that an abyss had been opened beneath her defenceless brother.

" Let me entreat you, for God's sake," she wrote to the King, " quickly to take some resolution to hinder this great mischief as well for your soule's sake as your body's."

She urged him with all her will to " hinder this new misfortune in our family." The King acted promptly, Henry broke off relations with his mother, even James (then serving with Turenne's army) sided with the young duke, and arrangements were made for Henry to rejoin the Princess Royal in Holland. On the way there, as though Heaven itself disapproved of his conduct, he fell seriously ill at Antwerp and was unable to travel until the end of January 1655 to meet his sister at Teyling. The States-General affected ignorance of his presence, but became uneasy when reports of royalist activity in England and on the Continent reached them. Besides, Henry was acting like a Stuart and ordering people about. He had a particularly odious habit of instructing his groom to bring his horse into the house so that he could mount at the foot of the staircase instead of in the yard. A private message was sent to Mary advising her to bid Henry depart. She took no notice. The States-General in conclave debated whether he should be arrested or forcibly banished from Holland. The King was warned by Lady Stanhope, and he immediately summoned Henry to his side at Cologne. The whole episode seemed to have concluded when he reached there in May, but it left complications. Charles's attitude, while it showed the world that he was no Papist, offended the Catholic powers. Henry's conduct deeply mortified his mother.

'Brother trouble' was no new thing for Mary. Around this time she had an angry exchange with the States-General over the sudden disappearance of the King from Cologne. The oligarchy at The Hague suspected she had concealed him in Holland—unlike Cromwell, who thought Charles was in England and ordered the arrest of one very surprised Thomas Sacheverell, who resembled the King in appearance, at his innocent house near Oxford. The insolent tone of the States-General's "very uncivil letter" to the Princess Royal, with its prohibition that the "Lord King do not repair within the power of their High Mightinesses," incensed Mary. She ordered the document to be preserved "that I may the better remember it, when maybe they will not desire that I should." In fact Charles had gone secretly to Middleburgh in Zeeland hoping to sail for England at the head of an invasion fleet, but the design withered on the branch, and Charles's resolution with it, and he returned disconsolately to 'Collen'.

There in August his miserable existence—his expenses were now cut to the bone and he had no more jewels to pawn—was brightened by the appearance of Mary, who on the way paused at Meurs to meet James, still campaigning with Turenne. One great blessing of her visit to Cologne was that Charles and his bedraggled and hungry retinue could live on her credit, as she kept an ample table around which the King could sport with ebullient and laughter-loving companions.

"You must not expect to hear from me often so long as my sister is here," the King apologised to a friend.

He added that they passed the time as well as people could who had no money, "for we danse and play as if we had taken the plate fleet". But in the midst of rejoicing Mary fell seriously ill. Thanks to the ministrations of the court physician she was well enough by the end of September to join with her brothers in the annual Frankfürt fair. They travelled under various thin incognitos so that they were easily recognised, especially when at Bonn they embarked on a pleasure-boat for Frankfürt.

"Their way of travelling was very convenient," recorded a contemporary scribe, "for, besides the greater, they had two lesser boats fastened to it. In one they conveyed all their beds, trunks, and wardrobes, and they made a kitchen of the other, which was a very fine accommodation for this water voyage that continued for four or five days, having all their victuals dressed at hand, and at table there was no state nor distinction among them, eating all together . . . to make the more merry."

Nicholas commented disapprovingly: " Young Princes think of nothing but pleasure."

The descent upon Frankfürt of the eccentric Queen Christina with a train of seven coaches and 200 attendants did nothing to alter his opinion. The Queen, who took the greatest delight in dressing as a man, had made some brutally sarcastic remarks about the Stuarts and, having rejected Charles and entered into a commercial treaty with Cromwell, could find no words of praise for the Protector too obsequious to mouth in company. But now she was on her way to Rome and Charles was much on her conscience. The King, who could not contain resentment indefinitely, agreed to see her. After a tête-à-tête their meeting was broadened to admit Mary, Henry and Rupert. Christina was particularly taken with Henry and threatened to carry him off to Rome.

" People talk," she said, " that I am going to Loretto to offer up a sceptre and crown to the Lady Mary there. I laid down these regalities in Sweden, and if I had any crown to dispose of I would rather bestow it on the good poor King of England."

The " good poor King of England " unbent to receive Christina, but he refused point-blank to have anything to do with his cousin Charles Louis, Prince Elector of the Rhine, who had repaid great kindnesses he had received at Whitehall by deserting Charles I on the outbreak of the Civil War and supporting the Commonwealth. On seeking a chance meeting at a theatre he was astonished when Charles and Mary fled at the sight of him, so speedily that he could not overtake them. Other Electors were kinder. In Mainz the royal visitors received " a very noble supper and good lodgings " on one occasion and were " nobly feasted for two days " free on another. Yet for all the hospitality the expedition cost a small fortune, and when they returned to Cologne the King's mind and pocket were scarcely improved when a well-wisher in England sent him a present of hunting hounds—" fourteen couple "—which cost him and the Princess Royal more to transport and to keep than they were worth. In Cologne after Mary's return to Holland the spirits of the little court were further downcast when the royalist Henry Manning, presumably out of pique at the King's indifference to him, busied himself spying for Cromwell. When he was arrested he denied that he had sent anything useful about the King's plans, but said he transmitted only unimportant details concerning " the Princess Royal's journeys hither " and other stories about the royalists which he had made up. Charles was so mortified by Manning's treachery and by his other misfortunes that he ordered Nicholas Armorer and James Hamilton to dispose of him. They took him on a two hours' journey from Cologne and shot him in a wood on the estate of Charles's friend, the Count of Neuburg.

Another source of irritation was Mary's projected visit of reconciliation to her mother in France—irritating because it threatened to unravel a whole web of royalist intrigue designed to win the practical goodwill of Spain, the enemy of France, for a possible reconquest of England from Flanders.

" Remember, Sire," said the Irish Jesuit Father Peter Talbot, when pressing Charles to gain Spanish favour by embracing the Roman Church, " that three kingdoms is worth a journey." (He prudently excluded Scotland.)

The grandson of Henry IV of France did not need to be told this, but his conscience had endured enough already, and he contented himself by trying to lure James away from the French service. The Duke of York had become deeply attached to Turenne, but when he was not playing a gallant part in skirmishes with Louis's foes he was leading a life of " ease and decency " at the French Court on a lieutenant-general's pay of 6,000 pistoles a year. James therefore had no particular wish to join his brother in some useless foray against England to add to the list of Stuart rebuffs, and he used as an excuse for prolonging his stay in Paris the imminent arrival of his sister.

Fifteen grief-laden years had passed since Mary and her mother had last met. Meanwhile their relations had been chilled by the Queen's attempts to convert her children to the Roman faith; but the youngest, Henriette, was the only child of Charles I to be brought up to Roman Catholicism. The situation had been further exacerbated by Mary's appointment of Anne Hyde as a maid of honour at The Hague. The Queen Mother's distrust of Charles's chief counsellor Hyde, Anne's father, was now notorious, and she supported every move to dishonour and ruin him. She heartily disliked Anne's close proximity to her daughter. But now the Princess Royal had arrived at years of discretion and was

anxious to appease her mother. Henvlieet shrewdly advised her
to delay the visit, but she spurned not only his counsel but
also the King's veto. Mary could be as wilful and perverse as any
other Stuart. It mattered not to her that this ill-timed expedition to France in 1656 threatened to thwart Charles's hopes of
Spanish aid. Mary remained a year in her cousin Louis's domain,
and it says much for her personality that she did not wear out
her welcome at the French court. But her disobedience offended
Charles, and when Mary broke her homeward journey at Bruges
she found him ill-tempered, for it seemed to him from that
distance that she and James in Paris had thrown in their lot
with Henrietta Maria and the Palais Royal set.

A most serious breach opened in a Royal Family in which,
jaundiced by misfortune, there was too little love to temper
folly. Mary now sided with James, but when the young lieutenant-
general decided to run away in January 1657 rather than break
with his pro-French friend Charles Berkeley, their friendship
was not so firmly established, despite the King's suspicions, as to
permit him to take her into his confidence. His " unimaginable
sally," so reminiscent of his flight from St. James's Palace some
nine years earlier, sent the King into a rage and he blamed his
sister for conniving at their brother's escape, a charge which she
as hotly denied because it was baseless. After lying low in Utrecht
for a week the runaway duke repented of his escapade and returned to Bruges. Family relations remained clouded. Mary was
so thoroughly unhappy that she cut short her stay and actually
looked forward for the first time since her marriage to returning
to Holland, where she arrived at the end of February. All three
brothers put a good face on her departure by riding with her as
far as Sluys, where the garrison were thrown into such transports
of joy when the royal party appeared that volleys were fired in
all directions. One soldier was shot through the head, another in
the neck, and a third in an undisclosed part of his anatomy.

At any rate this erratic welcome was more heartening than
the King's Spanish-assisted scheme to descend upon England
from Dunkirk, for once again fate turned against Charles. On
the dunes at Dunkirk the King and James exposed themselves
to fire from Cromwell's ships, but that was as close to England
as the brothers ventured. The year wore on. The King's heart
sank with the shortening of the days as, without money or

bottoms and almost without hope, he burst out morosely, " If this winter pass without any attempt on my part I shall take very little pleasure in living till the next."

The estrangement from his sister deepened his natural melancholy. Now there was fresh cause for dissension. At her brother's request Mary had two years earlier taken into her household the wife of the Earl of Balcarres—one of her chief occupations seems to have been helping lame royalist dogs over stiles; but when the earl intrigued with the Palais Royal the King sharply admonished her to banish Balcarres and his wife from Holland. In her devotion to Lady Balcarres the Princess Royal returned as sharp a refusal. She did not, she said, propose to dismiss people just because he happened to dislike them. Charles then accused her of having treated Balcarres " much better since I have been unsatisfied with him than ever you did before ".

This quarrel did not prevent the King that autumn from borrowing from his sister " a jewel " which he was able to pawn for £1,500 to provide arms for a royalist rising in England. The strange request had been preceded by an even stranger transaction between the three Stuart brothers and Mary to borrow money from John Webster, an English loyalist in Amsterdam, on condition that the loan would be repaid by whichever of the four eventually regained the throne; it was because this sum was insufficient that Charles begged Mary's jewel. His correspondence shows that he never readily tried to milk his sister's funds, even when she had plenty. Now, as he acknowledged, she was " not much better provided than myself. . . . I know you are without money, and cannot very easily borrow it "; and so he promised to return the jewel before Christmas. With a sense of duty which again throws a favourable light on her character, Mary concealed her injured feelings and released the jewel to him.

Surely sisterly love could go no further, yet the New Year of 1658 was barely a fortnight old when another babbling discord rent the Stuarts. The Dukes of York and Gloucester, with one of James's pro-French friends, joined Mary in " frolics " at Breda. Stories got abroad that Mary showed too much affection for the friend who, ironically, was Harry Jermyn, a nephew of that same future Earl of St. Albans whom James had accused of a guilty liaison with his mother. The King was livid when the scandal came to his ears, and he recalled Jermyn to Bruges. The slight cut Mary to the quick. She wrote to Charles protesting her " innocency " and condemning the " insolency " of the tattle-bearers. She begged him to " stop the malitious tongues " by sending Jermyn back to Breda, but Charles in reply thought it " very strange that you should think the continuing of that which is the cause of the report should be the meanes of taking it away." The only " meanes to shunne any future inconvenience " would be her going to him at Antwerp, where Charles was to set upon that course of rewarding importuning toadies with English titles. Mary joined fully in the revels which followed there, but the King's volatile and daring friend Rochester died at Ghent in the midst of the celebrations—" a happy departure out of this unhappy world ". His death caused no interruption. Before he was buried a last great ball was given, and the next day Mary, having publicly established the family's unity and distributed largess to needy royalists, left for Breda. But the breach over Jermyn was unhealed.

Even the pleasure the royalists took in the death, at last, of Oliver Cromwell was tarnished by the quarrel between Charles and his sister, who poured out her heart to Lady Stanhope after Amalia had maliciously spread tales of what her brother had been saying of her. Mary burst out that the King had ruined her fame. She even went so far as to say that if he were in his kingdom he " could not make her satisfaction," and that she would never have anything more to do with him, " what change soever should be in his or her fortune ". She was no more his subject, she was a free woman who might marry or " have kindness for whom she pleased " without anybody's leave. Mary did not deny that she was pleased to be loved by Jermyn or that she had a " kindness " for him.

Henrietta Maria was even more scandalised than the King by the cause of this dispute, for she had hoped to marry her widowed daughter to Louis XIV. But Charles really drove a dagger into Mary's heart when in the summer of 1658 he began to intrigue with her mother-in-law during a clandestine tour of the United Provinces, where he first heard rumours of Cromwell's death. As the Commonwealth and its treaty with the Dutch still existed, Charles only endangered the lives of his followers living in Holland by remaining there, but he contrived a meeting with the Dowager Princess of Orange and her two unmarried daughters, Henriette and Marie. The King and Henriette had long felt a mutual attachment (by this time Sophie had faded out), but Amalia aimed higher and infuriated Mary by discussing her daughter's dazzling prospects of marriage with better-heeled suitors. Amalia really had no objection to Henriette's marrying the King, but she was wary of the States-General, and Charles and his Dutch nymph met in secret. The King was back in Amsterdam when a messenger interrupted tennis to confirm news of the Protector's admission to that Puritans' paradise which had been so warmly waiting to receive him, so the royalists said. Charles at once wrote to Henriette asking her hand, following his letter with a personal appearance at the Princess Dowager's summer palace in Brabant.

With that remarkable lack of discretion which ever distinguished him, James at this time carried off his brother Henry on a surprise visit to Mary at The Hague. They arrived late one Sunday night after the Princess Royal had retired, but she rose and they gossiped until dawn, when she forced them to retreat hurriedly. James again startled his sister with another visit in October, but for his own safety she had him whisked off to Delfshaven before he was discovered, and joined him there later. She and her two brothers then wintered in Breda, but this time there was no " scandal ", only a a mood of rising exaltation. At the first intimation of Cromwell's death the States-General had begun to look with more favour on the exiled Stuarts, the stiff-necked French nobles rushed to congratulate Henrietta Maria, and Spain and Germany began to fawn. But yet again hopes " fel away like fruit blowne downe with winde ". Richard Cromwell succeeded his father. The States renewed their treaty. Charles dropped once more into his almost friendless condition.

Wretched indeed was the King's plight: estranged from his family, his bravest expectations dashed, purposed English risings aborted, his associates quarrelling and duelling among themselves day and night, enemies watchful everywhere, and himself languishing in " want and contempt ", reduced to eating off common pewter. Amalia turned the screw: she withdrew her consent to Henriette's marriage and betrothed the muddled girl to the Prince of Anhalt instead—which served her right. However, unlike some of her other actions, Amalia's intervention seems defensible. Charles's improprieties with the ladies were provoking the jealous interest of royal males throughout the Continent. While he was betrothed to Henriette of Orange he was wooing Beatrix de Catecroiz, mistress of the Duc de Lorraine.

Even King Louis, whose expertise in matters of morality cannot be questioned, was heard to remark that his cousin " should rather with tears seek to appease the wrath of God . . . than follow his amours at Brussels ". But Charles was not the first nor would be the last aspirant to an English throne to make love to more than one flattered woman at the same time.

In all the circumstances it seems miraculous that Charles should have regained his throne. But Richard Cromwell's Protectorate crashed and ' Tumbledown Dick ' fled to the Continent as Charles proceeded to leave it. Significantly Charles's ' declaration ' before the Restoration was made at Breda, little Prince William Henry's town, where, when the King and the Princess Royal had been on better terms, they spent some of their happiest times together away from the vexing importunities of the dour-visaged States-General. Significantly, too, it was at neither a French nor a Spanish port that the King embarked on his last sea voyage to assume the crown of his father's four kingdoms, but at Scheveningen in Holland. In the joy of deliverance the Royal Family were united in fact and not merely in fiction. Mary's contribution to this achievement should not be under-estimated. Despite the embittering quarrel with her brother, when she declared she wished no more to do with him, her loyalty to the whole Stuart clan never wavered. Her influence was paramount in Charles's choice of the Netherlands as a staging-post between exile and restoration. Otherwise brother and sister might never have met again.

An eager witness to the historic meetings at Breda in May 1660 was Prince William Henry, then 9 years old and very like his mother and his uncle Henry of Gloucester in features and temperament. All the exiles, including the Queen of Bohemia, gathered at Breda, except Henrietta Maria and her daughter Henriette, who remained in Paris. In the last days before his return in triumph to London, Charles with cynical amusement witnessed the squalid rush of pardon-seekers and place-finders who had snubbed or mischiefed the Stuarts in the days of eclipse. Some members of the States-General were of this high-principled company. Now they and the magistrates of the towns along the royal route from Breda to The Hague came out with generous offers of money, ships and hospitality. When Sir John Grenvile arrived with a chest full of English money for the King, Charles called Mary and James to come and gaze upon it; they had not seen so much for many years

Until now the bursting of the dykes would have caused little more consternation in the breasts of the States-General than a visit from Charles to his sister. Now the effusive thanks of a States deputation for the honour of his residence at Breda, and a warm invitation to The Hague, tickled his sense of absurdity. But he choked back his chuckles and by coach he went, with Mary and his nephew—who sat on his uncle James's knee— through squadrons of cavalry to Marvaeret, where they boarded yachts berthed at the quay. From thence to Dort the river banks were alive with shouting and cheering Dutch folk, the bulk of whom had differed from their rulers in the emphasis of their loyalty to the House of Orange. Seventy-two coaches, each drawn by six horses and preceded by State trumpeters clad in crimson velvet, carried them the several miles from Delft to the capital.

There a superb reception awaited. The thump of cannon marked Charles's progress to a mansion reserved for his occupation. Where he had so recently supped off pewter, now he banqueted off gold plate. At the head of the table the King was flanked by Mary and his aunt of Bohemia. Fiddlers diverted the royal guests and cannon boomed outside at the toastmaster's signal when some pompous burgher proposed " a health unto his Majestie ". The King had not eaten so well since Worcester. On his first night at The Hague he slept in a Paris-made bed artificed for Mary but never used, in a chamber from which the ancestors of Orange looked down upon him from gold frames. In one way and another the States-General laid out £30,000 to entertain the Stuarts. They also found presents of £60,000 for Charles and £7,500 each for James and Henry. As Charles in the noonday of victory committed the Princess Royal and his nephew to the tender care of the States-General, it seems inconceivable that another ten years was to elapse before William Henry was restored to his father's offices. But the oligarchy was already showing the same bigotry as was to distinguish the contemporary founders of the Dutch colony at the Cape of Good Hope.

The future of William and his mother was pushed into the background as English members of Parliament competed for audience of their King. A committee of Lords and Commons had swarmed upon Charles with protestations of love and loyalty, but, more important, with a useful addition of £65,000 to his treasury; of this James was to have £10,000 and Henry £5,000. Portly aldermen of the City of London buffeted into the royal presence with another £10,000 and could see nothing ridiculous in the light brush of the sword with which they received knighthoods from the monarch with the mocking lips. As Mary watched this grotesque performance she marvelled at her brother's restraint. But the time for recriminations had passed. Charles in a final act of family reconciliation restored the post of Lord High Admiral to James, who hastened to strike his flag on the former Parliamentarian vessel *Naseby*.

At the end of May the royal standard rose lazily above the foremast of *Naseby* as Charles, with his sister, nephew and aunt, passed over the dunes beyond The Hague to Scheveningen through dense files of people and, almost stunned by the cannonades, stepped aboard a sloop and was rowed across the water. Sailors aboard the English flagship almost fell overboard in their excitement when the King ceremonially rechristened the four ships at anchor. *Naseby* became *Royal Charles*, *Richard* was converted into *James*, *Speaker* into *Mary*, and *Dunbar* was substituted by *Henry*. Up and down, up and down the deck of the *Royal Charles* paced the King, the Princess Royal clinging tearfully to him as, followed by the young Prince of Orange, he moved to the poop deck. The ship began to roll and heave on the swell of the afternoon tide. A favourable breeze sprang up from the south-east. Through the summer haze the King took a long last look at Holland, from which he had received so much and so little and would never see again. Then he turned to his sister who, as the captain began to relay his orders, burst out sobbing. Charles took her tenderly into his arms and said through his tears, " Most dear sister, I beg you do not sorrow. Soon we shall meet again, and you must bring William with you, and we will make merry in Whitehall as we did at Spa and Cologne."

Mary protested that when she came to England nothing should ever part them again. Charles then embraced and blessed

The betrothed William II of Orange and Mary Princess
Royal, by Van Dyck

Mary II, Queen of William III of Orange, by Wissing

William III, King of England and Prince of Orange as a boy

William Henry " as if he were his own ". One last charge the
King laid upon Mary: to send a present to their sister Henriette.
At last, after much kissing and weeping, Mary and her son left,
anchor was weighed and the *Royal Charles* with her transformed
escort of neo-royalist oaken bottoms, sailed for Dover. The
crowds on the dunes watched the flotilla out of sight, but
long before that Mary and her son were at the Binnenhof. Not
once had the King's sister turned her head to watch the departing ships. There had been too many Stuart partings, too many
quarrrels and heartbreaks, too many pledges given and promises
broken. She did not wish to be reminded of those other occasions.

The Restoration marked an important constitutional stepping-
stone for Mary Stuart. With three brothers living, she had no
expectations of the throne, either for herself or her son, but now
William Henry was not only Prince of Orange but also the
nephew of the reigning King of England. Moreover, lest the
States-General forget it, the blood of Stuart, Bourbon and
Medici flowed in his veins. Indeed, it was the Queen Regent
of France, Marie de' Medici, once a refugee in Holland, who had
first drawn the attention of Charles I and Henrietta Maria to the
advantages of an alliance between the Houses of Stuart and
Orange. As the outcome of this alliance William Henry inherited
the proud but tragic histories of Stuart and Orange. His great-
great-grandmother was Mary Queen of Scots.

Indoors the puny little prince with the grave eyes and slight
figure had powerful enemies in Count William Frederick of
Nassau-Dietz, who coveted the Orange heritage, and the suave
lawyer De Witt, who was determined out of revenge for his ill-
used father to destroy Orange pretensions to kingship in the
United Provinces. But out of doors William Henry's very stature
brought out the protective instincts of the warm-hearted populace, and wherever he went he was greeted with Orange colours
and processions of small boys acclaiming his name and rhyming,
with political undertones which they did not understand:

> Though our Prince be very small,
> Yet he'll be Stadtholder after all.

As a pale, dark-eyed boy William Henry had been taken by

E

his mother to receive homage as Baron of Breda. In one way and another, although she left him for long intervals, the Princess Royal kept her son's name before the loyal public. She also never let it be forgotten that she was the Princess Royal of England with the style of Her Royal Highness, while her mother-in-law Amalia was merely Her Highness. The distinction, the legacy of a tragic Stuart monarch, did nothing to warm their collaboration as William Henry's guardians.

From her ' house in the wood ' outside The Hague the Dowager Princess of Orange kept a jealous watch both on her grandson and her daughter-in-law, whose cold demeanour and almost unbroken silence in the presence of Dutch politicians alienated many who might have befriended her son. William Henry grew up to hide his true feelings. He was almost as reserved as his famous ancestor ' The Silent ', so-called after he had been rendered speechless with horror at Henry III's disclosure of his plan for the massacre of St. Bartholomew. Throughout her son's early years the Princess Royal's policy, like that of the future Duchess of Kent in the case of the young Princess Victoria, was to display her son in public whenever she could, and thus openly to encourage the Orangists to accept the deprivation of his father's offices as only a temporary setback to their fortunes and his. They took the point. The Orange party struck a medal containing a bust of the prince, in his tiny cap and plumed hat, the whole encircled with a wreath of orange-blossom and beneath it the words *William Henry by God's Grace Prince of Orange.* A phoenix prophetically rose from the ashes on the reverse side.

In every way Mary sought to turn the grand climacteric in Stuart affairs to her son's advantage. A comprehensive plan of education had been drawn up for William Henry. It was based on solid Dutch principles and seasoned with the pure herbs of Calvinism. The programme, embodied in the *Discours sur la Nourriture de Son Altesse Monseigneur le Prince d'Orange,* established that William Henry was to be equipped for the offices filled by his Dutch forebears when they again fell to him " by the turn of the wheel of time ". At the Restoration the prince was a student at Leyden University, founded by William I, and Mary pressed De Witt immediately to reinstate her son in his father's offices. The Grand Pensionary evaded the demand. She threatened him with the displeasure of her brother the King and the revolt of the Orange Party: when Charles left Holland he had enjoined the States-General to cherish his sister and her son— " two persons peculiarly dear to us ". Mary had neither forgotten nor forgiven the insolent letter from the States-General and determined to let them remember it. After much haggling a compromise was reached. The State of Holland undertook to pay 40,000 florins for the prince's further education, to administer and maintain his still extensive properties, and to pay him a large annual pension to show " the greatest possible proof of the interest they would take in him," as De Witt explained. But as to restoring him to his father's honours, De Witt asked whether it was reasonable to expect a boy of 9 to assume great offices for which he might well prove unfitted. The Act of Exclusion was repealed, and William Henry seems to have been placed " on approval." Endless tiffs, fortunately not in front of William, although they had previously fought like vixens in his presence, brought Mary and Amalia to accept the general principles. Three Commissioners were appointed to supervise the prince's studies, on two conditions: they were to be appointed by Mary and they were not to interfere with the three family guardians, Mary, Amalia and her brother of Brandenburg

During these negotiations Mary used the change in the climate of opinion to draw her son further into the limelight. His readings at Leyden were not resumed until she had led him on a triumphal progress through Amsterdam and other cities in the first days of June 1660, through laurel archways and streets hung with banners, amid the pealing of bells, the firing of cannon and the blast of sennets. Tableaux were mounted to display Nassau and Stuart ties. Medici complicity in the tragedy of St. Bartholomew was discreetly omitted, but one *tableau-vivant* clumsily portrayed Charles I with his head on the block. Mary shuddered and wept at the sight, but it made little impact on the martyred monarch's grandson, who as he trotted around Amsterdam on horseback was voted " a pretty boy ", with his long chestnut curls and keen eye, like his father's. On his return to the Binnenhof he was gravely honoured to accept the title of ' general ' from a platoon of small boys in hats with orange-blossom who formed a guard of honour with wooden swords outside the palace. At William Henry's invitation they trooped indoors to be regaled with drinks and fruit and to receive from their host, as they left, a gingerbread cake each. The little ceremony, although he knew it not, marked the climax of William Henry's brief boyhood.

Some maternal premonition can be read with hindsight into Mary Stuart's businesslike approach to the question of her son's future. But having reached a settlement, and left the States-General unctuously building a luxury yacht as a present for King Charles (it was called the *Mary* but was wrecked in fog off Anglesey in 1675 and not found again until 1971), the Princess Royal eagerly prepared for the great Stuart reunion in London. Long ago Mary had told friends: " The greatest punishment in the world would be to spend my whole life in Holland." She also confided to Mlle. de Montpensier that she would return to England to live as soon as Charles was restored, for she had a " horrible aversion " to Holland. In September the Prince of Orange was again brought back from Leyden to embrace his mother before she left. A tremor of remorse and apprehension seized her as William Henry advanced into his mother's presence. He was not quite 10 years old! Roughly the age at which she had left England, a fretting child on whom homesickness weighed so heavily that she wept herself to sleep. In the eighteen years which had passed since then her brother's cause had been her own, all the perils and worry of it, the anxiety and the sorrow, the pouring out of money and jewels like so much sand thrown into a sea of want and longing.

The sight of her own son, so defenceless and so appealing, almost drove her to cancel her plans, but she looked forward so devoutly to this unique time, and had suffered so much to bring it to pass, that she must go on. She wept over him. In all the family leave-takings of her turbulent and unpredictable life this proved the hardest. From Helvoetsluys where she finally said farewell to William Henry on 29th September she wrote to the States-General making it clear that her son—" the being who is dearest to us in the world "—was now in Holland's care. Sailing was delayed by contrary winds, but finally all was ready for the great adventure. Mary's heart fluttered with excitement. But as she stepped aboard a message was handed to Lady Stanhope. In the ominous silence which fell upon the royal party Mary, suddenly pale, whispered, " In God's name, what has gone amiss?"

Amiss indeed. Her brother Henry had died of smallpox in London a few days earlier.

Was nothing ever to go right for her family? Mary wished herself dead. Throughout the stormy crossing she kept to her cabin. Once when the ship seemed likely to founder she uttered not a word; she seemed dumb with grief. Constantly a vision of the 20-year-old Duke of Gloucester rose in her mind's eye, alternating with that of the white face of little William Henry as he had kissed her good-bye. She arrived at Dover in deepest black, and after a sorrowful but affectionate welcome from the King and the Duke of York at Whitehall she again wrote to the States-General beseeching them to protect and guard her fatherless son, remembering how her youngest brother's disorganised life had been buffeted about by the whims of others. She even saw his death as a judgement on her mother for having tried to convert Harry to Rome.

Thus Mary Stuart returned to her homeland as she had left it, tremulous and in tears, and every bit as apprehensive of the future as she had been in 1642. Ironically she felt homesick for the Netherlands. The ' gay ' London of Charles II irked her, fear of smallpox haunted her, while the autumnal mists which brought strange poisons floating up from the wide, brackish and softly flowing Thames affected her chest. Clad in mourning weeds, she was reading the Bible in her apartments one day when despatches arrived from De Witt with a proposal that William should be transferred from Leyden to live at the Binnenhof under his new ' guardian ', the State of Holland, and that his governor shoud be replaced by another less attached to the House of Orange. The Princess Royal agreed to William Henry's residence at the palace, but absolutely forbade the removal of his governor, for she saw in that proposition the ever-avenging hand of De Witt, who lived with the memory of Lovestein to his dying day.

Mary's distrust of the State of Holland's chief administrator did not extend to the United Provinces as a whole, and when Dutch envoys came to seek her intercession in another matter she was more than kind. The emissaries sought a renewal of their former alliance with England and wished to quicken the negotiations. At their behest Mary dictated a letter to the King. She described herself as " a fellow citizen " of the United Netherlands and besought him in diplomatic phrases: "Most worthy brother, nothing is more conducive to the progress of religion, the increase of trade, and the power to keep back every enemy by water and by land, than the mutual friendship and the confidence of the two people; on the one hand, the first step towards war leads to destruction and ruin, on the other, by taking the path which I humbly pray Your Majesty to follow, we go on the good way which leads to all safety and prosperity and advantage, such as I can better conceive than express."

She was unsuccessful.

Charles treated his sister with warmth and compassion, and Londoners made much of her. But for the Stuarts troubles never arrived in single numbers. As though the shock of Henry's death were not enough, a few days earlier James had secretly married Edward Hyde's daughter Anne at the Chancellor's residence, Worcester House. The duke's chaplain, Dr. Crowther, officiated. Anne had been in Mary's household while James was visiting. At the time of her marriage she was eight months advanced with child and James, bursting into the King's presence, blurted out the facts on his knees. Charles was surprised, probably because he doubted the heir presumptive's ability to make love adequately to any woman of spirit; hitherto the King's view of his brother was that his priests had given him mistresses as a penance. But Hyde appeared even more dumbfounded than the King. He tore his hair, historians claim, and hoped Parliament would make an end of Anne by expediting her execution, a sentiment which convinced many people that he was mad, as the marriage was thought to have been of his conniving. James with a regrettable lack of chivalry affected to believe that Anne had been unfaithful with other men. The King was the only one who acted with any sense in this crisis. He not only visited her in her confinement but also created her child Duke of Cambridge when the baby made its short-lived appearance on the world stage in October, and he created her father Earl of Clarendon. There nevertheless seems to have been some truth in reports that Anne was inconstant.

Mary arrived on the scene between the marriage and the birth and viciously denounced the bride-mother as a whore, swearing that the child was the bastard of James's equerry, Charles Berkeley. In her passion for character-assassination she was presently joined by Henrietta Maria—now " a very plain, old woman " at the age of 51—who arrived soon after her unwelcome grandson's birth. The two royal ladies, united in their hatred of the Hydes, did everything in their power to wreck the marriage, which the Queen Mother condemned as " a foul disgrace to the Royal Family ". She vowed that " whenever that woman should be brought to Whitehall by one door, she herself would leave the palace by another and never enter it again." Mary declared she would " never yield precedence to a girl who had stood as a servant behind her chair ". One historian has remarked dryly that after these unedifying and ineffective examples of royal grace, harmony was restored in the Royal Family by the sudden deaths of Henry of Gloucester—and of Mary.

The controversy had barely faded when towards the end of December 1660 the Princess Royal fell into a burning fever. In a few days she was delirious with the smallpox. On Christmas Eve, between bouts of unconsciousness, she confessed that she had lied about Anne, Duchess of York. Having removed that stain from her conscience, for she remained a devout high Anglican to the end, she composed herself for death, but even in the calm before her soul flew she uttered never a word to confirm or refute the story of her own marriage to or liaison with Harry Jermyn, and their exact relationship remains a mystery to this day. Nor did she send any personal message to her son, who, unaware of her condition, sat at his desk the day before she died composing his first Latin epistle to his Uncle Charles, whom he praised as " a Prince who is the paragon of our age, a Prince who is my Uncle and guardian, and who now holds my precious mother in his treasure-house ". When the letter reached the King his sister had followed their brother Harry to the Stuart tomb in Westminster Abbey, where they would be followed just over ten years later by the maligned Anne Hyde. One of the elegies written in the Princess Royal's memory was from the pen of the young John Dryden at Cambridge University. The Queen ·of Bohemia broke the news to William Henry, who sorrowed so grievously that a subsequent attack of asthma nearly killed him.

All Mary's possessions at Whitehall were faithfully catalogued, down to her black velvet Bible-bag, but at her places in Holland the English servants before they sailed back to England ransacked her personal effects. The Dutch people genuinely mourned their late Stadtholder's proud and haughty but respected wife, whose life since childhood had been lived more under the shadow of tragedy than in happiness.

" All heere from the highest to the lowest ", wrote Elizabeth, " are verie sorrie for her. I shall neuer forgett her memorie; we liued almost 20 yeares together and always loued one another."

Whether the " all heere " embraced Amalia is doubtful, for no one now stood between her and the course she had plotted for her grandson. Yet neither she nor her daughter-in-law foresaw that William Henry would become Stadtholder of the Netherlands ten years later and occupy the English throne with James's daughter—Clarendon's grand-daughter!—eighteen years after that. Lord Craven wrote to Queen Elizabeth two months after Mary's death that she was as much forgotten in Whitehall " as if she had never been ".

But Charles remembered. How could he ever forget? In her will the Princess Royal had enjoined the King and their mother to take upon them the care of her son, and when the Prince of Orange ten years later visited Mary's tomb the King found him startlingly like his mother.

Anne of Orange

I

FORTY-EIGHT YEARS elapsed between the death of the first and the birth of the second Princess Royal. The Hanoverians had not yet succeeded to the English throne when in their ancient German capital the Electoral Princess Caroline, on 9th October 1709, presented the future George II with their third child and first daughter. Named Anne after her godmother, England's reigning queen, she was destined to be treated no more kindly by historians than had been her Stuart predecessor, whom she resembled in over-weening pride and hatred of Holland, which was also to be her adopted country. As a maiden she wished her elder brothers, the unfortunate Frederick Lewis and the Duke of Cumberland, out of the way so that she might succeed as Queen Regnant.

" I would die tomorrow to be Queen today," she informed her astonished mother.

To the lower orders she yielded nothing of grace and little of favour. While she was yet quite young Anne used to make a lady-in-waiting stand at her bedside every night reading aloud until she fell asleep. One night the Princess Royal was so long falling off that her lady swooned with fatigue in mid-chapter. Queen Caroline, who in her wisdom found much to deplore in the Hanoverian whom she had wed and some of the children they had bred, called Anne to her bedside the next night and asked her to read to her.

" No, no," she said as the Princess Royal reached out for a chair, " —read to me standing. . . . I can hear better."

From time to time Anne paused from tiredness or dry throat, but the Queen urged her on. " It entertains me." " Continue, pray continue! " " I am not tired yet of listening."

At last the princess sobbed, " I feel very faint."

A homily followed but, as historians have sadly observed, Caroline's disquisition on the penalties of selfishness were ignored; Anne carried her vexatious ways to the grave. After all, in childhood and youth she was surrounded by some rather dubious characters at Kensington Palace and Hampton Court. It was not surprising that she turned out to be more unpleasant than most of those who influenced her life.

For instance, she could scarcely have benefited from contact with her grandfather, George I, who had locked up his wife, Sophia Dorothea, in a fortress at Ahlden, probably because she had infected him with the pox, although the facts behind his inhuman treatment of her remain obscure. Her son never spoke of her. Indeed, the second George never spoke of his father if he could avoid it, either. George I had entertained, but later discarded, a plot to kidnap his son and send him to America rather than allow him to succeed to the English throne. George II liked the regal state. Anne was in her eighteenth year when he acceded. She was presumably created Princess Royal almost at once. She was old enough to appreciate her father's pleasure in kingship of a dual monarchy as he puffed and pouted about his business, red in the face, inclined to stoutness, a rather comical figure who suffered from piles but was honest in his dealings, even in the meticulous detail with which he reported to his long-suffering Queen why mistresses were so essential to his peace of mind. But his heart was never in England, always he longed to visit Hanover, which he frequently did, and once when his bishops bothered him about the Quakers Bill he spluttered, " I am sick to death of all their foolish stuff, and vish mit all my heart zat ze Devil may take all your bishops, and ze Devil take your minister, and ze Devil take ze Parliament, and ze Devil take ze whole island, provided I can get out of it and go back to Hanover."

As a father he barely tolerated his offspring—" I did not love zem when they were young; I hated to see zem running into my room." Later he came to love them " as vell as most fathers ", although he was apt to kick his hat and wig around the room if they annoyed him. Anne inherited his selfish and stubborn nature and possibly his conceit and that streak of sadism which ladies-in-waiting had plenty of opportunity to study at first hand as they attended their mistress.

Queen Caroline, an amiable woman generally regarded as one of the finest consorts any king ever had, endured not only her family but the gout. But George hated illness either in himself or in others. No one must admit to feeling unwell. Sickness was to be walked off, or thumped out of the system, or ridden out of sight and mind on a good, strong-boned horse. Whenever he wished to walk, all must walk, too. One day when the Queen was in the agonies of gout she plunged her hot, swollen feet into cold water to reduce the swelling and get into her boots in time to trail around with the royal master. George firmly held that Charles II had been governed by his mistresses, James II by his priests, William III by his ministers, and Queen Anne by her women. And he craftily inquired who governed now. Who, indeed? For everyone knew it was the clever Queen, through the even cleverer Robert Walpole, who had invented the cult of the Prime Minister—*primus inter pares*, forsooth!

Few more indulgent women than Caroline ever lived. George had a passion for mistresses. Having collected them, he ran them off their legs. His daily walks with Mrs. Howard, later Lady Suffolk, were part of his life. In Hanover he loved Madame de Walmoden, whom he created Duchess of Yarmouth; and Lady Deloraine, his children's governess, solaced his English days for a time. These and others Caroline tolerated, concealing her distaste. She had always her dear, precious Hervey to comfort and amuse her and say witty things and write witty little sketches to please her. If George II is remembered for little else his remark at Caroline's deathbed when she urged him to marry again—" No, I shall have ze mistresses "—will ever be regarded as a quaint commentary upon the vagaries of royal companionship. The Queen, whose early education had been influenced by men of learning in Berlin, could curse like a trooper. As a rule she found plenty to curse about. After all, she could have married Charles, the future Emperor of Austria. But if there was one thing even more dreaded in Hanoverian Protestant circles than an abdication or a royal birth out of wedlock is was conversion to or marriage into the Roman Catholic Church. So Catholic Charles fretted his way out of her life and she stepped into George's in 1705 when he was Electoral Prince of Hanover. All their married life Caroline subordinated her inclinations to her husband, for as Hervey remarked: " For all the tedious hours she spent alone in watching him whilst he slept or the heavier task of entertaining him whilst he was awake, her single consolation was in reflecting she had power."

When she died the King was inconsolable—" I never yet saw a woman worthy to buckle her shoe." He loved Caroline so devoutly that her coffin was left open-sided so that when his own time came his own open-sided casket might be slid in beside her. These high sentiments did not prevent his begging Anne to send Madame de Walmoden to him from the Continent to comfort her father on his sad loss.

In the pursuit of love, if that is what it can be called, the King never paused to consider the effect of his comical amours on Anne and her sisters. They loved their mother, a warm-hearted woman, whose love was put to a remarkable test early in her motherhood when Lady Mary Wortley Montagu on returning from the Near East in 1721 remarked on the beneficial effects of inoculation for the smallpox, which had carried off so many members of earlier royal families. Six criminals under sentence of death were spared on condition that they allowed themselves to be pocked. When this experiment succeeded Anne and her sisters were inoculated by Dr. Mead.

Yet Caroline, the loving mother in so much else, abhorred her first-born son and obdurately rejected him to the day of her death, possibly because she felt she had to support the King, and the King's view of Frederick Lewis, Prince of Wales, is best expressed by his comment when Caroline died. Refusing the heir apparent permission to seek his dying mother's blessing and pardon, the King said, " I always hated the rascal, but now I hate him worse than ever."

The extraordinary antipathy which poisoned relations between the King and his father George I was reproduced in George II's reign and was to be projected into the reign of his grandson George III. It was said that George II cared no more for his son than he did for a louse. He cut his annual allowance to £24,000, although he himself as Prince of Wales had enjoyed an income nearly four times that sum. Anne loathed her brother as much as her parents and her sisters are said to have done. Their aversion extended even to culture. George II hated all writers and artists, whom he called puppies and fools, but he liked Germans. Anne admired Handel and frequently patronised his appearances at the Haymarket theatre. This was enough for Frederick Lewis to denounce the composer and for the King and Queen to side with Anne. Her brother formed a rival musical circle at another opera house. The sycophants around him, taking a chance on future favours when he should succeed his father, crowded around him at the opera house in Lincoln's Inn Fields, while Anne and her parents sat " freezing constantly at the empty Haymarket opera."

Walpole tried vainly to reconcile father and son, although the only present he ever received from the King for his pains was a diamond which he later found to be cracked. But he came to the conclusion that Frederick Lewis was " a poor, weak, irresolute, false, lying, dishonest, contemptible wretch, that nobody loves, that nobody will trust, that nobody believes, and that will trust nobody by turns, and that everybody by turns will impose upon, betray, mislead, and plunder." Money, or the deprivation of it, was probably a root cause of the estrangement between monarch and heir. Frederick Lewis was never really allowed to love his pig-headed parent, who ordered him to be left behind in Hanover when Anne and her younger brother and two younger sisters were transferred to England by their parents in the wake of George I. Then again, when George II reigned in England, the Prince of Wales was replaced by his mother as Regent during his father's absences in Hanover. It was enough to try the patience of a more saintly character than Frederick Lewis. While Lady Bristol found him " the most agreeable young man it is possible to imagine," Hervey remarked that it was his fate to be detested by his father, despised by his mother, betrayed by his sisters and oppressed by his brother Cumberland.

This Duke of Cumberland was to gratify his eldest sister, with her delusions of majesty, by effectively terminating the Stuart resistance to the Hanoverians. In the process of eliminating the claims of Bonnie Prince Charlie the Duke was blamed for the large number of Scottish prisoners of war who were put to the sword. He denied the slander, but went down in Jacobite history as the Butcher of Culloden. Three years earlier at Dettingen he had retired wounded from the field on which his father earned such distinction when, his horse having fled without him, the King flourished his sword at the whole French army with consummate aplomb.

The court of George II was inexpressibly dull, and upon the Sovereign's five daughters the dullness pressed heavily. Three of the princesses—Anne, Amelia Sophia Eleanora (sometimes called Emily) and Caroline Elizabeth—were born in Hanover between 1709 and 1713; Mary, in 1723, and Louisa, in 1724, first opened their eyes in England. Marriage released the youngest pair and their eldest sister from the stifling formality of life at Kensington Palace and Hampton Court, but for the unmarried Amelia and Caroline there was no escape from the iron routine imposed by a well-meaning King who talked on every topic interesting to him, or played at commerce or backgammon, while Queen Caroline knotted and yawned, and courtiers fawned. Amelia and the future Frederick the Great were betrothed in their cradles, but the negotiations, proceeding on and off through the reigns of George I and his son, eventually broke down.

In some ways Amelia was almost as arrogant as the Princess Royal. Even the great Nash had to dance attendance on her and her little court at Bath. When she became Ranger of Richmond Park she closed it against the public until a lawsuit forced its reopening. She was deterred from closing St. James's Park by Robert Walpole, who, when she asked him what it would cost, replied dryly, " Only a crown, Madame." Deprived of marriage, she grew into an eccentric spinster with mannish airs, accentuated by a German riding habit in which she was wont to stamp about her room as she swallowed the breakfast chocolate or coffee. The only real light in her life came from a love affair with Charles II's grandson, the Duke of Grafton—" almost a slobberer, and without one good quality," as Swift so generously described him —but marriage was out of the question. They frequently hunted together and sometimes contrived to ' lose ' their attendants in Windsor Forest. Amelia outlived most of her family and in old age kept to her London house in Cavendish Square; as her grand-nephew George III feared her tongue she was discouraged from attending his court. She was buried near Mary Stuart of Orange in Westminster Abbey.

When Princess Caroline was 2 years old the Queen offered the poet Gay a post of gentleman-usher to this baby. The ludicrous proposal was demolished by Swift. Caroline was the loveliest of the sisters and superior to them all in sweetness of disposition. It was her misfortune to fall in love with one of the most elegant opportunists of the day, Queen Caroline's ' pet '—John, Lord Hervey of Ickworth, who at the age of 24 married a woman of the court, Mary Lepell, and procreated eight children. Mrs. Hall in her book castigates Hervey as a man who won the heart of young Caroline—" this fair young creature "—to gratify either his vanity or his ambition. In other words, this " painted child of dirt," as Pope out of malice called his ' Sporus ', repaid the Queen's patronage by exciting her daughter's hopeless attachment, and when he carried off the bold and pert Lepell he undoubtedly shortened the princess's life. She declined into melancholy after Hervey's death in 1743, and yet found some consolation for her lost love by virtually adopting his children. The grave closed over her at 45. In her will she left " my dear sister Anne" an enamelled case " and two bottles of the same sort ".

Life treated Anne's sister Mary even more harshly than Caroline. At the age of 17 Mary married Frederick Prince of Hesse-Cassel, who turned out to be a regular viper in the Hanoverian bosom, for he converted to Rome, upon which it is said " his bad temper increased ". Victorian writers in particular have been most scathing about this particular Frederick, for it is no light thing for a girl of nice Protestant scruples to find herself in bed with a man who turned out to be, in George II's words, " a brutal German, obstinate, of no genius ". Mary withdrew to the white palace of Rumpenheim on the River Main near Frankfurt after her husband's intolerable defection: the retreat was built for her, and after her time it became a meeting-place for the Hesse-Cassel family and their numerous relations.

Anne's youngest sister Louisa married Frederick V of Denmark, who gave her four children and plagued her with his mistresses. But she accepted her burdens philosophically, never complained to her family and died meekly at the age of 27 from the effects of neglected rupture, the same malady from which her mother perished.

Blessed with two sons and five daughters, George and Caroline should have been happy indeed, but they were not. The King's lamentable punctuality—his custom of arriving at assignations watch in hand so that he should be neither exactly early nor exactly late—was allied to a suffocating etiquette which sorely taxed the nerves of his equerries. Escape from this atmosphere became the ardent desire of all his daughters as they grew up. They dreamed of marriage, they talked of marriage, they planned marriage. The younger ones looked imploringly to sister Anne to make the first move and release them from unendurable bondage. But the Princess Royal could not marry just anybody. Her station in life forbade it. Queenship, as we have seen, was her target. At 16 her heart soared at the mention of Louis XV's name. A marriage contract was actually drawn up. All seemed settled. Then the inconstant French suddenly insisted that the bride should first be received into the Latin Church. Thus died Anne's hopes of presiding over the fortunes of France. For her Paris was not worth a Mass, and after salvaging her wounded pride she settled down to await a suitor whose religion would be no bar to marital felicity.

Such a swain was at length discovered in the modest person of William IV of Orange, a grand-nephew of William III through the Friesian branch of the House of Nassau. Portraits of the young royals were exchanged and the fourth Earl of Chesterfield, author of the famous Letters, who was British ambassador at The Hague, beavered away to bring about a union with—so the King later assured Parliament—" a family and name always dear to this nation ". But the King had privately warned Anne that William was " the ugliest man in Holland ". That he was not the most handsome the Princess Royal was well aware, and she did not care.

" If he were a Dutch baboon I would marry him," she replied.

This pretty little interview ended with the King's promising that she would " find him baboon enough ". The egocentric Hervey could see no joy at all in such a wedding, if only because Chesterfield had had a hand in it. Where Hervey had shifted his ground to win Caroline's lasting favour and the confidence of the King and Walpole, the earl had backed the wrong horse in Mrs. Howard when her lover was Prince of Wales, and consequently had incurred the Queen's undying enmity and Walpole's indifference. Hervey made the most of William's wry neck and halting gait, and of his comparative penury, to disparage Chesterfield's diplomacy. At that time the Prince was 22, but his character has been distorted by Hervey's malicious description of him

Anne of Orange,
Princess Royal

William IV of Orange

Caroline of Ansbach,
Queen to George II,
from the studio of
Jervas

John Lord Hervey of
Ickworth, from the
studio of J. B. Van
Loo

and by his glancing blow at the Princess Royal in this passage of his rambling memoirs:

The Prince of Orange's figure, beside his being almost a dwarf, was as much deformed as it was possible for a human creature to be; his face was not bad, his countenance was sensible, but his breath more offensive than it is possible for those who have not been offended by it to imagine. These personal defects, unrecompensed by the *éclat* of rank or the more essential comforts of great riches, made the situation of the poor Princess-Royal so much more commiserable; for as her youth and an excellent warm, animated constitution made her, I believe, now and then remember she was a woman, so I can answer for her that natural and acquired pride seldom or never let her forget she was a Princess; and as this match gave her very little hope of gratifying the one, so it afforded as little prospect of supporting the other.

He alleged that Anne accepted William because marriage was better than unmarriage—that she had to decide whether to be "wedded to this piece of deformity in Holland, or die an ancient maid immured in her royal convent at St. James's", where she would be at the mercy of her elder brother and his wife, Augusta of Saxe-Gotha, when they should become King and Queen. These passages irresistibly suggest that Hervey at one time chanced his arm with the not unattractive Princess Royal and was spurned. Chesterfield was much kinder to her Dutch suitor and, reporting on an interview with the Prince of Orange, said: "I think he has extreme good parts. He is perfectly well bred, and civil to everybody, and with an ease and freedom that is seldom acquired but by a long knowledge of the world. His face is handsome; his shape is not so advantageous as could be wished, though not near so bad as I had heard represented. He assumes not the least dignity, but has all the affability and insinuation that is necessary for a person who would raise himself in a popular government."

Government in a popular or democratic sense was destined to be a stranger to William, who was by breeding an aristocrat, and to that extent Chesterfield gravely underestimated his character. But not even the elegant earl could pretend that the mention of William's name was calculated to send a Lombard Street merchant into transports of joy. His estate was lumbered with debt and he could scarcely lay his hands on a round £12,000 a year, a

F

bagatelle compared with the vast incomes commanded by the House of Orange in the previous century. Holland had fallen into sad decline after William III's death. The fourth William had become Stadtholder of Friesland at the age of 7, and later of Groningen. He was still a minor when the Treaty of Utrecht ended the War of the Spanish Succession in 1713. Colonial revenues had withered, and as a result of unwise speculation many formerly rich families had been bankrupted. The Dutch had slowly gone soft, the great merchant princes had been replaced by guilder-grubbing retailers, and one author commented: " Nobody thought now of portraying the Hollander as the rough, round, horny-handed seadog, but rather as the prosperous seller of cheeses, with a Gouda pipe in his mouth and hands in his pocket, calmly collecting or enjoying his profits."

A daunting prospect indeed. But, as Hervey implied, Anne's choice lay between Holland and Hell, and as a good Protestant she was prepared to embrace the one to avoid the other. In the long run it seems to have made little difference to the course of British history.

So this " miserable match both in point of man and fortune ", in Hervey's phrase, went forward during 1733. Parliament voted Anne £80,000, double the previous rate for this kind of jointure. The outlay was covered by the sale of lands in the little-known island of St. Christopher, and as these moneys had not been appropriated by Parliament it was a simple matter for the nation's legislators to be generous. The decision incensed the Frederick Lewis set. The Prince of Wales, beholden to his father for every grudged groat, naturally considered that as the Sovereign's eldest child he had a prior right to a parliamentary allowance. His partisans threatened to demand £100,000. The threat came to nothing but it contributed to the turbulence of a session in which the affairs of the South Sea Company since its provident rescue by Walpole played no small part, and everyone, from the King downwards, sighed with relief when at last Parliament got up at the end of June. On the day before this useful and overdue exercise William was given one of three vacant Garters —the other two went to the Duke of Devonshire and Lord Wilmington—and the day after Lords and Commons dispersed the Royal Family departed to Richmond and thereafter to Hampton Court.

From then and for the rest of the year, with Parliament up and no visible mischief being done, the prevailing topic from cottage to court and from crofter's hearth to country mansion was the impending marriage of the Princess Royal.

II

It HAD taken an unconscionable time to arrange, thanks to " the dilatoriness of the King, the indifference of his Ministers, and the tardy phlegm of Dutch negotiators ", according to Hervey; and autumn fell before Horace Walpole, the Prime Minister's younger brother and not to be confused with his tattling nephew of Strawberry Hill, was dispatched to The Hague to escort William to England aboard an English yacht. Walpole at the age of 55 was hardly cast for the role of Cupid, but he was by eighteenth-century standards an honest and straightforward diplomat, and the Prince of Orange arrived without incident at Greenwich on 7th November and was lodged at Somerset House in the Strand.

Now for the first time the public were able to testify the truth of rumours that the King was opposed to the match, which he considered to be beneath his daughter's dignity. It explained the long delay. It explained why not one single salute gun was fired, why not one soldier appeared on parade. Lord Lovelace waited at the landing-stage at Greenwich with a modest coach from the royal mews. On the night of William's arrival the King was persuaded with the utmost difficulty to send Hervey to present his compliments to the prince. On his return from this mission the faithful chamberlain was summoned by Queen Caroline, who wished " to know without disguise what sort of animal she was to prepare herself to see." Hervey assured her the prince was not as bad as he had imagined—" that she must not expect to see an Adonis, that his body was as bad as possible but that his countenance was far from disagreeable and his address sensible, engaging and noble; that he seemed entirely to forget his person, and to have an understanding to make other people forget it too."

On the other hand, the Princess Royal had some claims to beauty, including a lively clean look and a very fine although faintly cicatrised complexion. However, at the age of 24, slightly older than her bridegroom, she was rather inclined to embonpoint or, as Hervey chivalrously exaggerated, showed " a great propensity to fat." Anne reacted to the arrival of the betrothed more calmly than the rest of the Royal Family. She made no move to greet William, but remained in her own apartment at St. James's playing the harpsichord with musicians and singers from the Haymarket opera. The Queen observed that her daughter had been as easy all that afternoon as she had ever seen her.

" For my part," said Caroline, " I never said the least word to encourage her to this marriage or to dissuade her from it; the King left her, too, absolutely at liberty to accept or reject it. . . . She was resolved, if it was a monkey, she would marry him."

When later Hervey confided his personal impressions of William to the princesses, Caroline playfully referred to her future brother-in-law as " the animal ". But from ordinary Londoners the Prince of Orange received a more respectful welcome than the one accorded his predecessor William II nearly a century earlier. Next day when he set out for the palace he passed through streets throbbing with cheers. Men and women of fashion thronged the courtyard of St. James's. Some were unaware of the King's incivility to William or they would have been less anxious in that age of sycophancy and corruption to be seen bowing the knee and curtseying to Anne's chosen. But a wedding was a wedding and fashionable London was prepared to do it justice. Tailors and dressmakers were drawn unprotestingly into the service of the great ones invited to the ceremony, which was to take place in the French Chapel at St. James's Palace on the Monday after William had submitted himself to inspection by the Royal Family. All was ready by the Sunday, a small fortune having been laid out in wax candles to drive away the November gloom, when a messenger galloped across the western suburbs with the news from Somerset House. The prince had been taken ill in the night with a fever and in no circumstances could he leave his bed.

The wedding was postponed.

Inconsiderate critics have suggested that his illness was brought on by the glacial atmosphere of the London court and that he contracted an almost fatal chill from the frosty glares of his future in-laws. Whatever the cause, William tossed for some weeks between life and death. He was unable to leave his room before Christmas.

" During this tedious and dangerous illness," Hervey reported, " no one of the royal family went to see him. The King thought it below his dignity and the rest, whatever they thought, were not allowed to do it."

The prince's Dutch retinue loudly inveighed against this infamous treatment; but William, reminding them that beggars cannot be choosers, accepted the indignities which the Hanoverians knew so well how to inflict upon those of lesser rank and glory. The general feeling at St. James's was that Anne had chosen a dud, and as he might die at any moment there was no more to be said. It is inconceivable that the Princess Royal did not cause daily inquiries to be made of his progress, and as soon as he was well at the end of December she invited him to visit the palace incognito. There he probably even embraced his fiancée, but as Hervey was not present we shall never know; and he followed up with a simple game of cards in which Anne, Frederick Lewis and their sisters Amelia and Caroline participated. These performances were repeated. Some gaiety was thus injected into the staid life of George II's court, and even the King unbent sufficiently to play backgammon with the young people, though it was also said that when he heard that William had dined with his daughters he told them to break off that highly venturesome practice.

William was sent at first to Kensington for the air and then to Bath for the waters. What was Anne's attitude to all this flummery? Hervey had something to say of it: " On his arrival in England—and the day for the marriage being appointed— on its being put off—on his illness—on his recovery—on his being in danger—or on his being out of it—the countenance of the Princess Royal to the nicest examiners appeared exactly the same; which surprised everybody so much the more as she was known to be of a temper to which nothing was really indifferent, whatever it appeared."

After a month's tasting of the waters, and lionising by dear

Mr. Nash and the ladies of Bath, the Prince of Orange in February drove to Oxford, where he dined and wined joyfully and was given an honorary degree. At last a date for the wedding was fixed—24th March 1734—and the beau monde breathed more easily. It had been a racking interlude, especially as Frederick Lewis had added to the perplexities of royal life with his caballing: the rupture between him and the King was now so serious that there was never any prospect of restoring harmony while George reigned. The Prince of Wales also galled his mother. Somehow without meaning it he " tore the flesh off her bones with hot irons ". The gulf between them widened unbridgeably. She denounced him as " a nauseous beast and the greatest liar that ever lived."

Parliament had assembled again and was gratified to hear from Hervey, moving the Address in the Lords, that England was " prosperous at home and considerable abroad," largely because of the King's caution, prudence and foresight. Indeed, George II seemed to have only one disgruntled subject, and she was the widow of the Duke of Marlborough. Sarah Churchill had found the postponement of Anne's wedding unbearable. Among the street ' furniture ' erected for the occasion a boarded gallery had been set up the previous November close to the windows of Marlborough House in The Mall. The hideous red-brick mansion, gloomy enough on the brightest summer's day, was starved of even the slight infiltration of winter's light to which is was clearly entitled.

" I wish the Princess would oblige me," swore the formidable forebear of Sir Winston Churchill, " by taking away her *Orange chest.*"

From October when the original wedding day was arranged until almost the day of the postponed ceremony in March the Irish peers engaged in a running battle about precedence with the English and Scottish members of the Lords. The dispute arose mainly because Irish earls and viscounts refused to walk behind inferior English barons in the nuptial processions. Finally order was restored. The processions through a covered way from the palace to the chapel were timed for seven o'clock on the night of 24th March. By that hour the bridegroom and all the males had assembled in the Great Council Chamber and the bride with all the ladies in the Great Drawing-Room like so many bees about to swarm. The King and Queen with the Royal Family and the court hirelings waited in the King's Lesser Drawing-Room. William, almost choking on his new Collar of the Garter, wore a rich suit of cloth of gold and, Hervey noted, was " a less shocking and less ridiculous figure in this pompous procession and at supper than one could naturally have expected such an Aesop, in such trappings and such eminence, to have appeared." The reference is obviously to the Greek fabulist's traditional ugliness and deformity and not to his fables. Hervey further noted that William had " a long peruke like hair that flowed all over his back, and hid the roundness of it; and as his countenance was not bad, there was nothing very strikingly disagreeable about his stature ".

Anne with her shining blonde hair beneath a twinkling coronet was a radiant bride in " virgin robes of silver tissue, having a train six yards long." Ten virgins attended her, the daughters of dukes and earls—Fanny Manners, Caroline Campbell, Louisa Bertie, Caroline and Anne Pierpoint, Betty Seymour, Ann Cecil, Di Gray, Caroline D'Arcy and Fanny Montagu. All were sheathed in silver tissue. The processions to and from the chapel were " splendid and magnificent," led by the bridegroom's, preceded by " a numerous and well-appointed band ", with the sergeant-trumpeter at their head. The band filed off at the chapel entrance to return for the later processions, those of Anne and of the Sovereign and his Consort and their retinues. Within the candle-bright chapel, whose scarlet-draped galleries held 4,000 of the favoured, everyone was seated according to rank.

Even Gulliver could not have done justice to the scene. A throne had been erected to the right of the elaborate altar, with two chairs of state for Their Majesties. Next to the throne was a canopy of state for Frederick Lewis, Cumberland, Amelia and Caroline. The two younger princesses were cordoned off from the lesser order in a gallery. Two chairs of state faced the throne and on these, after the Bishop of London had performed the rites of holy matrimony " according to the Church of England ", the newly-married couple sat enthralled listening to an anthem composed by Anne's music master, Handel, for the occasion. Organ music, brilliant dresses and uniforms, regimental airs from a band posted in one of the galleries, and the multi-branched chandelier spreading their glow over the animated but reverent scene, completed one of the most superb royal wedding pageants London had ever seen. George II had certainly done well for his eldest girl, they said, considering how parsimoniously he usually behaved towards her. No doubt he considered that a magnificent wedding was sufficient compensation for her marriage to a ' baboon '. It had cost him a pretty penny, and so he merely gave her as her portion " a thousand kisses and a shower of tears, but not one guinea " out of his own pocket.

On their return to the Lesser Drawing-Room the bride and bridegroom knelt to receive the blessing of the King and Queen. At eleven o'clock the Royal Family supped in the Great State Ballroom, the King and Queen under a canopy at the head of the table, with Frederick Lewis, Cumberland and the bridegroom at the right hand and the bride, Amelia, Caroline and Mary at the left. Two hours later William and Anne retired to the bridal chamber and were later discovered, according to the singular custom of the day, sitting up in bed " in rich undress " while the whole company passed before them in review. Custom stopped short at inviting the guests to remain while the marriage was consummated, but Hervey made much of William's nocturnal raiment.

" When he undressed," he noted, " and came in his nightgown and nightcap into the room to go to bed, the appearance he made was as indescribable as the astonished countenances of everybody who beheld him." From the shape of his brocaded gown and the " make of his back " he looked behind as if he had no head, and before as if he had no neck and no legs.

Hervey slept little that night, and next morning he dashed away to exchange confidences with the Queen. Speaking tearfully in French, Caroline expatiated upon the sight of her poor daughter in bed with " that monster "; but Hervey consoled her, " Oh! madam, in half a year all persons are all alike; the figure of the body one's married to, like the prospect of the place one lives at, grows so familiar to one's eyes, that one looks at it mechanically, without regarding either the beauties or deformities that strike a stranger."

The princesses also chattered vulgarly about William. They spoke " with horror of his figure and great commiseration of the fate of his wife." Amelia, knowing not that celibacy stretched timelessly before her, said nothing on earth would induce *her*

to marry " the monster ", and even the kindly Caroline thought
the whole thing " very bad ". Yet, as Hervey recalled, the
Princess Royal behaved to William as though he had been an
Adonis. She " made prodigious court to him, addressed everything
she said to him, and applauded everything he said to anybody
else ".

At this stage doubts about history's accepted judgement of the
Prince of Wales begin to creep in. Hervey, who can never be
regarded as an unbiased witness, thought Frederick Lewis
" forced himself to be tolerably civil " to William, but alleged
that he hardly ever spoke to Anne either in public or in private.
Yet a few days after the wedding William and his bride, with
the princesses, called on Herman Van Der Mijn, the portraitist
from Amsterdam, at his house in Cavendish Square to view his
paintings. William was so impressed with the work of the artist,
who was to become immortal for his *Peter Denying Christ*,
that he ordered a full-length canvas of himself to be painted in
Garter robes. The artist, who was in the habit of charging 500
guineas a time, a useful revenue even in those days, paid regular
visits to the Princess Royal's apartments at St. James's, and produced such a remarkable likeness—that is, he flattered William
—that the Prince of Wales was persuaded to sit for his portrait.
Anne was herself an artist of no little skill, and when Frederick
Lewis " as a mark of condescension and esteem " asked her to
draw the artist she " obligingly performed the drawing with a
delicate and masterly execution ". For a whole week afterwards
Frederick Lewis, although he was " not particularly pleased at the
Princess Royal having married before himself ", escorted his
brother-in-law to all the sights of London. The fact may be that
the heir apparent, to spite his father, took the despised brother-
in-law under his wing and tried to make his sister look ridiculous
by encouraging her to paint a painter. The more charitable view
is that in his journals Hervey tried to justify himself before history as one of the great figures of the age and did not much mind
whose character he blackened in the process.

Another of Hervey's butts was Lord Chesterfield. When Parliament passed Addresses congratulating the King and Queen on
their daughter's marriage, Chesterfield apparently thrust himself into the limelight, standing upon his right—" the greatest
impertinence "—as the eldest peer to deliver the message and

speak to the Queen, whom he had not seen " since he was turned out " of court. The Queen was to receive the document in her bed-chamber with " nobody present but the three messengers, her children and the servants in waiting " —and, of course, Lord Hervey, who reported: " Lord Chesterfield's speech was well written and well got by heart, and yet he delivered with a faltering voice, a face as white as a sheet, and every limb trembling with concern."

The earl's discomfort could be traced back to when Caroline was Princess of Wales and Chesterfield was in the habit of " ridiculing her with bitter jests, which stick long and deep in the memory of the great ". However, she had warned Chesterfield that she had " a most bitter tongue, and would certainly put him into debt of that kind with the most exorbitant interest ". And one can imagine the thin little upper lip moving beneath the sharp little nose in a vixenish leer. Hervey also construed messages from the City of London, Oxford University and other " disaffected towns and incorporated bodies " as pieces of impertinence in the guise of " complimental addresses " soaked in irony and satire. The tenor of them all, said Hervey, was to express their satisfaction in this match " from remembering how much this country was indebted to a Prince who bore the title of Orange; declaring their gratitude to his memory, and intimating, as plainly as they dared, how much they wished this man might follow the example of his great ancestor [sic], and one time or other *depose his father-in-law* in the same manner that King William had deposed his [James II] ". The lyrical quality of the City of London's address may be savoured from the lines:

> We therefore hope that young Nassau,
> Whom you have chose your son-in-law,
> Will show himself of William's stock,
> And prove himself a chip of the same block.

Hervey goes on to point out that these rude addresses reflected the general unpopularity of the court and that Frederick Lewis, who supposed himself the idol of the people, was fully as unpopular as his parents. The Prince of Wales was therefore dismayed when, on escorting his brother-in-law to theatres and operas, the galleries " only made a little clapping " when he entered, but burst into peals of shouts and huzzas when William appeared. The King also felt irked when, glancing through his window at St. James's Palace, he saw his son-in-law on opera nights ushered out through Holbein's entrance with "incessant halooing", while his own chair followed at a decent interval "through empty and silent streets". In fact the people had not entirely thrown off their Jacobitism—the Forty-five was yet to come—and so detested a King who seemed to prefer Hanover to his island domain that they might have wished "another William" to supersede him on the London throne. George was also uneasy about the outcome of the pending parliamentary election, and with good reason.

Much of the King's time was therefore spent in devising means to get William and his bride out of the country. Parliament was persuaded before the dissolution to rush through a bill naturalising the Prince of Orange and to approve the King's intention to settle £5,000 a year on Anne for her life or until her father's death. But William had problems at home. Like William III at the same age he was Stadtholder only of a small part of the Netherlands—Friesland, Groningen and Guelderland—and the State of Holland was as much opposed to him as it had been to his great-uncle. Messages reached him at St. James's conveying the hope that he would not think to pass through Holland to Friesland, but would go direct there by sea, as there was the danger of a populace rising in his favour. Horace Walpole secured permission for William and Anne to land at Rotterdam and to proceed to Amsterdam "with the utmost expedition and privacy" in order to re-embark there for Friesland. The generous impulses of the leaders of Holland were severely taxed even to offer a military guard to Anne should she pass through The Hague on any future journey to England, but they shrank from extending a similar courtesy to William. Poor Horace, whose wife shouted and stank, which made her "offensive to nose and ears", did the best for his royal client.

But Hervey, perceiving that the King, in his anxiety to be rid of his daughter and her husband, now treated William with a little more civility, veered towards the Prince of Orange and secured his consent to stand sponsor with the Princesses Amelia and Caroline to his latest baby daughter, who was consequently christened Emily Caroline Nassau and lived to be 80 in spite of it.

III

THERE ENSUED perhaps the most remarkable exhibition of filial affection in the annals of the Hanoverian dynasty. Anne, after the first flush of nuptial ardour, found the tug of parting from her family too much. The Queen wept for three whole days, it was claimed. On 22nd April the bridal couple embarked at Gravesend for Holland and on the Queen's orders Hervey saw them off.

"Never was there a more melancholy parting than between her Royal Highness and all her family, except her brother [Frederick Lewis], who took no leave of her at all, and desired the Prince of Orange to let her know his reason for omitting it was the fear of touching her too much."

The yacht was windbound in the river and Hervey had plenty of time to observe the proprieties and to discuss international politics and other weighty matters with the Princess Royal. The chances of a Continental war, if possible with Spain or one of the other non-Protestant nations, always aroused the liveliest expectations of victory and profit in the breasts of the early Hanoverians, and one could never tell just when the Jacobites would launch out on some squalid expedition to reclaim the styles and titles which the Stuarts still oddly believed to be theirs. Now that Anne had reached the great divide in her life, and the prospect of Holland's being drawn into war could not be disregarded, she thought that if William were to campaign with the Imperial forces this would provide an excellent excuse for her to return to London.

Hervey's sensitive nature was revolted by the Princess Royal's cast of thought: that if Europe should be engulfed in " murder, rapine, distress and calamity " all the better, for then William would stand a better chance to be Stadtholder. It was that kind of sentiment which secured for her an unenviable reputation as a self-centred and calculating woman. The peace-loving Hervey reflected with alarm on the fate of half Europe which might be influenced by the Queen, and how much influence Anne had upon the Queen, and how the interplay of feminine emotions and loyalties might thus involve the lives of many thousands and encompass the destruction of many cities. In fact, Anne neither at the time of her marriage nor later had any influence over her parents. As for the bridegroom, Hervey found him in a surprisingly cynical mood. In the five months he had sojourned in England he had learned, like Gulliver, a great deal about the Lilliputian society of which Lord Hervey was so noble an exemplar. William was full of droll Dutch chaff about his brother-in-law Frederick Lewis, and when some of his shafts made Hervey uneasy he turned lightly to a subject with which the Vice-Chamberlain never dreamed the prince was acquainted—the disputed parentage of Fitz-Frederick Vane, who had been born illegitimately to Miss Vane, a maid of honour to the Queen and the Prince of Wales's mistress. While Frederick Lewis was generally supposed to have fathered this bewildered boy, both Hervey and Lord Harrington also believed him to be their son. William, who knew well that the true cause of the quarrel between Hervey and Frederick Lewis was Miss Vane, mockingly urged Hervey not to be too proud of the child, since he had it on good authority that he was the son of a triumvirate. Hervey quickly begged him to change the conversation.

Much to Hervey's relief the royal party sailed at length. On the same day the King and Queen repaired to Richmond. Parliament had been dissolved and the country was in the throes of a general election. As every result came in the news was carried to Richmond, where George and Caroline waited " with as much anxiety as if the crown had been at stake ". After three weeks the Princess Royal " seemed as much forgotten as if she had been buried three years "—a phrase reminiscent of Lord Craven's remark after the death of Mary Stuart of Orange. While Robert Walpole refreshed himself with the charms of Miss Skerrett at Houghton, his Norfolk seat, the Princess Royal and her husband were on the bosom of the deep, and as the little vessel bumped across the Zuyder Zee the King of England's daughter kept to her

bed and so avoided the worst effects of sea-sickness. Miss
Dorothy Dyves, who attended Anne in Holland, described their
progress from Harlingen, where they had to wait aboard for three
days until the faithful citizenry could muster a suitable welcome.
Thereafter the party made a splendid progress in a fine open
coach drawn by eight horses. Guards made a lane for them
from the gate into Leeuwarden " quite up to the drawing-room "
of the Stadtholder's residence, and fired past their noses so close
that they broke several windows. After a great fireworks display
Anne retired to bed at two in the morning, and next day held a
drawing-room where her graciousness enchanted the Dutch
notables.

" There was no kissing of hands. She stayed with them—
about 40 women and more men—about half an hour and then
retired, as in England."

Anne sat that her ladies should sit; the men had to stand. But,
free of parental restraints, she now reverted to those petty
tyrannies which had made her so disliked at home, displaying
that same lack of consideration for servants as Mary Stuart
before her. The Princess Royal supped with William at nine
o'clock, therefore Miss Dyves could not reach her bed until near
midnight after her royal employer had retired for the night. One
of Dorothy's duties was to read to the princess. One day she read
five hours.

" I am quite happy that she is pleased with my reading," wrote
Miss Dyves to her aunt; " I do not find that it is at all troublesome to me, but it makes me have little time for anything
else."

Mr. Chevenix, who had taught Anne to speak French, had been
engaged as her chaplain at " £100 a year clear ", and that was all
he had. But he considered " the honour of serving the Princess
Royal will, I hope, be thought a reasonable earnest of some
future preferment " Hervey's commentary on Anne's early life
in Holland opened typically: " How the Princess Royal was
received in Holland or what she did there is little worthy of any
particularising account. . . . She felt, I suppose, as unabated
pride generally feels in diminished grandeur; and as she did not
care to let down that pride to cajole the people of the country,
nor the people of the country care to do anything to gratify
it, she neither pleased there nor was pleased. She passed a

solitary life, with music and books, and found no consolation for having quitted England but the prospect of soon returning hither."

Horace Walpole strove to make the Dutch people as acceptable to Anne as he wished her to be to them, but hardly a month had passed before she was hankering after England. During that month a rumour based on an ancient prophecy swept Holland that all Protestants were to be massacred by the Papists. In that same month of May the prince and his bride decided to visit The Hague. The authorities mobilised a strong guard and had every part of the town patrolled. Their presence did not deter several hundred people from surrounding William's coach with loud acclamations and huzzahs, shouting that they wanted to see him as Stadtholder and asking if they should go off and set fire to the houses of anti-Orangists. William was "forced to reprove them for what he secretly thanked them". Soon afterwards he joined the Emperor's army of the Rhine, and Anne began seriously to consider her condition.

She was pregnant.

Immediately her doctors had confirmed her own diagnosis she set her household to the task of packing her baggage, some of it as yet unopened. She had no intention of bearing a child on Dutch soil. Ever present at the back of her scheming mind was the thought that a son of hers might one day inherit the thrones of England and Hanover and she would not wish the fact of his foreign birth to weigh against him. She swore her attendants to secrecy, and three months after her arrival in Holland she was back in England, leaving the perplexed Dutch, who until then had no inkling of the reason, to ask themselves why they should be blessed with a part-Stadtholder who spent so much of his time in Vienna and a consort who was here today and gone tomorrow. Anne reached Kensington Palace at two o'clock in the morning of 2nd June, precisely fifty days after her arrival in Holland, or seventy days after her wedding.

To do unexpected things in grand style, to throw others into turmoil and inconvenience, to treat the hired hands as though to manage them with kindness were to give them ideas above their station, was the Princess Royal's notion of her exalted state; but the King, who had half-forgotten Anne's existence, was by no means gratified to be roused from his slumbers in the middle of the night to be told his married daughter was gone with child but two and a third months and was posting up to the palace gates. Queen Caroline took refuge in tears, there were embraces all round, and the King, having been assured that his crown was still on his head and that Jacobites had not broken loose in the palace gardens, went back to sleep. In due course William received news of his bride's flight, and as he was in no position to do anything about it he expressed the hope that she would have a good holiday. But as the summer passed and she remained in England he began to wonder.

Anne showed little understanding of her husband's position and wrote asking Horace Walpole for advice. The ambassador, who at this crisis seems to have been the only one of the King's representatives capable of using honest common sense, replied from Holland gently urging her to return voluntarily so that she would be back when William returned from his military camp, instead of forcing him to send for her. Anne " cried the whole morning after receiving Walpole's letter, and as soon as ever she read it, carried it with red eyes and wet cheeks to her mother." The Queen at first took Anne's part. She wrote to Walpole begging him to mind his own business and, half in jest, asked him whether he thought her daughter had nothing better to do than be crossing the seas for his pleasure so that he could drive away his boredom playing whist with her. In the end Horace's wisdom prevailed, but he was overruled when he suggested that to avoid partisan broils at The Hague the baby should be born in Leeuwarden, the Friesian stronghold so devoted to the Orange cause. The King and Queen decided that it would be better for the Princess Royal's dignity and interest to lie in at The Hague.

William had now left camp, was touring Germany, and sent one of his gentlemen, Monsieur Grovestein, to London to let Anne know that he would be at The Hague in a fortnight to meet her. On receiving this affectionate message the Princess Royal burst into tears of mortification in such floods as made Victorian chroniclers of the Hanoverians doubt whether she was right in the head. She concealed her emotion from Grovestein, but gushed like a little fountain in the quiet of her apartment. Her first going to Holland and her returing home again had been sensational enough. But the circumstances of her second departure for her husband's country would probably not be surpassed even by the manner in which Mr. Lear's fabulous Dell, the daughter of the King and Queen of the Pelicans, left home for the Great Gromboolian Plain to dwell by the streams of the Chankly Bore. The door-knocker at Kensington Palace was busy for the next day or two as a stream of physicians and midwives flowed up the stairs to examine, prod, cough and advise. They were followed by a whole quarter-deck of admirals called in to chart her voyage. Long consultations resulted in a firm decision to convey the pregnant princess by coach to Colchester, where she was to lie overnight, and thence to Harwich for the embarkation. It was now October and the period of the autumn gales, and the Princess Royal required careful handling. As the fateful day of her journey approached " the Queen was most unaffectedly concerned to part with her daughter, and her daughter as unaffectedly concerned to leave England, and exchange the crowds and splendour of this Court for the solitude and obscurity of her own ", so Hervey remarked. Anne's fancy had concentrated upon Augustus Schutz, the elder son of a German baron who had come over with George I and settled in England. Augustus held a trusted position at court and the Princess Royal would have no one else to escort her to her coach. She insisted on his writing to her regularly, especially about the progress of her old music-teacher, Handel, who was doing so well in England and, with a last injunction to Hervey to " look after Augustus ", was hauled away in tears along the Gore toward the City.

The dust thrown up by the coach wheels had hardly settled when Hervey was back at the palace, where he found the Queen and Princess Caroline weeping together into their hot breakfast chocolate—" drowned in tears and choked with sighs ". At this delicate moment the gallery door stealthily opened and the Queen, who was expecting the King, on hearing that it was the revolting Frederick Lewis come to offer loving commiserations on the departure of Anne, clasped her hands to her head and, the tiny upper lip trembling, burst out maternally, " Oh! my God, this is too much!"

The agitation of Anne during the next few hours while the familiar scenes of her youth passed before her through the carriage windows was enough to defy the imagination of any Whig historian. Tears welled afresh as she thought of those whom she had left behind and the unknown into which she was going: dreaded childbirth, the possibility of death in an alien land among people who wore Dutch bonnets, baggy trousers and clogs, smelt of cheese and ate cake for breakfast. Was this the life for a decent German? Quarrelling with Frederick Lewis were better than all this uncertainty. Thus it was with unmitigated joy that when the coach clattered into the courtyard of the inn at Colchester she was handed letters bearing the seal of the Prince of Orange.

"My dearest," he wrote in effect, " I shall be at The Hague later than expected and therefore not in time to meet you there. But I will make haste and long only to clasp you in my arms," etc.

A sign from Heaven! Dear God, her prayers had been answered! While the innkeeper and his menials bustled about in mingled apprehension and excitement, Anne paced her room turning over in her mind the question: to go forward—or back. By the next morning she had determined to return to dear Kensington, to the parents and sisters who loved her, even the brother whom she hated yet who seemed preferable to the detested Dutch. Perhaps now she could have her baby in comfort in the bosom of her family, who had grown dearer to her with every mile she travelled from London, and dearer still with every mile she travelled back to it. Thus on 22nd October she suddenly appeared again in the West End of London, and those who had marvelled at her going could now hardly believe that she had returned. This time the King was up and about, just setting forth to take a turn in the gardens, when Anne fell into his arms. The unpredictable George, who had been annoyed at her first return, was pleased at her second: he probably realised that he was soon to become a grandfather. The Queen " received her with a thousand kisses and tears of joy ". In after years Anne frequently ' bragged ' of this reception, for she had no idea how she would be received.

Probably the King would have been cooler in his embraces had he guessed at Anne's attitude to Lady Suffolk, his mistress. It was at this time that the Queen's opposition forced Lady Suffolk from court into the comparative oblivion of her Palladian riverside mansion at Marble Hill. Apparently George counted on his eldest daughter's understanding affection. He thought she might save his favourite. But Anne sided with her mother. " She spoke of him disrespectfully (and with good reason) as though she even despised him and thought him tiresome, requiring always novelty in conversation from others but never having anything new of his own."

Anne's pent-up exasperation with her father vented itself one day. " I wish, with all my heart," she exploded, " he would take somebody else, that mamma might be a little relieved from the *ennui* of seeing him for ever in her room!"

Such ingratitude was enough to send George II into yet another of his attempts to abdicate. It certainly outraged the nice feelings of Mrs. Hall, a Victorian expert on English princesses. " What a remark, and from a Princess of England!" she expostulated. " We would gladly have been spared recording such a sentiment from a child to a parent."

However, Lady Suffolk continued complacently to receive £3,200 a year from the King, and at that price no wolf was ever known to loiter afterwards at her door.

After nearly a month of borrowed time in England the Princess Royal was again on her way. But as the little ship left harbour to breast the November challenge of the North Sea she claimed to be in convulsions. The master, aware that he might be endangering not only a frightened woman and the whole destiny of England, as well as jeopardising his prospects of a ribbon or two, prudently put back to port. There seems to have been no limit to the Princess's ingenuity to ensure, in her parturient state, that William's seed should be securely transplanted in England. For the third time since the summer all was again confusion and uproar at Kensington. Messengers were posted to London while Anne waited for calmer weather at Harwich. But the King smarted still from his snub over Lady Suffolk and refused further sanctuary to his daughter, whose importunities had become a plague, a bore and a pest. After all, *she* had decided to marry this ' monkey ' from Holland and she must put up with it.

Meanwhile William, out of consideration for his bride, had suggested her taking the shortest sea route via Dover to Calais. There he would meet her and they would proceed quietly by road through Flanders to Holland. The King peevishly forbade Anne to approach the Presence. She was to come no closer than London Bridge, and this she must cross as quickly as possible and *never* come back to England " in the same condition of health ". Well might he complain, thought Mrs. Hall, for Anne's five months' stay had already cost him £20,000 and he knew of monarchs who had become grandfathers at considerably less cost. On 6th December the Princess Royal was safely back at The Hague. All the fuss had been futile, for William told Miss Dyves and other courtiers that he was " much surprised " that Anne did not lie in in England after all that Dr. Douglas and Dr. Tissue had told him—and as English court physicians never lied, a simple Dutch prince had no option but to believe them. However, he seems to have been delighted, for Miss Dyves and her colleagues received half a year's salary soon afterwards. And Anne gave birth to a son.

In this sorry affair the Princess Royal's passions and her calculations " entirely got the better of her reason and her understanding ", but she gradually settled down with her ' baboon '. Horace Walpole, who alone seems to have written temperately of her, praised her accomplishments in languages, painting and especially in music. But " the pride of her race, and the violence of her passions, had left but a scanty sphere for her judgement to exercise itself." She had a ready wit, but in the arrogance of youth and of her exalted station in an age when ' bottom ' or guts was a quality more highly regarded than brains, she often deserted logic for impetuousness. William, in Walpole's view, was no fool but was rather vain; he was a " trifling lover of show, and not master of the great lights in which he stood ".

In December 1736 the King returned through Helvoetsluys after one of those visits to Hanover which state business and the charms of Madame de Walmoden rendered essential to the good of the two kingdoms. Four days earlier Anne had gone into " a terrible labour " with a second child. Hervey says she was in great danger of her life when she was " brought to bed at The Hague of a daughter, which Dr. Sands, a very eminent man-wife sent from London by the Queen, had been obliged to squeeze to death in birth to save the mother ". The King must have remained extraordinarily bitter towards his daughter, for although he received the message he refused to turn aside to call on her. His whole trip had been derided in England, partly because of his callous indifference to his daughter's illness, for a trick which was played on him in Holland, and for an advertisement which

was nailed to the gate of St. James's Palace when he left for the Continent: "LOST OR STRAYED out of his House, a Man who has left a wife and six children on the Parish. Whoever will give any tidings of him to the Churchwardens of St. James's Parish, so that he may be got again, shall receive 4s 6d reward.
N.B. This reward will not be increased, nobody judging him to be worth a Crown."

On his way to Helvoetsluys the King's carriage broke down and he and his attendants were obliged to take refuge in a shabby village inn where the only refreshment was coffee and Schiedam. But when the bill was produced the innkeeper had the audacity to demand £100. The King flew into a temper and one of his gentlemen was told to ask whether coffee and gin were rare articles in those parts.

"No," the innkeeper replied, "but kings are."

George is said to have "laughed heartily" at this sally, which in the robust reportage of the period meant the reverse. However, any laughter soon died in his throat. As he could not spare the time to see his daughter he arrived at Helvoetsluys just as one of the worst winter gales of the year was blowing up. The King wished to get home for Christmas, and he swept aside the warnings of Sir Charles Wager, commander of the royal fleet, and ordered him to sail. The vessel almost foundered in the North Sea. It was blown back and forth until, being four days overdue, word reached St. James's that it had been lost with all hands and passengers. Even as George was praying fervently to "Our Father Vich is in Heaven" the Cabinet met at the Duke of Devonshire's prepared to proclaim King Frederick I. The Queen and her family prayed for the King's deliverance at a service of intercession in the Chapel Royal. In some way or another the ship struggled back to Helvoetsluys and a messenger arrived at St. James's to tell the Queen so while she was still on her knees. Robert Walpole immediately took to the bottle—an exercise not beyond his competence—and became "very childish, for he drank more than he should . . . and felt something of the gout that same night", wrote Princess Amelia to the Prime Minister's brother who was on the ship and arrived with the King when the storm died down. "I thank you, dear Horace, for letting me know so exactly what my sister does," Amelia added. "I am very happy she is so well."

The Queen told Hervey that the agitation she had been in twice during the fortnight, first for fear of her daughter's dying in childbed and next for fear of her husband's being drowned, had left her so stupefied that she could not recover her wits.

Before her death in 1737 the Queen had to brace herself for the final break with Frederick Lewis and her fatal operation for hernia. The Prince of Wales and his wife Augusta were living on sufferance at Hampton Court. The princess was with child. Augusta went into labour. Her husband refused to have any child of his born under his father's roof. He rushed her into a carriage and started at a gallop for his apartments in St. James's Palace, pursued some hours later by a wrathful King and a palpitating Queen. Details of Augusta's night ride were said, even by Hanoverian standards, to be too disgusting to describe. No preparations had been made for the princess's confinement. The hunt for doctors and midwives continued into the small hours. Augusta was put to bed between two tablecloths. By the time Queen Caroline arrived little Augusta had been born. The Queen, after whipping her son with all the scorn and fury of which her tongue was capable, crooned over the whimpering mite. " Poor little creature, you have arrived in a disagreeable world."

No doubt this was true, but with the tenacity of her father's race the child managed to cling to it for nearly eighty years, during which she became the mother of the future George IV's unfortunate Queen Caroline. As a result of this episode the King ordered his son from court, and Frederick Lewis formed his own establishments at Kew and at Norfolk House, St. James's, and finally moved to Leicester House, where the rivalry of the previous reign was paralleled, to the disgrace of the father, the shame of the son, and the disgust of the nation. The royal parents were moved not so much by the Princess of Wales's plight as by the fear that some Jacobite nursling might be insinuated between the tablecloths. Hanoverian babies looked so much like Stuart ones that one could never tell.

Queen Caroline died of a strangulated hernia, preceded by pain, vomiting and abdominal distension which the Court physicians failed to diagnose and correct in time. In her last days, between doses of snake-root and bouts of sickness and purging, the Queen refused to see the heir apparent. The surgeons successfully paved her way to the tomb and George Selwyn crept under her bed the more minutely to examine the corpse when the royal undertakers had departed. The King sent a message to the Prince of Orange telling him that the Princess Royal's presence was not required, and that if she pressed to visit London he must stop her. Anne was not to be restrained. On the pretext of ill health she sailed home after the Queen's death, presumably to try to take her mother's place. The King saw through the ruse, and after she had spent only one night in London he sent her to Bath, the place for invalids, whom he could not bear and never acknowledged—the root cause of Queen Caroline's early mortality. Soon Anne was back in Holland, unforgiven by her father for having stood up for the rights of wives against mistresses. So far as he was concerned she was temporarily outside the pale.

During the next few years Anne repressed her longing for England and threw her talents into family life and her husband's advancement. Soon Holland was menaced by the War of the Austrian Succession, which, after a long period of peace, embroiled England and France in those mutual hostilities which had contributed so much to the enlightenment of mankind. The tides of war rolled into Germany, George II ensured his fame as the last monarch of England to fight in the field, and Holland was saved from invasion by the intrepid exertions of English foot and horse at Dettingen which drove the French out of Germany; but the Dutch were menaced again a year or two later when the the French invaded Belgium and defeated Cumberland and his troops at Fontenoy. The King blamed the duke for the defeat. The usual family recriminations were followed by news of Bonnie Prince Charlie's rising in Scotland, whither Cumberland was dispatched, with results which so many historians have with uncanny skill and accuracy explained.

Events pressed upon the Prince of Orange, but by 1747 the percipient Dutch, impelled by external forces to unite against the French, turned once again to the House of Orange and called upon William at the age of 36 to become Stadtholder over all the United Provinces. So far his career had borne some resemblance to that of William III. His ambitions were fostered by his wife, who thought she might soon become Queen of the Netherlands. The remaining years of William's Stadtholdership were

marked by strong autocratic tendencies which were not to help
his son when he succeeded his father, especially as the Peace of
Aix-la-Chapelle which ended the war, although the Dutch regained most of their lost possessions, seriously undermined the
morale of the nation when the people realised how they had
fallen, and how far they had fallen, from power.

Blow after blow fell upon George II and his eldest daughter
in 1751. " This has been a fatal year to my family," mourned
the King. " I lost my eldest son—but I am glad of it; then the
Prince of Orange died and left everything in confusion. Poor
little Edward [his grandson the Duke of York and Albany] has
been cut open for an imposthume in his side; and now the Queen
of Denmark is gone." Then he chided himself, in the words
quoted earlier about his failure to love his children when they
were young. Frederick Lewis had taken to drink, and he died
at the age of 44, although ostensibly from a blow on the head
from a tennis or cricket ball. Horace Walpole's literary namesake
and nephew thought " cricketalia " was responsible: Frederick
Lewis had played frequently at Cliveden and he probably had a
thin skull. Whatever the cause, his devoted father was " glad
of it "; the Princess of Wales had proved fruitful despite the
almost fatal dash from Hampton to St. James's, and the future
George III was dearer to the King than Frederick Lewis could ever
be. Anne grieved for her youngest sister, Louise of Denmark,
who wrote to her affectionately a few days before she died from
the same ailment which had killed their mother, having concealed the fact that by stooping, when she was advanced in
pregnancy seven months with the first of her four children, she
had started the fatal rupture.

By the autumn of 1751 the Princess Royal was a widow.
William died at the age of 40 from an imposthume or purulent
abscess in the head, probably a brain tumor, although Ambassador
Walpole thought he had been killed by the waters at Aix-la-
Chapelle. The Princess Royal had been established Regent some
time earlier, " but as her husband's authority seemed extremely
tottering, it is not likely that she will be able to maintain hers.
Her health is extremely bad, and her temper is neither in-
gratiating nor bending ". The King, appalled by these family
tragedies, sent Lord Holderness to The Hague " to learn rather

than to teach " and with letters of sympathy. But Anne remembered with deep revulsion her father's neglect to visit her
when she lay at death's door, and also his surly objection to her
condolences when Queen Caroline died, and she treated his envoy
with hauteur and with so many insults that the King angrily
recalled him. Presumably she saw no members of her family
again. Over the years she had come to love her misshapen but
cultured and tolerant husband. " He had not improved in beauty
since his marriage," wrote Walpole, " but increasingly ugly as he
became, his wife seemed also increasingly jealous of him. Im-
portunate, however, as the jealousy was, it had the merit of
being founded on honest and healthy affection."

According to the same source William had not been an un-
qualified success as Stadtholder during his three or four years
of power, but his son was to prove a disaster. As Walpole
observed, it had " become the peculiarity of the House of
Orange to have minorities ". When his father died William V
was a child. Anne took oaths as his *gouvernante*, but in this
exalted position, the nearest she would ever come to queenhood,
she proved in general incapable either of ruling or of accepting
that impartial advice which might have enabled her to reign. She
was drawn towards France by the influence of Dubacq—" a little
secretary "—against the counsel of Bentinck and Greffier, who
favoured friendship with England. But Dubacq's links were broken
when, on William's death, he was excluded from a Council called
by Bentinck at that same ' house in the woods ' where so many
family conflicts disturbed the rural peace during the time of
Mary Stuart and her mother-in-law.

In the seven years of her widowhood Anne turned the tables
on her ' correctors ', and averted a breach between England and
Holland over the British capture of many Dutch vessels carrying
supplies to the French settlements. As she lay dying at the end
of 1758 she summoned strength to make one final and decisive
contribution to the Orange succession by signing a marriage contract between her daughter Caroline and the Prince of Nassau-
Walburg, and writing to ensure the sanction of the States-
General. For her son she could do no more. The political power
of the republic waned rapidly under the rule of this last of the
Stadtholders, war broke out with England in 1780, opposition
to the House of Orange revived, the French Revolution precipi-

tated William's flight to England in 1795, and he died an exile in Brunswick in 1806. But the son of Caroline grew up with all the royal qualities of his proud grandmother, who, deprived of queenly status herself, would have rejoiced to see him elected the first King of the Netherlands in 1815. But by that time she had been in her grave fifty-five years.

Anne died on 2nd January 1759, and this time no regrets and no messages went forth from the white-haired, unforgiving old King at St. James's, who had another twenty-one months before he expired in his water-closet to make his 22-year-old grandson King George III. And if England remembered Anne it was probably in the vein of the unfeeling verses written after ' poor Fred ', her hated brother, had died in the arms of his dancing-master:

> Had it been his sister
> No one would have missed her.

Charlotte of Württemberg

I

QUEEN IN fact Anne of Hanover never was, but her successor as Princess Royal in the next reign compensated richly for that disappointment by developing into the largest consort in the Europe of her time. Princess Charlotte, Anne's great-niece, was the eldest of the six daughters who, with nine sons, made up the quiver of George III and his Queen, Charlotte of Mecklenburg-Strelitz. The eldest daughter's importance was impressed upon her brothers and sisters early in their lives: they called her 'Royal'—for instance, "What is 'Royal' going to wear for the Kew ball?" or, " ' Royal ' had only three chins before Austerlitz; now she has five, poor dear."

The first thirty-one years of Charlotte's life were spent in Britain and the last thirty in the German state of Württemberg, of which her husband became King in Napoleon's time. The greater span of her life, the forty-eight years between 1785 and 1813, was overshadowed by war: the French invaded Germany fourteen times in those three decades. For nine years after the Treaty of Amiens ended the Princess Royal was completely cut off from her family in London. Her German husband Frederick William steadily drank himself into the mausoleum. Napoleon considered him a "drunken brute". Charlotte produced no children. The eccentricities of her brothers and the irregularities of some of her sisters came to her ears across the ' iron curtain ' at second hand; these reports left her sorrowing, but it was difficult for her to realise that they were usually spiced with malice. All this time she endured the pangs of exile. But, unlike Mary Stuart and Anne of Hanover, having made her bed she was not afraid to lie upon it. Accordingly she seems entitled to more tolerance than historians bestowed on her predecessors.

On 29th September 1766 this unfortunate princess followed into the world, then pirouetting sedately around the new Buckingham House, those three excellent princes—" three royally promising boys "—who afterwards rejoiced the hearts of romancers as George IV, the " grand old " Duke of York and William IV. In due course the question of marriage arose. Then a pedigree princess could only wed a pedigree prince. The celebrated courtier Madame Schwellenburg (the two-headed ' Cerbera ' of Fanny Burney's fanciful journal) joined with other English patriots, and none in those days was more patriotic than the foreign immigrant, in advancing the matrimonial cause of the young Charlotte. At the age of 15 the Princess Royal was well up in French art and all the accomplishment of privately tutored royal youth. At early as 1781 her name had been linked with the Emperor of Austria's, but a Roman Catholic potentate in Middle Europe stood no chance of marriage to a Protestant princess.

To be fair, the Hanoverian embargo extended also to Protestant suitors in Denmark, Holland, Sweden and Brunswick. Here the obstacle was not so much religion as the suitor-scaring hauteur of Charlotte's inflexible mother. Queen Charlotte, with her mulatto looks, her passion for snuff (equal only to that of Catherine the Great), her habit of interjecting " Zo! " in a guttural German splutter and her Lutheran sense of duty, in varying degrees distorted and in some cases blighted the romantic hopes of her young. History has dwelt long and disapprovingly on the tendency of the first three Georges to hate and suppress their sons; but it is even more remarkable that Charlotte of Mecklenburg-Strelitz reproduced almost exactly some of the worst defects of her husband's grandmother, Caroline of Brandenburg-Anspach, as the mother of daughters. Of Queen Caroline's five girls, two, as has been recounted, had unhappy love affairs and died unmarried. Three of Queen Charlotte's six remained unwed but not untouched by those grand passions the existence of which even Miss Burney seemed unaware. George III's unsatisfactory mental condition overshadowed the childhood of his oldest daughters and their brothers. The Queen's freezing grandeur, although she showed tenderness to her daughters when they were younger, frightened off potential candidates for marriage into the Hanoverian ' Sisterhood '. The Princess Royal, who as a teenager was by no means unattractive, at last at the age of 30 when she was inclining to embonpoint escaped the rigours of Windsor by marrying the first man she could get.

Frederick William Charles, Hereditary Prince of Württemberg and nephew of the reigning Duke, was ten years her senior, but he came upon the scene just when the Royal Family had become unhappier than any in the land through the escapades of the Prince of Wales and his brothers. Charlotte tenderly loved the ' Brethren ', but felt that she had no chance of ever marrying, and consequently had " fallen into a kind of quiet, desperate state, without hope and open to every fear." Her doctor, Sir Lucas Pepys, thought marriage offered the only chance of " saving her life or her understanding ". Frederick began his wooing from afar, by letters and pictures, but it was hard going. Neither the King nor the Queen raised a hand to advance the match. Only the Prince of Wales used his influence to liberate his sister from the stifling influence of her parents. His diplomacy served only to incense his already unstable father, for George III had the gravest objections to the marriage. Frederick was a middle-aged widower with three children whose mother had died after a mysterious scandal which racked the royal salons of Europe. The dead wife, Augusta of Brunswick, was a cousin of the Princess Royal and sister of the ill-starred Caroline who was to become the unwanted Queen of George IV.

When Frederick married the unhappy Augusta in 1780 he entered the service of Russia. This was not too difficult. His sister Sophie had married the snub-nosed future Czar Paul, who during brief intervals of mental brightness used to splash the dessert from his dining table about the room for his servants to scoop up. Augusta was apparently as flighty and feather-brained as her sister Caroline. Her conduct encouraged her husband to beat her cruelly, especially when she was unwise enough to become the mistress of a discarded lover of Catherine the Great and indiscreet enough to have a child by him too long after she had left Frederick to be able to attribute it to her husband. German princesses have ever had disquieting experiences in Russia, and Augusta was no exception. Catherine sent her to the prison fortress of Lhode on the Baltic, and Frederick and the children returned to Germany. Two years later the loving husband, who on one occasion had thrashed his wife in the Empress's presence, heard from Catherine that Augusta had died of " a putrid fever ", although some said a haemorrhage. The exact cause was never established, for the disease was apparently so infectious that she had to be buried the same day as she died. No post-mortem was held. The manner of her death gave rise to the legend, firmly believed by Augusta's mother, that she had been exiled to Siberia. Taking all in all, therefore, Frederick's reputation was hardly untarnished when he came to seek the Princess Royal's hand. Apart from anything else he was almost inaccessibly stout, a difficult man to shake hands with.

The King caused searching enquiries into the circumstances of Augusta's death before he approved " a match which seemed requisite to his child's happiness, at least, in her own judgement ". It was not until March 1797 that Frederick received from the King a portrait of Charlotte. The following month he was suffered to cross to England to claim her. Even then, like his predecessors in this series, he was treated more like a robber than a lover, and instead of visiting London immediately he was hurried incognito on a short tour within a hundred-mile radius of the capital, and then smuggled to Sir Joseph Banks's place at Isleworth. Under the marriage contract Charlotte received £80,000 from the Commons; any children were to be brought up in Württemberg but might not marry without the consent of the reigning monarch of England. The whole marriage portion was to be invested in British funds and paid to the Princess Royal half-yearly, but if her husband predeceased her she could return to England with " the whole of her paraphernalia ". When Frederick landed in England his fiancée was " very fussed and agitated " and " almost dead with terror ", but the Royal family united in a special effort to put the substantial bridegroom at ease.

On 18th May the King gave away the bride in the Chapel Royal at St. James's. And who do you suppose had made the wedding dress? asked Mrs. Hall. None other than the Queen! This remarkable revelation was confided by Princess Augusta to Miss Burney in these words: " You know what a figure she used to make of herself, with her odd manner of dressing herself; but Mamma said, ' Now, really, Princess Royal, this one time is the last, and I cannot suffer you to make such a quiz of yourself, so I will really have you dressed properly.' "

Charlotte asserted herself sufficiently to embroider her wedding robe with her own hand. Over her white satin gown, with gold (instead of silver) embroidery to denote that she was marrying a widower and not a bachelor, the bride wore a scarlet mantle. Her hair was arranged in long ringlets under a crimson velvet coronet with a broad band and a plume of diamonds. The Russian Order of St. Catherine decorated her bosom. The Duke of Clarence in brown and Prince Ernest (Cumberland) in the Hanoverian uniform supported their sister, who was attended by two daughters of dukes and two of earls—Frances Somerset, Mary Bentinck, Caroline Damer and Mary Howe. But she was outshone by the bridegroom, who almost hid the altar from view in a peach-coloured suit of silk, shot with gold and silver richly embroidered, with gold and silver flaps and cuffs, beneath his coat the Order of St. Catherine, and over one shoulder the blue watered ribbon insignia of the German Order of the Golden Fleece. Once again the spirit of Handel was invoked and the organ pealed forth his overture to *Esther*. A startling impact was made by the Prince and Princess of Wales, the handsome Florizel in a sky-blue suit embroidered down the seams and set off with a diamond star and epaulettes, Caroline in " a silver tissue train, with purple, lilac and green trimmings."

In the crowded chapel the heat was so intense on that fine summer's day that several women collapsed and one bridesmaid was " with much difficulty" restored to consciousness. But Charlotte faced the Archbishops of Canterbury and York in a " perfectly collected and unembarrassed" manner, unlike her sisters, who " shed tears of sensibility and affection" while the King and Queen also " discovered an excess of parental feeling ". After a drawing-room the court drove to Windsor. Five days later the Queen gave a great fête at Frogmore in honour of the nuptials, which for some reason excited the humorous talent of Gillray. In a cartoon entitled " The Bridal Night " he showed Frederick smothered in orders (one of them is hanging from the ribbon of his tie-wig) and his splendid proportions are explained in the nickname, " The great Belly-gerent ". In after years Napoleon was heard to declare that God must have created Frederick to show the utmost extent to which the human skin could be stretched without bursting.

Despite the crude jokes of the day, Frederick was by no means

H

the monster he had been painted. As soon as he could disengage himself from business he wrote to his daughter Catherine that " since Thursday the 18th you have a new mother " and gently enjoined her to love Charlotte very much. He also ordered a painting of George III after Gainsborough to be sent ahead to Württemberg so that it would be hanging in the bride's suite when she arrived. Apparently Frederick also gave his father-in-law a solemn promise never to become a Roman Catholic like that other German reprobate who had so deceived the King's late Aunt Mary. The assurance came as a great relief to all who heard it, for George III was already having so much trouble with bastards in his family that he had no wish to be plagued with apostates as well so soon after the Reformation. For his part Frederick secured the King's undertaking always to support the House of Württemberg, a promise which it was not hard to make as England was at war with France and there was little chance that anybody would be able to keep such a pledge for as far as could be seen ahead.

All the royal ladies from the Queen down dissolved into floods of tears when on 2nd June the bridal procession left St. James's for Harwich. Tucked away in the Princess Royal's trousseau were two sets of baby clothes, one for a boy, the other for a girl. But she was never to need them and they were sold at her death. At the parting, in her blue riding habit and straw bonnet, the Star of St. Catherine clinging to her breast as though it had nested there, she " endeavoured to appear cheerful; but the faltering accents with which she bade her attendants and the surrounding multitude farewell bespoke her agitated feelings ". The King could scarcely stammer the one word *adieu*. No French warship dared approach the yacht, thanks to its naval escort, and the party arrived safely but shaken at Cuxhaven after a rough passage which made the bride feel miserably giddy and faint. They were greeted by Frederick's son Prince Adolphus (Dolly), whose hair had grown so long that his father felt impelled to comment adversely upon it. Württemberg was reached via Hanover.

" In all the places we came through," wrote Charlotte to her father, " the Peasants inquired which was their King's daughter, and then came up and spoke to me, entreating that I would persuade your Majesty to come among them."

The Court of Württemberg was the great snob court of Europe, feudally maintained by its hereditary duke in a baroque palace at Stüttgart with its blue marble columns, painted ceilings and prolific sculptures, and at the Versailles-type palace of Louisbourg (Ludwigsburg), standing amid avenues of limes and chestnuts. To this latter haven came the Princess Royal. She was greeted affectionately by her step-daughter Trinette, as Catherine was called—" a very handsome girl, the very image of her father ", though, of course, somewhat smaller and slimmer. At dinner that night musicians played " God Save the King ". Charlotte was almost completely tone-deaf, and music caused her actual physical suffering, but she recognised the tune when the rest of the party stood—" I own that I required all the Strength in my power not to burst into Tears," she noted of her feelings as the band struck up. All her letters home at that time exuded perfect bliss—sheer delight with her new home, the blazing cornfields, the mountains, the sleek fat cattle, the Spanish sheep grazing on the clovered lawns. Indeed, she never betrayed any unhappiness with Frederick, whose knowledge of natural history, geography and sciences complemented her not inconsiderable artistic talent. Her early impressions of this paradise were probably modified as her husband's enormous liver fought a losing battle with the wines of the country, but at the outset she was in love with him, especially when he fell from his horse in August this same year.

Out of consideration for Charlotte he ordered that she should not be told until he had been carried up to bed because his " Arm was broke ", as she told her father. " When I came to him he forced himself to appear chearfull." Though in dreadful pain he talked with her for three hours, and when she had gone he fainted away—a remarkable demonstration of courage as well as of affection: he did not wish to upset her because she was expecting a child. In the few months she had been among the Germans they had come to admire and even love her. Meanwhile the old Duke had died at Stüttgart, leaving Frederick his title and a fortune which included a library of 100,000 volumes, with a unique collection of 9,000 Bibles of different editions and in fifty-one languages and dialects, to say nothing of 2,000 volumes all printed before the Reformation and a complete collection of all sovereigns, families and towns from earliest

times. So when the new Duchess was brought to bed in April
1798 the churches were filled with tearful peasants all praying
for the safe delivery of an heir and making ready for the greatest
celebrations the duchy had ever known.

On 5th April Frederick and Charlotte took the Sacrament
together, but on 27th April after a long and hazardous labour
Charlotte gave birth to a dead child—" *une grande et belle
fille* ". The Duke wrote: " Our dearest hopes have been
dashed." A week later Charlotte was writing doggedly to her
father: " I trust that I feel this as a Christian, and submit with
resignation to the will of the Almighty, but Nature must ever
make me regret the loss of the little thing I had built such
happiness on."

Frederick, who had " suffered cruelly ", was kindness personi-
fied. By early June his wife was spending most of the day at
Louisbourg in a little flower arbour he had made for her, and he
was planning a small farm " in the English style " and a cottage
" covered with moss " to make her feel more at home. Both were
also eagerly awaiting " a pair of Cangaroos " for which Charlotte
had asked her father. But by the time they arrived great changes
had come about.

Originally the Austrians were committed to protect Württemberg against the French, and when Charlotte first took up
residence in her Swabian demesne she noted how the fields had
been scored by their cannon wheels. But the Austrians instead
of maintaining themselves were living off the land when in March
1799 the Princess Royal heard the distant growls of the French
artillery. Refusing to flee, she wrote her father begging him take
the duchy under his protection and to send money to raise and
equip troops to fight alongside Austrian forces. But the spirit
of the French Revolution had permeated Germany, Napoleon
was about to advance on Louisbourg, and Charlotte complained
that *égalité*, to say nothing of *liberté* and *fraternité*, had so be-
mused even the nobility that it would be difficult for her " to
find Ladies " for the court, as clearly ' Peasants ' were unsuitable.
Excursions followed alarums, and sudden flights ended with
shamefaced returns; and then in May 1800 the Duke and Duchess
found themselves exiles at Erlangen in the Franconian lands of
the King of Prussia, having been abandoned by the unreliable
Austrians. The French demanded a payment of £6 million in

specie or plate to indemnify them for their having been put to the trouble of taking Württemberg, and Charlotte prepared not only to sell her jewels but also to beg a loan from her father.

Thus painfully Duke Frederick William suffered the inconvenience imposed by Austrian friends who charged him for making off with his portable property and French enemies who charged him twice as much for putting it back. In the midst of these complications the two kangaroos sent by his kind father-in-law somehow got to Erlangen in the summer of 1800. It had taken them two years to reach their destination, and a year later they produced two young ones—" which are great Beauties ". As the shadow of Napoleon deepened across Württemberg the occupants of the royal palace at Stüttgart took stock. Up to 1805 the Princess Royal's letters revealed her as a mature woman of a cheerful outlook and cultivated tastes. Her speciality was painting on porcelain: she had an oven for baking china at Stüttgart, and there she created vases, bowls and pots with landscapes and garlands delicately traced upon them in monochrome. Most of her pieces were signed at the bottom with her initials and some were afterwards preserved at Frogmore House. She designed a broth-cup for her father and wrote him volumes about her activities in Württemberg—farming, theatres, sledging and her education of the young people in whose company the childless princess always delighted, especially that of Trinette, whose tuition she supervised on the system she had inherited from her German tutor at home. As a stepmother Charlotte filled most of the gaps in the lives of Frederick's three motherless children. Dolly was perverted by " wicked, intriguing men ", fell foul of his father and grew up to marry three times; but Charlotte always found excuses for him and finally reconciled father and son. Her favourite stepchild was " little Paul . . . a very comical Boy "; yet he, too, turned out to be a bad father. Frederick accused Charlotte of spoiling his children, and she lived long enough to spoil his grandchildren, too, for she virtually brought up the two daughters of her " very comical Boy ".

Nevertheless her heart beat for England. She followed the war news avidly and regarded Nelson's victory of the Nile as the first rift in the clouds since those " odious Philosophers " had started the sad decline of human values in 1789. When English friends visited Württemberg during the Amiens breathing-space she was transported with joy: she felt "like an infant" as she listened agasp to all Lord Minto's news from home. Alas for Frederick, he was by now a puppet of Napoleon. His little eyes, almost immured in the folds of florid fat to which his original features had surrendered, darted suspiciously from Charlotte to anyone with whom she conversed in English. The general air of distrust increased after 1803, when, then completely under Bonaparte's influence, Frederick was promoted Elector of Württemberg. By that time the Peace of Amiens—"of which everybody was glad and nobody proud"—had come and gone and Charlotte was deprived of contact with the family in England, although she managed to slip her father some painted flowerpots of her own design before the Grand Armée filled Württemberg with its clatter.

As early as 1801 Charlotte had tried secretly to persuade her father to mediate with Russia on Württemberg's behalf. In this way she hoped to spare Frederick the indignity of subservience to the foreign conqueror. Nothing came of these overtures, and she had to prepare to face her father's enemy on his own terms. The new emperor was sweeping all before him when in 1805 he advanced on Ulm, south-east of Württemberg before the Battle of Austerlitz. Some 60,000 Austrians surrendered at Ulm, on the eve of the Battle of Trafalgar. In St. Helena years later Napoleon told Dr. O'Meara: "I had the pleasure of interfering to her [Charlotte's] advantage when her husband, who was a brute though a man of talent, had ill-treated her, for which she was very grateful to me."

Whether Frederick was a brute or not, he was certainly more and more like the Vicar of Bray and in his Germanic way subjected the Princess Royal to insults because she was her father's daughter and on the other side. Napoleon did not require him to beat his wife, but he did require him to supply troops and to join the Rhenish Confederacy. In payment for these modest acts of political backsliding the Emperor of the French elevated Frederick to kingship. The new King Frederick William of Württemberg and his consort were crowned on 1st January 1806. There afterwards appeared on the roof of the Stüttgart palace a gilded crown of such a size and ornateness that it excited the derision even of Napoleon.

Charlotte behaved with great dignity in the presence of the

Emperor, who arranged for her to get at least one letter across the Channel to her mother after she had become Queen. It was in French, which suggests that part of it at least was dictated by one of Napoleon's aides on the Emperor's orders, and it began: " My dear Mother and Sister ". What an explosion! Queen Charlotte, senior almost when off in a cloud of snuff and her " Zo!" could be heard ricocheting down the corridors of Windsor for some time afterwards. Even when it had still been possible for the Princess Royal to write freely she had upset her mother, according to Dr. O'Meara, by praising Napoleon to her: she described him as having " so bewitching a smile "; and Harriet, Countess of Bessborough, declared: " Think of the King's eldest Daughter writing to her mother a letter full of praises of Bonaparte, saying he is much belied!"

However, it is possible that both these letters, subject as they were to censorship, were written under duress. Years after the war Miss Frances Williams Wynn heard Charlotte explain her relationship with Napoleon. " It was of course very painful for me to receive him with civility," she said, " but I had no choice: the least failure on my part might have been sufficient pretence for depriving my husband and children of this kingdom."

In other words, she had to make the best of a bad job, but it is unlikely that she could ever voluntarily have praised Napoleon's " smile " She found the Emperor's manner brusque even when he was being polite. And to avoid the pillage of her treasures she was forced to lie about them. " I made them myself," she told the Emperor. As he knew so little of art he did not doubt it. Napoleon was " pleased " with Charlotte and, according to him, she " soon lost whatever prejudices she might have entertained against me."

One evening whilst Charlotte was playing whist with Napoleon against the King and Trinette at the royal card table, in which a convex opening had been cut to accommodate the King's paunch, Frederick stopped the Emperor just as he was about to pick up a trick belonging to him and his daughter.

" Sire," he said dryly, " one doesn't play here to win."

Both Napoleon's empresses visited Stüttgart, where *The Judgement of Solomon* was presented to Marie Louise in a freezing theatre. The Empress, who seemed to mind nothing provided she could ride her horse and eat four or five square meals a day, took an instant dislike to all the Royal Family except Charlotte and Trinette.

The climax of Bonaparte's association with the Princess Royal fast approached. Having made himself Emperor, he began to bestow crowns on his brothers and sisters, a process facilitated by his territorial conquests. The zenith of power was achieved with the Peace of Tilsit in 1807; Napoleon's deal with Czar Alexander I embraced the dismemberment of Prussia and the reorganisation of the rest of Germany to include the creation of the new kingdom of Westphalia. The crown was to be conferred on his youngest and prodigal brother Jerome, fifteen years Napoleon's junior and the most frivolous yet most adored of the Bonaparte tribe. In 1803, during a naval cruise under Admiral Joyeux, he had jumped ship to savour the fleshpots of America, where he married the daughter of a Southern shipowner, a Miss Elizabeth Patterson, known as ' The Belle of Baltimore '. As he omitted to inform his brother, Jerome was ordered to dispense with the lady, who sought refuge in England, where her baby was born. The marriage was declared null and void, Mrs. Bonaparte received a handsome Imperial allowance and she seems to have lived happily ever after. Jerome enjoyed some success as commander of a frigate, and on his return from a nine-months' campaign in the autumn of 1806 was greeted like a hero and informed that he was to marry Princess Catherine of Württemberg.

At that date Catherine had grown into a " short, round doll-like figure " with a profile as near classical perfection as can be imagined. Charlotte resisted the sacrifice of her loved step-daughter to Napoleon's ambition, but Frederick was in no position to protest. The parvenu Bonapartes could now claim equality with the regal families of Europe. One can only imagine how the news was received by Queen Charlotte at Buckingham House. As for the Princess Royal, she watched the progress of the marriage with pangs of fear and anxiety. Jerome lived like a king at his luxurious mansion of Napoleonshöhe in Westphalia, filling it with expensive treasures and even more expensive mistresses—court ladies, actresses, whores, all were welcome. Jerome loved Catherine in his way, but she was far more in love with him, and so long as he had no regular favourite she tolerated his infidelities. But she could do nothing to check the reckless extravagance which rapidly reduced Westphalia to penury. When in 1812 Jerome reluctantly left his seraglio to command a wing of the Grande Armée in the invasion of Russia, he travelled like an oriental mogul, bathing in rum on rising and in milk before retiring. From early 1813 the bankrupt kingdom was torn apart by Czernitchev's Cossacks. But Jerome was too preoccupied to care. Princess Lowenstein, his current mistress, was expecting a baby and all his efforts were concentrated on divorcing Catherine. The Czar offered peace to spare the further humiliation of his kinswoman, but Jerome sent back a haughty rejection —" the brother of the Emperor would never admit his defeat ".

Jerome fought bravely at Waterloo. Only when he finally deserted Trinette did she turn once again for comfort and sympathy to her ever-understanding stepmother. Napoleon's assertion that Charlotte " contributed materially towards effecting a marriage " between Jerome and Catherine should be treated with reserve. The Princess Royal seems to have played no part, either, in another family marriage forced by Napoleon—that of Frederick's son Adolphus to Princess Charlotte of Bavaria.

II

AFTER WATERLOO the Queen of Württemberg expressed the hope that her brother the Prince Regent would unite prudence with lenity and allow Napoleon—" this extraordinary man "— to live out his life as a state prisoner under his protection. She showed much the same compassion as, a century later, Queen Mary was to show for the deposed Emperor Wilhelm II of Germany; and she claimed that Napoleon had never failed to speak of the Prince Regent in other than handsome terms.

With the resumption of relations between Britain and Württemberg in 1813 she had made the strongest representations to her brother on Frederick's behalf, explaining in a long memorandum why he had acted as he did and seeking British support for the claims of his kingdom at the Congress of Vienna. The memorandum was probably dictated by Frederick or his advisers. Charlotte's loyalty to her ambivalent spouse emerges among the purifying and wholesome factors left in the conqueror's wake. Ultimately the King, as anxious to disown Napoleon as he had ever been to welcome him, was allowed to keep his toy kingdom and his palace with the great golden crown and to fade into history in a miasma of tainted honour. But his time was come.

In 1815 Adolphus and Paul went to London to celebrate Waterloo year. Their visit filled the Prince Regent with " fuss, fatigue and rage ". The old King George III appeared to be hopelessly mad and his grand-daughter, Princess Charlotte, was then in the process of rejecting the Prince of Orange in favour of Leopold, the future " dearest Uncle " of Queen Victoria. The chances of the Dutch suitor, although he became the first King of the Netherlands, were scarcely enhanced, and Princess Charlotte's choice may have been influenced, when Prince Paul got him " remarkably drunk " at Carlton House. These frivolities tore at the nerves of King Frederick William, and the royal morale also suffered a sad setback when Napoleon escaped from Elba. During the Hundred Days the monarch suffered a hundred years of the agonies of Hell, but at last it was over, and Charlotte was glad to bowl him back to Stüttgart away from Vienna, where the air and possibly the amusements had a pernicious effect upon him. But beneath the humiliated Frederick William simmered the feudal Frederick William. His precarious escape from the war stiffened his autocratic tendencies: he refreshed his dignity by abolishing the 1771 constitution and substituting a less reasonable one which the stout Württembergers immediately resented.

The fierce polemics engendered by Frederick William's statesmanship were at their height when the monarch suddenly died on 30th October 1816, within a week of his sixty-second birthday. Heavy drinking and compulsive eating had undermined his health, which failed to withstand the successive shocks of allied diplomacy and Napoleonic strategy. Charlotte was left prostrated by her loss and encumbered with debt. She had grown " very large ", not rotund like Frederick William but " shapeless and like a figure of snow ". Usually she appeared with a turban of soft material on her head, which heightened the snowman simile, and her hair was frizzed and powdered above " a pleasant, good-humoured face, without any pretensions to beauty ", but such looks as she had in widowed middle age were soon overwhelmed by obesity. She became grotesque: the size of her hips and stomach, given full rein beneath a billowing evening dress which she invariably wore in the daytime, was said to be " something quite extraordinary ". Criticism of Frederick William after he was dead evoked all the fierce loyalty with which she had defended him when he lived. At almost the same time as Napoleon for his own purposes was describing him as a brute Charlotte wrote reproachfully to the Prince Regent: " Believe me, dearest Brother, never could I have been as happy as I was had not our minds been congenial. . . . You have wounded my feelings by attending to the idle Reports of those whose only object must have been to do mischief and who ever wish to blame the Conduct of all Sovereigns."

Old Queen Charlotte had no reason to love her German son-in-law, but she decreed that she and the 'Sisterhood' should wear black " bombazin " for a month as a mourning gesture. By royal standards the Dowager Queen of Württemberg's financial position was more than delicate, but when she asked her eldest brother for help he sent her a medallion of himself with apologies for his inability to do more. As he was up to the neck in debt his parsimony is understandable, and the Queen replied meekly that she would have " avoided being troublesome " had she known of the bankrupt state of the British finances and the cry for " Œconomy ". Such virtues were now being practised by her stepson Dolly, the new king. Among other ways of raising the wind Adolphus sold some porcelain which Charlotte had painted for her father. Gradually Charlotte recovered her spirits: she found refuge and consolation in her religion. To keep her husband's memory fresh she celebrated his birthday every year with a service at which a sermon in praise of the late monarch was preached by an expert; she afterwards prayed beside his tomb in the family vault, foreshadowing that sombre practice adopted by Queen Victoria on 'Mausoleum Day' half a century later.

In Württemberg her popularity reached new heights as she plodded ponderously but good-naturedly among her husband's people, supporting all good causes and ever inquiring kindly after the 'Peasants'. But her thoughts more and more drifted to the land of her birth which she had not seen for twenty years and from which she had been completely cut off for nine years. She had wished to make the journey as soon as Napoleon had been packed off to Elba, and when communications were resumed in 1813 the Prince Regent, to do him justice, tenderly invited her to Britain, but the 'arrogance' of Frederick William barred the way. Apparently the king of Württemberg, who sometimes acted as though he had created the Danube which rose in his kingdom, took umbrage because the invitation was addressed to the Princess Royal and not to him. He was also miffed because of all decorations in the world the Garter was the most desirable, and yet he was denied it. But there is little doubt that the ill-treatment of a devoted wife and dubious dealings with the mortal enemy of his father-in-law disqualified Frederick William from membership of Europe's oldest order of chivalry.

Word of the German monarch's impudent attitude reached London, and in December 1813 the Prince Regent sent his Gentleman Usher of the Black Rod to Stüttgart. Sir Thomas Tyrwhitt, one of those rare courtiers who from time to time served the monarchy without perceptibly harming it, was known to the Royal Family as 'The Dwarf' ('*Der Zwerg*') or 'The Twenty-third of June' because he was, according to the court punster of the day, the shortest (k)night. As Charlotte's first human contact with home since the Peace of Amiens, he filled her days with news of her parents, brothers and sisters which alternately alarmed, puzzled, shocked or delighted her. Tyrwhitt also looked into the Princess Royal's personal finances, only to discover that her marriage allowance had been woefully reduced by the manipulations of Continental exchange jugglers. The £5,000 which was always punctually transmitted from England every year had by 1805 fallen to £190, and between then and 1813 it had never exceeded £1,333 in any one year. But when Sir Thomas raised the question of a visit to Britain the Princess Royal contrived to cough " in a very violent and painful manner ", at which the King, who had instructed her to do so, would exclaim, " Vot did I tell you? She is not in goot condition to travel. Ve vish not for her to go." Whenever Tyrwhitt reopened the question the King flew off into one of those passions which Castlereagh had heard of when he described Frederick William as " a tyrant both in his public and private character ". Yet when Charlotte's brother Edward of Kent visited Stüttgart in 1816 he noted that 'Royal' appeared to be " perfectly happy ".

After Frederick William's death Charlotte, who had found a " most melancholy comfort " in talking over with Tyrwhitt the " dreadful situation " of her beloved father, lost interest in voyaging to England. She preferred to feed her imagination on the facts supplied by the diminutive Black Rod, after whose mission to Stüttgart she wrote to the Prince Regent: " Your angelic conduct towards him [George III], my dearest Brother, to my Mother and Sisters, is a theme Sir Thomas kindly loves to dwell on, as he sees how much it soothes my mind to be acquainted with every circumstance of your dutifull Behaviour to our Parents; and your affectionate kindness to my Sisters, whose situation would have been melancholy and unpleasant had your good heart not induced you to step forth and have such handsome establishments settled on them."

But soon she was writing in her beautiful copperplate hand with a heart full of grief to console her brother on the death of Princess Charlotte, that dynastic convulsion which sent the Princess Royal's morganatically disposed brothers chasing off in search of respectable royal brides in the so-called 'race for an heir'. When her aunt left home in 1797 little Charlotte had been only eighteen months old, and from time to time she sent dolls' china of her own making, and other dainty gifts, to her "Little Beauty". From afar she lavished upon her niece the love she would have reserved for her lost daughter, much as her sister-in-law, the future Queen Adelaide, filled with love for the little Princess Victoria the void left in her heart by the death of her infant daughter who might have reigned as Queen Elizabeth II.

Visits from William and Adelaide brightened the early days of her widowhood, but her brother was horrified by the way she had ballooned into a travesty of youth. How very different from those days when she was attractive and slim and had excited a romantic passion in the breast of Thomas Stone! Poor Thomas was the son of a Shaftesbury floor-cloth painter. He had been trained as a solicitor, his parents having ideas beyond their station, but something must have gone to his head because he conceived a plan—anticipating a future Chancellor of the Exchequer—for paying off the National Debt. This admirable idea was then regarded as evidence of lunacy, and when Thomas began to pay court to the King's eldest daughter he was deemed to be incurably mad. In 1787 Stone was 32 when he wrote to Queen Charlotte proclaiming his warm affection for her daughter and promising, should their Majesties approve, that he and the Princess Royal would make a "very happy couple". As no reply was returned to this letter, Mr. Stone naturally assumed that the princess had accepted him, and he accordingly presented himself at St. James's in his Sunday best, only to find to his mortification that no one had heard of him. He then pursued the beloved to Kew. There he was arrested and told to turn out his pockets, which were found to be full of love poems addressed to Charlotte, whom he claimed he had loved for three years since, one night at the theatre, she had looked up at him in the two-shilling gallery. Thomas immortalised the occasion in the imperishable words.

> Thrice glad were I to be your willing slave,
> But not the captive of the tool or knave;
> With woe on woe you melt my sighing breast,
> Whilst you reject your humble would-be guest.

Thomas and his sighing breast were returned to London, and he found himself a would-be guest not at the court of George III but in Bedlam, the hospital where so many other misunderstood subjects of the King were to end up in a plight not far different from that of the King himself.

The bonds of love between Charlotte and her father outlasted his life but in the early years were sorely strained by his sickness. He called her Matilda after one of her names and considered her the true ' governess ' of her three younger sisters, Augusta, Elizabeth and Mary. The childhood of all these was overshadowed by the King's plight, but Charlotte, his inseparable companion, felt the responsibility more than any other member of the Royal Family except her mother. An attempt on the King's life in 1787 by the unhinged Magrater Nicholson shocked her profoundly, and she was the first to notice the sudden deterioration in her father's condition in the autumn of the following year. The King and his daughter had been out for an airing in the royal chaise. Outwardly he was all smiles and grace, but words suddenly began to tumble from him in a torrent, confusing the postillions, who were called upon to stop and start and repeat the exercise before the King, who stepped out of and back into the chaise twice during this exercise, calmed down sufficiently to avoid alarming the ' Peasantry ', who doffed the cap and touched the forelock at reassuring intervals all the way back to Windsor. The Princess Royal kept calm and gave her mother in German a comforting version of the drive. But that night there was a terrifying scene at dinner, and for three weeks afterwards the King babbled incoherently. His doctors refused to allow Charlotte to accompany him to Kew, and she did not see him there until Bastille year was sixteen days old, by which time he was playing picquet with the Queen and lusting after Lady Pembroke, a love of his youth. Between them the three eldest princesses " wept pools ", but none more than ' Royal ', when the King eluded his doctors to smuggle a copy of Colman's adaptation of *King Lear* into his apartment and give his three daughters a touching account of it from a personal point of view.

" It is very beautiful, very affecting and very awful," he said. " I am like poor Lear, but thank God I have no Regan, no Goneril, only three Cordelias."

Yet when the King recovered he showed no disposition to arrange marriages for his Cordelias—" the beauteous boast of Britain's Isle " in Peter Pindar's graphic phrase. When they entered the Presence he saluted them with a few shrill blasts on his flute, spoke vaguely of taking them abroad to meet German Protestant princes, but seemed to place anyone of lesser rank or religious persuasion on the same footing as the court hirelings. Yet the ' Sisterhood ' were not unhappy, and ' Royal ' during the years of exile in Germany often recalled happy times, not least at Weymouth, where the Royal Family first took up residence during the King's convalescence. There she and her sisters " bathed frequently, and received much pleasure from their ablutions ", and also from visits to men-o'-war at Plymouth, where one of the ships' cutters, escorting the royal barge, was rowed by six " Devonshire mermaids " and steered by a seventh, all in loose white gowns and black bonnets with sashes of royal purple across the shoulders inscribed in gold letters with the legend: " Long Live Their Majesties ".

Meanwhile the court gossips were keeping a fairly close watch on the adolescent sisters, loyally committing their impartial impressions to diaries and journals. Mercifully their contents were hidden from Charlotte, for most of these records conflict in their assessment of her nature. Fanny Burney attributed to her almost supernatural qualities, but revealed her human side as well, for she records that the Princess Royal once asked her, " Pray, is it really true that in your illness last year you coughed so violently that you broke the whalebone of your stays in two?"

Both Mrs. Harcourt, who was related to the Queen's Master of the Horse, and Mrs. Papendiek, another lady overwhelmed by the privacies of court life and the need to divulge them, thought Charlotte " timid ". Probably this was because the Princess Royal stood in awe of the Queen. The whole family did, for that matter; but Charlotte seemed " a different being " when

Charlotte of Württemberg, Princess Royal

Frederick William, Duke and later King of Württemberg

Queen Charlotte and the Princess Royal, by West

she was away from her mother, whom she is said to have described as a silly woman because of her ludicrous absorption in etiquette. On the other hand, Mrs. Hall in her book claims that all the princesses became " exemplary, accomplished and high-minded women ". Lady Louisa Stuart noted compassionately Charlotte's deep love for her sick father. She was the King's " comfort and darling " and resembled him in many ways. She also had " sense, though not brilliancy, a thoroughly right mind, and real dignity ". Lady Mary Coke considered Charlotte " the best humour'd Child that ever was " after having seen her " a good deal try'd by her brothers, who pull'd her about most unreasonably ".

Charlotte's first public appearance was on the Queen's birthday in 1782 when she was 16. To commemorate the occasion she opened the ball with the Prince of Wales, who wore a waistcoat of the Queen's own embroidering. But for all her good humour, sense and dignity Charlotte really was a little clumsy long before she put on weight. We have seen that she had no clothes sense, but she could command the best dressmakers and she appeared at another ball in " white and gold with a green spot, the beautiful manufacture of England ". Yet she had taken no more than a few steps in a gavotte when the fringe of her petticoat became entangled in her shoe buckle. Charlotte blushed with embarrassment, but blushed even more when one of those wits of whom the Hanoverian royals were always the defenceless target rhymed:

> Tho' well she tripp'd,
> The lady slipp'd,
> The Princess lost her shoe.
> Her Highness hopp'd,
> The fiddlers stopp'd,
> Not knowing what to do.

She was rescued from the abominable predicament by the gallant Lord Hertford, who flew like lightning to unbuckle the royal shoe.

Memories of this and other events of her youth came flooding back as Charlotte toyed with the idea of revisiting England. But her mother died, the King became incurably mad, the ' Brethren '

I

were whizzing about after royal brides, and the 'Sisterhood' had their problems.

Long before communications had been restored between London and Stüttgart those "much supervised young women" had revolted against the strictures of court life imposed by Queen Charlotte and applied by those twin dragons of propriety, the governesses Miss Goldsworthy and Miss Gomm. Towards the end of the war which 'the Monster' Napoleon had inflicted upon Europe the Queen's nature, austere at the best of times, had been warped by the tensions springing from the King's heart-rending sickness. She was driven almost berserk herself by reports that the princesses had been visiting their brothers' apartments without chaperones. There had been dreadful scenes about this kind of romp, so little Tyrwhitt told the Queen of Württemberg, who reacted with consternation to delicate hints that her sisters were not all that an innocent and virtuous British public had the right to expect them to be.

Her second sister Augusta, for instance, who had once shocked a simple Windsor cleric by claiming the sky to be her parish, was considered to be an old maid, but was more likely a widow. She was thought to have contracted a secret marriage with one of Wellington's generals, Sir Brent Spencer. The third sister Elizabeth, known as 'Fatima', suffered in common with other members of the 'Sisterhood' from chest complaints and spasms, and these every nine months or so necessitated her removal to a quiet house in Kew. The Princess of Wales, who among other testimonials to a thoroughly unstable marriage pleaded that she had been forced by her husband to smoke a pipe, promised to list "the offspring of the unmarried Princesses" for public consumption if she were driven to it. The artistic Elizabeth, who suffered from the family tendency to hard-upness and was usually in debt, apparently had shown her etchings to Ramus, a member of the household, who rewarded her with his passion. From this unsuitable connection she had been rescued by the Princess Royal, at whose suggestion she was married in 1818 to the garlic-eating Hereditary Prince of Hesse-Homburg—"an uglier hound, with a snout buried in hair, I never saw", according to one witness; while Lady Jernyngham reported that he was immersed several times in a warm bath to make him clean before his wedding day. Frederick Joseph's vice was smoking—five pipes a day—at a time when drunkenness in gentlemen was regarded as a virtue. The garden-loving Elizabeth, perhaps the warmest-hearted and most typically English of George III's girls, made the best of her marriage but, like Charlotte, bore no children.

The Princess Royal's third sister Mary, known as ' Miny ', was the Aphrodite of a family remarkable in early life for good looks. She too, suffered from cramps and spasms, but her love live was unblemished, although more than one early suitor whom she rejected died of a broken heart. Ultimately she married a child-hood sweetheart, her cousin the Duke of Gloucester. The match was tempestuously opposed by the King, partly because William Frederick's mother, Maria, Countess of Waldgrave, had been an illegitimate Walpole. A prodigious effort had been made by Trinity College, Cambridge, to coax the duke's brain into action, and in sheer desperation he was made the present of a Master of Arts degree. Among his limited accomplishments was an ability to tuck a violin under his chin and scrape the strings with his bow. A visitor once asked his tutor if he played much. " Not much," was the reply; " only God save his Uncle, and such little things."

Gentlemen, even old ones, were never tolerated to sit in his presence, and when he took coffee, he expected the ladies of the party to hand it to him on a salver and to remain standing while he imbibed. Mary survived this and the other disadvantages of a man who seemed to have married her for himself alone, and she lived long enough to hear of the birth of Queen Victoria's last child Beatrice—' Little Bee '.

In March 1814 the Queen of Württemberg had written to Tyrwhitt: " I fear that you will find poor Sophia sadly altered." Indeed he had, for there had been plenty to change her fourth rather elfin and gipsy-like sister from the ' Sea Nymph ', as the Prince Regent called her, into a sour spinster of 36. Char-lotte's tale-bearing as a teenager at her father's court had fallen harshly upon Sophia, who seemed " a little more gay " after her eldest sister had departed for Württemberg. But there was plenty to sneak about. Sophia became involved with, and was probably married to, one of the King's equerries, General Thomas Garth, by whom she had a son, also Thomas Garth, in 1800. The Court was again at Weymouth, frolicking in the sea from ' huts ' which resembled miniature parlours cut out of the royal

apartments at Windsor, when Sophia suddenly developed
' dropsy ' but as suddenly got rid of it two or three months later.
General Garth had been innocently described by Princess Mary,
who never suspected the liaison, as " the Purple Light of Love "
from the strawberry birthmark which disfigured his features.
Sophia's marriage to Garth, who was thirty-three years her
senior, was not unhappily the end of the story. After the birth
of her child, whom she supported for the rest of her life, a
hideous legend circulated that he was in fact the product of an
incestuous union between Sophia and her brother Cumberland.
All this came about, it was said, because the brothers and sisters
defied their mother's orders and were always hopping in and out
of each other's rooms. The probability is that the legend was
invented by the Princess of Wales, who had suffered so much
that she cared little whom she maligned.

Of all Charlotte's sisters the youngest, Amelia, born after two
of the King's nine sons—Octavius and Alfred—had died in infancy, was genuinely devoted to the Princess Royal and unwilling
to hear her criticised by Mary and Sophia. When Charlotte left
for Württemberg in 1797 Amelia had written to her favourite
lady-in-waiting: " Oh, my dear Angel, my Heart is so full with
parting with my dear Sister that I can scarce write. Pray say
everything that is kind to my dear Royal . . . how sincerely I
love her."

Amelia's brief life was brightened by a romance with General
Sir Charles FitzRoy, descended through the Dukes of Grafton
from Charles II. When she died in 1810 in her twenty-seventh
year rumours ascribed several children to her by FitzRoy, whom
she regarded as her lawful husband, although he was twenty-one
years older. But she was also said to have died giving birth to
a child or twins, sired by Edward Phelps, a friend of the Prince
Regent. Her young life was blighted by incurable tuberculosis
complicated by St. Anthony's Fire. All she had was left to
" beloved Charles FitzRoy ", but apart from a few pieces of
plate from which her executors discreetly erased her monogram,
he was deprived of his legacy by the combined opposition of the
Prince Regent and the Duke of Cambridge.

Sad indeed was the news from home after the close of the
war, and as Charlotte's stepson, the new king, treated the
Dowager Queen shabbily and sold some of her treasures, she was

not too happy in the land of her adoption. But between 1819 and 1821 there were compensations. She was overjoyed to receive her sisters Elizabeth and Augusta, who found her immersed in charitable works—paying rents or finding work for indigent Württembergers, educating their children out of her own purse, training apprentices and carrying out a variety of eleemosynary assignments. But she forbade anyone around her to speak of her charities under pain of instant dismissal. Augusta was appalled at the change in her physical appearance in quarter of a century—" very large and bulky ", " face very broad and fat . . . three or four times larger than it was ", " a great deal of lower stomach ".

All this great load of flesh was forgotten when her brother George alighted heavily upon the Continent soon after his coronation and she hastened to greet him; and in the summer of 1822 brother William of Clarence and sister-in-law Adelaide descended upon her Hercynian forest retreat at Louisbourg and joined in a general wassail, singing and dancing, while donkeys raced and contests peculiar to the neighbourhood were dutifully organised by " the inferior Peasantry " The Clarences brought Charlotte news of little Victoria, to whom the Princess Royal stood sponsor at her christening in 1819, with her sister Augusta acting as proxy. William again visited her in 1825, when it was noticed that she not only brightened up but actually took some exercise, the lack of which had contributed to her immense girth.

Dropsy was beginning to take its toll. Charlotte also suffered exceedingly from gout. She ate sparingly, never touching meat but refreshing herself with a daily glass of Malaga, yet she continued to deteriorate until at last she was so short of breath that she had to be hauled up and down stairs in a chair. This was her condition when, early in 1827, her brother the Duke of York died, and, amid general manifestations of sorrow, deprived England of yet another future King Frederick. His eldest sister bemoaned " this severe Calamity ". Sister Augusta had meanwhile been gently pressing her to visit London, not only to see the relations before any further tragedy struck them but also to consult the surgeon Sir Astley Cooper. " Though I am a very stupid old Being I am a gratefull one," she replied, and she hoped her dear brother would " have patience with my infirm-

ities "—as indeed he should, for George IV himself was much
altered, so billowed out and grotesque around the lower body
and legs that he had the streets cleared before he would take
a drive, or else he travelled under cover of darkness so that
none of his loyal subjects should see him. Before her journey
Charlotte made an heroic attempt to reduce her weight by
taking thirty medicinal baths at Teinach. Even so she could not
face the sea passage without begging the King to have her drawn
up the side of the royal yacht in a chair, as she could not
possibly climb a ladder, her great fear being that she might
alarm everybody with " one of my Suffocations ".

A special operating theatre was equipped in deepest secrecy
at St. James's Palace, and Sir Astley began tapping the whale-
like figure of the Dowager Queen of Württemberg to reduce
pressure on the bloated abdomen. This temporary relief awakened
hopes of a cure, but Charlotte soon began to swell out again
and moreover suffered from erysipelas. There seemed no alternative for her but to say her farewells and go home to Germany
to die. Yet she enjoyed her stay, the crowds shouted with joy
when she appeared in the streets, her brothers and sisters were
kind to her, her little god-daughter Victoria paid her the
most flattering attention, and she spent many happy hours
with the King. Parting from her family proved as hard for them
as it was for her, and it was in a highly emotional state that
she embarked for Germany.

On the second day out the yacht was overtaken by a violent
storm near the mouth of the Thames. The Princess Royal lay,
sick but undaunted, in her cabin and prayed for release. She was
a model of courage to her ladies, and when they expressed
alarm she told them, " I am here in the hand of God, as
much at home as in my bed."

The storm abated and soon she was back at Louisbourg, but
as the months passed the dropsy spread to her brain, which
after her death was found on dissection to have been damaged
by the disease. Yet only three days before she died on 6th
October 1828 Charlotte kept up a cheerful conversation for
nearly two hours with her guests, the Earl and Countess of
Shrewsbury who had come to dinner, and was as affable as
ever.

Every Sunday her English maid read a sermon to her. On

the day before her death she listened attentively and then said, " There, my dear, you have done, and I thank you—you will never read me another."

When she felt herself slipping away she sent for the King of Württemberg, whom she called " my son ", and after a long talk asked him to bring his wife and children next day, but when they arrived she had gone blind—" I can hear your voices, but I cannot see you any more." Lady Louisa Stuart recorded that she was putting out one hand to the King, and his little boy, upon whom she doted, was kissing the other when her vast form shuddered and then subsided in death. The inconsolable child clung to his ' grandma ' until he was forcibly removed.

Charlotte was buried alongside her husband in the vault of Ludwigsburg and she was mourned in Stüttgart and throughout the kingdom. As she had made her will as early as December 1816 many of the legatees had died. Even her unreconciled brother Ernest, Duke of Cumberland, whom she would never see in Germany because of his " dirty tricks and his freedom of speech ", and whom she had not met since she left London in 1797, remarked, " One cannot help feeling deeply when one branch of the old tree drops off."

The Empress Frederick

I

" FROM DEAR Papa I can learn more than from anyone else in the world," wrote Victoria, Princess Royal, the future Empress Frederick, to her mother Queen Victoria in the days of her courtship. The adored Papa was meanwhile writing intimately to Fritz, her future husband, Prince Frederick William of Prussia: " From the moment you declared your love and embraced her the child in her vanished. . . . Vicky has learned many and divers things. . . . If I find that she has misunderstood something I make her work it out in writing without any help, then she brings it to me for correction."

Vicky was affectionately nicknamed ' Pussy ', by her fond parents, and she was then translating from the German a tome on the Duke of Saxe-Weimar—her fiancé's grandfather—and German politics. And the Queen wrote to her future son-in-law: " You must be always closer to us parents than our own son." Vicky was thinking of her " precious madly-loved Fritz " night and day.

To the Queen her daughter's suitor wrote just before their engagement: " I shall count the months eagerly until I can return to this dear family." On the Prince Consort's last birthday on earth Vicky wrote to Fritz of her father. " There is no one like him on earth, there cannot be another." Before Frederick William took her away to Germany she rested her head on Papa's bosom and he said, " You hardly know what a blank you will leave behind in my heart." The Queen wrote to Fritz: " You dear, kind person, you have torn a piece of our heart away." After her marriage Albert went through Vicky's wifely duties with her point by point, and when she came of age the Prince Consort, soon to die, wrote prophetically to her: "Good-bye . . . you old, twenty-one-year-old child!"

Rarely have four more loved or loving royal creatures stood more clearly revealed before history than in these excerpts. Queen Victoria loved Albert with a depth of feeling matched only by the mutual passion of Frederick William and the Princess Royal; but the Queen's romantic heart swelled at the sight of her daughter's handsome sweetheart, and in her way she fell in love with him, too. Albert, disappointed in his son Edward (Bertie), lavished love and talent on his first-born daughter, and Vicky rewarded him by developing an erotic father complex. To Frederick William he was a second father: Albert was particularly gratified by the sober-minded German prince's expressions of naïve astonishment at the wonders of the Great Exhibition of 1851, the product largely of the Prince Consort's fertile brain. Vicky was only 10 years old then, but she spoke good German and was a pretty little girl. The blissful domestic life of the Royal Family, so different from the rigid discipline of Potsdam, where Frederick William's unbalanced uncle, King Frederick William II, was striving to erect the monarchy into an instrument of Divine authority, overwhelmed the young prince. He left for home powerfully impressed by Britain's grandeur and greatness, the indestructibility of the Crystal Palace, Albert's genius, Queen Victoria's matronly charms, and above all Vicky's sweetness—"I keep thinking of beautiful Osborne and London where I spent so many happy hours with you," wrote Frederick William, then a stripling of 19, to the clever little girl in lace-fringed knickers who had temporarily shaken his philosophical mind from its normal pursuit of the serious.

There was much to be serious about. The Prince Consort as a German yearned to see the German states unified under the hegemony of Prussia, the largest and most capable of the three dozen or more disparate elements which had made up the Holy Roman Empire, dismembered with the ending of the Napoleonic wars. Should Humpty-Dumpty be put together again? Or should the "ill-joined conglomeration of disunited peoples"—in de Tocqueville's pregnant phrase—be welded by a group of feudally-minded Junkers controlling 17 million Prussians into a second all-German Reich, formidable in military power and impatient of democratic forms of government? For forty years since Waterloo the statesmen of Europe, France especially, had contrived to keep Germany divided. Now they began to ask, the British in particular, who should take the first shock of any threatened onslaught from the east. For the Russian giant had awakened and was reaching out towards those countries of the Balkan peninsula which were about to slip from the enfeebled hands of Turkey, the sick man of Europe. Despite all the advice which Albert in his good nature had pauselessly poured upon his wife's ministers about the Eastern Question, war became inevitable between the arrogant and tyrannous Czar Nicholas I on the one hand and Victoria and her new ally Louis Napoleon III, who had proclaimed himself Emperor of the French in 1851, and in whom the Queen, once so frightened out of her middle-class respectability by stories of his unbridled lust, now found sweet merit.

One would have thought that after her dear Albert's *vigorous* championship of the Germans they would have taken the side of the Western Allies in the Crimean War. But they remained neutral, so unlike the Prussia of good old Blücher, and this ' cowardly ' conduct left much to be desired. The British, not for the first time, trembled with anti-German anger. It was all most distressing, but even more incredible was the accusation hurled against the Prince Consort that he was a Russian spy—

> And little Al, the royal pal,
> They say has turned a Russian.

He was even said to have been arrested for high treason and clapped in the Tower. The story improved in the telling: the Queen had joined him there and large crowds had gathered outside the grim Norman fortress to see summary justice dispatched on Tower Hill. But as the Queen remarked some years later, after the Princess Royal, her dearest child, had been snubbed by the Czar's daughter, who would even consider consorting with Romanoffs? Such an inferior breed! " You are the eldest daughter of the Queen of England with a title and rights of your own, fifth in succession. . . . Our Princesses never admitted the Grand Duchesses of Russia having precedence over them; the Romanoffs are not to be compared with the houses of Brunswick, Saxony and Hohenzollern."

For good measure she added that although such matters appeared to be trifles, " the honour and dignity of one's family " did not allow them to be overlooked. No, it was certainly not Russians who preoccupied Papa's last years; it was Germans. If only he could get that industrious and talented conglomeration to coalesce under the Prussian king! Frederick William II it is true, was a dreamer who looked to be slightly off his rocker, but he was childless, and coming up behind him were his younger brother William, who was happier on a war horse than in any company of intellectuals, and William's Saxe-Weimar wife Augusta, a woman of solid German virtues. The Crown Princess had been brought up in Weimar, that most enlightened of German states, and had blossomed under the influence of Göethe. Hers had been an arranged marriage: as a young man William had been refused permission to marry Elise Radziwill, the daughter of a ' protected ' Polish princeling, but William had been 33 before his advisers had turned him from his resolve to dedicate his life to the army and had convinced him of the perils of celibacy. In the revolutionary ferment of 1848 William fled to England: young Frederick William still remembered with shame his father's sending him for a scissors to snip off his whiskers the better to disguise himself. Six years later William fell out with his brother and was banished to Coblenz because he opposed Prussia's neutrality on the Crimean issue. Augusta inclined to liberalism, but she pushed her views rather too forthrightly even for Albert, who found it necessary to chide her after she became his favourite daughter's mother-in-law: " I have today impressed upon her that people can only be controlled with and through love."

William was the Prince Consort's cousin. Prince Frederick William was the elder child of William and Augusta, who completed her marital functions when a daughter, Louise, was born. When it is added that Queen Victoria's omniscient uncle Leopold of the Belgians, as well as the revered Baron von Stockmar, urged that the best way to amalgamate the German states under Prussian leadership would be to bring about an Anglo-Prussian matrimonial *coup*, and that the Queen and Augusta were simply showering each other with letters on the subject, it is plain to see, in the afterglow of events, how some of the best brains in Europe conspired with some of the second-best to bring about the great tragedy of the Empress Frederick. For in the wings lurked the snuffy, wine-swilling, baleful figure of Bismarck, whose policy of ' iron and blood ' is so often blamed for the world wars of the twentieth century and who can certainly be said to have turned a happy young English princess into a tragic wife and an even more tragic mother and widow.

In August 1855 the Queen and Prince Albert visited Paris. The meeting of minds of the Monarch and the Emperor had a soothing effect on Anglo-French relations, although France would have no great reason for gratitude fifteen years later when she found herself alone at war with Prussia. The true significance of the Paris *entente* lay in the presence of the little known Bismarck, who in his ambassadorial capacity was presented to the Queen and found Albert regarding him with " a certain ill-disposed curiosity ", for which poor France, and in the long term poorer Britain, would pay a heavy price. When Napoleon and Eugénie returned the visit two years later the Princess Royal, now her father's most efficient little secretary and companion, feasted her eyes on the Empress—" my *beau idéal* of a woman ", she remarked. But with unusual perception for a maiden of 16 she felt Napoleon III was sitting on a volcano and wondered what would be Eugénie's fate.

Between these two state occasions the Crimean War had ended—not without some assistance from the Prince Consort, who anticipated history by denouncing the donkey-like generals as a bunch of " esses ". Secret plans were going forward for the marriage of the Princess Royal and Frederick William. The preparations had to be secret: a strong conservative faction in Berlin feared Prussia would go to the dogs if the known liberal instincts of the British royals and their prospective son-in-law and his mother were thus encouraged. The King of Prussia suspected his nephew might be infected by the ' English disease ' of which the chief symptom since 1832 had been a painful swelling of the head when British statesmen extolled the virtues of a wide-ranging electoral franchise (from which only a few million of the labouring classes were at that time excluded) and of a parliamentary system democratically manipulated by the old aristocracy. Indeed, during his last term at Bonn University before he joined the Prussian army Prince Frederick William and his English tutor, Mr. Perry, had amused themselves writing imaginary letters to Lord Palmerston and other English leaders. *The Times*, too,

would be frightfully upset by any kind of alliance with Prussia,
and indeed was; for when news of the engagement leaked in 1855
the Thunderer expostulated fiercely: was it expedient that " a
daughter of England should take her place upon the throne of
Prussia " or be pushed into a position where devotion to her
husband must be " treason to her country "? The newspaper
sighed for poor young ' Pussy ' and wished her " some better
fate ": it was a nice thought which even nicer people than the
leader-writer of *The Times* could scarcely have improved upon.
The Prussians, and especially their monarch, feared the prince
would be marrying beneath him, for Albert was a nobody. But
it was the effect on Bismarck that was to shape events.

" Is it really true ", he asked the King's adjutant-general " that
they are pressing on with this English marriage?"

He thought it would " introduce English influence and anglo-
mania without our obtaining anything similar in England ", where
anti-German feeling was increasing. Bismarck foresaw the court
at Potsdam " surrounded by English influence ", especially as
Stockmar's son Ernest was being sent to Berlin as the young
couple's adviser: obviously the fellow would be employed there
as a spy. The ' English ' in the marriage displeased Bismarck,
though the ' marriage ' might be quite good.

" If the Princess can leave the English-woman at home and
become a Prussian, then she may be a blessing to the country.
If our future Queen on the Prussian throne remains the least
bit English, then I see our Court surrounded by English influence."

He deplored his countrymen's current admiration for British
customs. " What will it be like ", he asked, " when the first lady
in the land is an English-woman?" And when Bismarck realised
that the Princess Royal was her father's ardent disciple he
became her foremost enemy.

Albert perceived that if reactionaries took over in Germany
the monarchy would be threatened. But how odd those ' progressive ' English royals looked to the straitlaced Prussians! The
future Field-marshal von Moltke, who in early life had obligingly
promised to translate the whole of Gibbon's *Decline and Fall of
the Roman Empire* for £80, visited the newly-completed Gothic
castle at Balmoral with Prince Frederick William and found the
household's lack of formality unnerving—only one minister at

hand, no doorkeepers, no swarm of flunkeys, not even an armed guard. The Prussian mind boggled.

"Nobody would guess that the Court of one of the most powerful states resides here, and that from these mountains the fate of the world is determined."

Von Moltke was profoundly shocked. And Fritz, concerned only with his own fate at that impressionable time, felt the world falling to pieces around him when the Queen and Albert gently asked him to wait for two years before proposing to ' Pussy ', and not to broach the subject to her until her seventeenth birthday.

On 20th March 1856 the Princess Royal was confirmed. Her younger sister Alice wept copiously. Otherwise the ceremony was distinguished only by an address from the Archbishop of Canterbury which the second (and slightly deaf) Earl Granville thought would have been incredibly dull had it not been inaudible to him. In the two years before her marriage ' Pussy's ' education was pressed forward: among other things she learned to swim. She was " growing fast and her figure developing ". Clarendon, the Foreign Secretary, praised her " highly cultivated intellect ", which, with a well-trained imagination, led her to " saying and doing the right things in the right places." She was also becoming a dear little compulsive writer, brightly chattering off one folio after another: after one of his later visits to London her fiancé received through the diplomatic pouch an epistle of some forty closely-penned pages, which more than compensated for his joyless return to Berlin. But a few months after her confirmation he was horrified to hear that while Vicky was sealing a letter to him she had been severely burned when the sleeve of her muslin dress came into contact with an oil lamp. She might have burned to death but for the swift action of two of her staff, who threw a rug over the flames, although not before the princess's right arm had been burned from elbow to shoulder. Fritz wrote: " Through this accident you have really been given to me a second time, but please, please be more careful in future."

Weeks later she was still writing left-handed with results, as she apologised, worthy of Bertie's parrot. But she soon revived. According to the United States ambassador she was now " all life and spirit, full of frolic and fun, with an excellent head, and a *heart as big as a mountain* ". When she smiled it made one feel " as if additional light were thrown upon the scene ". The Prince Consort found her intellect " quick and thoroughly sound in its operations ", like a well-tuned clock. Lady Paget, a German lady married to an English diplomat and high in Queen Victoria's esteem, thought ' Pussy ' very young for her age. Her eyes were remarkable—" the iris was green like the sea on a sunny day, and the white had a peculiar shimmer which gave them the fascination that, together with a smile showing her small and beautiful teeth, bewitched those who approached her ". The little turned-up nose contrasted with a small chin which apparently showed " a lack of determination ", but her very gentle and almost timid manner belied the impression of stubbornness. She spoke English and German " with a slight foreign accent " in a carefully modulated voice. Nevertheless the princess had certain defects of character: the violent fancies she took to people led to " bitter disillusion " when their conduct fell below her own standards. A creature of violent prejudices, she tended to judge people on first impressions. A mispronounced word or a slight trick of manner turned her against them for life. She was " no judge of character ", Walpurga Paget thought, " because her own point of view was the only one she could see."

In part Walpurga was right about the Princess Royal, but she misjudged Frederick William when she considered him to be " undeveloped for his age " and likely to be led by his wife. She was not alone in this opinion, but in practice he turned out to be the most enlightened and progressive of the Hohenzollerns. He was tall and handsome. The Empress Eugénie had raved about him when, after the prince had visited Russia for Alexander II's coronation, at Albert's prompting he paid a countervailing visit to Paris. He was almost a head taller than Napoleon III. " He is slim and fair," enthused Eugénie, " with a light yellow moustache—in fact a Teuton such as Tacitus described, chivalrously polite, and not without a resemblance to Hamlet." She added, as she later had good reason to test in the crucible of experience, that the Germans were an " imposing " race. Louis Napoleon, who was to figure as King Florestan in Disraeli's Endymion, in which Bismarck is portrayed as Count Ferrol, thought they were the race of the future. The Empress hurled this aside—" Bah, we are not there yet." Fritz anxiously explained

Victoria, Princess Royal,
the Empress Frederick III

The Emperor Frederick
William III of Prussia, by
Lawrence

The Empress Frederick with her son, later Kaiser William II

to his Imperial host that neither his trip to Moscow nor his marriage would imperil Franco-German relations, and he sincerely believed it.

On 14th April 1857 Queen Victoria gave birth to her ninth and, as it proved, last child, Princes Beatrice. The Queen had every hope of bearing at least one more baby, but for the present, while with one hand she rocked the cradle of her youngest daughter, with the other she signed orders and programmes for the nuptials of the eldest. The wedding was to take place on 25th January 1858 at the Chapel Royal, St. James's, the scene of her own unforgettable wedding. As the day approached Vicky, like the three Princesses Royal before her, began to dread the ineluctable parting from her parents. She only hoped that she and Fritz would be as happy as they after seventeen years of wedded bliss. The prelude to the ceremony was, however, none too propitious. At home the pleasure taken by the British people in the first royal marriage in a generation was overcast by the Indian Mutiny, and then Fritz, who felt every day " unbearable " that he had to spend away from his beloved, was caught up in his first constitutional crisis when the uncertain intellect of the Prussian king suddenly dimmed and his brother William became Regent. On the brighter side, this period saw Queen Victoria's dearest wish gratified: the Beloved One was created Prince Consort. But when all was nearly ready the monarch suffered the most profound shock. The Prussian Court stood firmly on protocol and indicated that the marriage should be solemnised in Berlin. Rarely had the Queen been so indignant.

" It is too absurd, there never was even the shadow of a *doubt* on *Prince Frederick William's* part as to *where* the marriage should take place. . . . Whatever may be the usual practice of Prussian Princes, it is not *every* day that one marries the eldest daughter of the Queen of England. The question must therefore be considered settled and closed."

And settled and closed it was. Prussians really were the most difficult people. Stingy, too. Albert worked himself into a pet over the " shabby " state of Pussy's marriage settlement: not one penny from Prussia. The Berlin set assumed that their future heir apparent had married a rich wife who would maintain him out of her own substantial English dowry. Meanwhile the object of their generous thoughts was in Berlin trying out what he

K

called the " gilded monkey cage " in which he and his bride were to enter his uncle's capital. On the evening before the ceremony the Princess Royal cut off a few strands of her golden hair and placed them in a locket, which she handed tearfully to the Queen, begging her always to wear it against her heart in memory of her sad little daughter.

Loyal Londoners lined up next day to hail their monarch and the Royal Family along the route between Buckingham Palace and St. James's. The ceremony was less elaborate than those of the Princess Royal's predecessors and there were fewer histrionics except when, the rings having been exchanged, the Queen who had re-lived her own wedding throughout the proceedings, on an impulse pressed the bride and bridegroom to her bosom, but could find no words to express her feelings and, probably for the first time in her life, was speechless with emotion. The honeymoon was to be spent at Windsor Castle; the boys of Eton College whooped at the sight of the royal couple, unharnessed the horses, and dragged the bridal carriage up to the castle.

" I think it will kill me to take leave of dear Papa," said ' Pussy ' as the time for her departure approached.

' Baby Bee ', then nearly nine months old, tugged at her finger as though reluctant to let her go. But she went, and on her way to the coast the rough draymen of Barclay and Perkins's brewery shouted to Frederick William, " Be kind to her or we'll have her back! "

" What a dreadful moment! " exclaimed the Queen when the royal yacht *Victoria and Albert* finally bore Pussy away from Gravesend. Albert's mouth opened. No sound came forth. The Prince Consort was what the Cockney costermongers call ' choked '. But in all this there was a certain gain to posterity. The faithful Alfred Tennyson composed a stanza to be added to the National Anthem—" Farewell, our England's flower ", it began, predictably, followed by the unforgettable epithalamium—

> God bless the Prince and Bride!
> God keep their lands allied,
> God save the Queen!

II

THE CHILDLESS condition of the paralysed King Frederick William ensured among ordinary Prussians a welcome for the Princess Royal which the political and social snobbery of her bride-groom's enemies in high places denied her. The Hohenzollern line, like the Hanoverian line forty years earlier, was in danger of demise. The 'Englishwoman' was expected to produce heirs. Her readiness to do so could be in no doubt: she was beyond expression in love with Fritz, as he was with her. Between January 1859 and April 1872 she bore him four sons and three daughters, but the fourth child Sigismund—'dear little Sigi'— died in infancy in 1866. His death tore her heart-strings. But worse befell. With the birth of her youngest son Waldemar in 1868 she realised with horror that, as had her mother before her, she had transmitted to her family the scourge of royalty, haemophilia. Waldemar bled to death when he was little more than 10 years old. The cause of his death was reported as diph-theria.

Child-bearing did not come easily to her. Even her tender and understanding husband underestimated the pangs of bringing young into the world! Vicky held that women—" we poor creatures "— were born for men's pleasure and amusement. Even dear Papa, shining paragon of all that was pure and saintly in manhood, was not quite exempt—" tho' he would not admit it." Holding this view, she did not surprise her numerous future biographers by an apparent lack of mother feeling, and they inferred from her clinical attitude to the processes of parturition that she would have fared better, and so would her adopted country and the world, had she paid more attention to her young family and less to politics. But the same criticisms could have been levelled at Queen Victoria. It is only because the monarchy survived in Britain but fell apart in Prussia in the twentieth century that this criticism has stuck. She was essentially a family woman, her heart was torn with compassion for her eldest son with his poor withered arm, she was a true sister to her parents' other children, and she did her best, as she saw it, for the future Edward VII. But Bertie was a vexing trial.

In the last months of her first pregnancy Bertie visited Berlin, preceded by written admonitions from his parents to his sister to try to bring out his good qualities. According to Prince Albert, the heir apparent at 17 had a gift for social life but no intellect. ' Pussy ' was divided between preparations for the birth of her first baby and her natural worry about relations between France and Austria, the sinister machinations of Russia on the one hand, and the unseemly conduct of Bertie towards his valet on the other, as her father reported it—" pouring wax on his livery, throwing water on his linen, rapping him on the nose, tearing his ties, etc. etc." Never had dear Papa met " such a thorough and cunning lazybones " as Bertie, not a thought in his head (except apparently about sex), refusing to read anything but trashy novels which he picked up at railway stations. And when he came of age at 18 the Prince Consort was grieved to think that at any moment his son might be summoned to " take over the reins of government in a country where the sun never sets [sic] and its progress is identified with the civilisation of mankind ". It was in these circumstances that ' Pussy ' bustled around trying to find a bride for her brother and contrived to engage him to Princess Alexandra of Denmark—a doubtful political blessing, for Alix was to bring into the Royal Family an abhorrence of Germany which alienated the Princess Royal and in after years curdled Anglo-German relations.

The first few years of the Princess Royal's married life set the seal upon her destiny. From the first her relatively liberal outlook upset the dying King and his wife Elisabeth. They resented her English brashness. Then she flung open the windows of her first home, the Old Schloss at Babelsberg. Her only aim in this was to drive away the foetid air which had not been changed since Fritz's grandfather had died in the room next to theirs years before, but she was accused of introducing foreign

habits insulting to the Prussian Royal Family. With lover's blind-
ness Fritz deluded himself into believing his whole family to be
' enchanted ' with his wife. His father-in-law showered her with
advice, urged her to parcel out the hours so that she could find
time for every duty; he even offered to supervise her household
budget. The Queen insisted on her writing a letter a day.

Soon the reams of prose were followed up by personal visits,
first by Albert and then by Queen and Consort together, who
arrived at Babelsburg ' semi-incognito ' but with old Stockmar
and three ministers in train. This really was too much! Who did
these arrogant English think they were! A Captain Macdonald,
of the British Army, soon found out. He was bundled by Prussian
police from a train at Bonn after some dispute about his seat
and, after cooling his temper in jail for a few days, was fined a
few thalers. But the public prosecutor took the opportunity to
say: " The English residing and travelling [abroad] are notorious
for the rudeness, impudence and boorish arrogance of their
behaviour."

Lord Palmerston rushed to the defence of the unfortunate
Macdonald and his fellow-countrymen, and the Diet and Parliament exchanged such ill-natured abuse that ' Pussy ', then re-
covering from the birth of her eldest daughter Victoria Augusta
Charlotte, plumbed the depths of misery, comforted only when
dear Papa wrote her a little homily on diet and the best way to
restore " the animal forces ".

Dislike of the princess grew, especially when at her receptions
she gave precedence to bourgeois intellectuals over blue-blooded
bigots; the narrow-minded Junker élite who controlled Prussia
never forgot the stigma. When King Frederick William II died
on the second day of 1861 his brother undoubtedly meant to
reign as a progressive monarch. But William I shed his liberal
intentions with his regency. The few modest reforms he had
initiated during his brother's idiocy faded out. Fritz, who had
now become Crown Prince Frederick, and his 20-year-old Crown
Princess watched with dismay as the new monarch succumbed
to the camarilla of Junkers who fiercely resisted any concessions
to the democrats. This was only a dozen years after the revolutionary turmoil of 1848. Quarrel after quarrel sundered the
Royal Family whenever political affairs were broached. Personally
William was the kindest father-in-law, but he was not going to

suffer a young English chit, however brilliant, telling him how to run his country. She should stay at home and dedicate herself like other German *hausfrauen* to the three K's—*Kirche, Küche* and *Kinder* (church, kitchen and children). Pussy found it ' difficult ' to get on with him. He said *such* rude things about Papa, who, after all, was only trying to help. Germany, said Albert, pursuing his ideal of an alliance with England, needed a great, liberal and generous policy before she could achieve such a partnership or lead a united Germany and become " renowned in arms ".

Absolutism was William's goal. His ministers were " mere clerks ". At his coronation at Könisberg the 64-year-old monarch allowed no ordinary man to crown him, but, placing the diadem on his head, asserted his belief in the Divine right of kings. The Princess Royal paid homage to the new King with " exquisite grace and intense emotion ", according to the Foreign Secretary, whose account gratified her parents. Lord Clarendon was " astonished " by the statesmanlike and comprehensive views she took of Prussian policy and of " the *duties* of a Constitutional King ". But William was the first professional soldier to rule Prussia since Frederick the Great and naturally Prince Albert felt a twinge of alarm. He warned his daughter: " The days are past when a single man could expect millions of educated, thoughtful people to trust their entire welfare and existence to the judgement and hands of *one* man " even if he were " an angel descended from heaven ", an apotheosis which students of William's future actions found improbable. To her worries about the King and the state of Prussian-British relations the Princess Royal now added family anxieties, notably the need to find her brother Bertie a suitable wife, the sickly condition of her infant son Wilhelm and, transcending all other worries, the failing health of her overworked father, who compared himself with a donkey—an " ess " —running around in circles and torturing himself about " the wretched people in the world, the confused state of Europe ", and not least the " set of rogues " whom Napoleon III had gathered around him in Paris.

When her grandmother the Duchess of Kent died of cancer in March 1861 the Princess Royal slipped across to London without King William's permission. This was almost *lèse-majesté* to a monarch so boiling over with self-importance, and Albert pleaded hard with him before he would forgive his daughter-in-law. Who ever had such a wonderful father? On her return to Berlin she wrote to the Queen: "Really there is not a thing I hear or say or do that my first thought is not 'What would dear Papa say, what would he think!'"

But the Consort was beginning to talk morosely of "the end". For the first time in her life the Queen knew terror. As though the family outlook were not black enough, Bertie had entrusted the more pleasurable part of his education at Cambridge to a pretty young actress of whom Buckingham Palace had never even heard. Her charms were infinitely superior to those of the prince's tutors, and he progressed so favourably under her tuition that some details of the curriculum leaked into the newspapers—so unlucky!—just when *The Times* itself was thundering away against Prussia. All this caused Albert "much worry and great sorrow", but it did not alone cause him to "give up the struggle" and before he died on 14th December 1861 he forgave his son—"the past is past". The Princess Royal was almost as inconsolable as the Queen when she realised that the Beloved One was no more. "Oh, dear Papa! How good, how great, how faultless, my whole heart and soul was devoted to him. How terrible to have to say he *was*!"

At the other end of the scale there were bounders like Lord Orford who could rejoice that "at least one foreigner [was] safely out of the way". But despite Pussy's grief she could not permit the Queen to continue blaming her unfortunate brother for her father's fatal illness. She intervened strongly on his behalf, although his indiscretion might have wrecked her own maturing plans to marry him to Christian IX's "*unverschämt hübsch*" (outrageously beautiful) daughter. The Queen, bearing her terrible cross, drew some comfort from her daughter's first moving letter after the calamity, and she carried this about with her together with the Consort's watch and chain, a golden cord with his keys, and his red pocket handkerchief. For a time she could not gaze on her son without a shudder, but under Vicky's gentle pressure she softened towards him, although she could not desecrate her saintly husband's memory by permitting Bertie and Alix to marry at St. James's on that hallowed spot where *He* had taken her to his wedded wife twenty years earlier and where darling Pussy and Fritz had been united. The royal homes became great 'vaults' presided over by the stricken Queen in white cap and widow's weeds. When Vicky visited Osborne before her brother's wedding she grieved to find her mother weeping. "Mama had so desperately longed for another child," she told her husband. Now the shepherd was missing. "We wander around like sheep." Horrible year! It witnessed not only the death of blessed Papa and the old Frederick William, but also the attempted assassination of William I at Baden Baden.

Fortunately for the Princess Royal her husband was hale and their marriage had been "made in heaven". But all was not well with little Wilhelm. Prussia had rejoiced in 1859 when he was born on Mozart's birthday—27th January—but in the process he nearly killed himself and his mother, who was held in her husband's arms throughout a prolonged labour. The birth pangs left her so spent that for a long time she was too weak to write to "dearest Mama" but had to dictate her letters to a secretary. The struggle for life—Wilhelm had to be slapped for nearly an hour before he uttered a cry—had left him with a contused left shoulder and the probability, later a certainty, that the arm would never develop. The misfortune was kept secret in the hope that the arm would somehow 'come right', and at Windsor the Princess Royal's younger brothers and sisters ran around calling themselves 'uncles and aunts' and strongly objecting to a notice in the royal schoolroom insensitively describing them as 'children'.

Forty-two godparents sponsored Wilhelm at his baptism. His grandfather Albert had mused upon his future. Would history embellish his name 'the Conqueror' or 'Rufus'—even 'the Great'? Not 'the Silent', surely, though he hoped the boy would not grow up to be a chatterbox. "May God bless our efforts to educate our son to be worthy of the love which he has been so heartily shown," declared Prince Frederick William. And Queen Victoria thought her first grandson might be "born for great deeds and for great times" She urged her daughter to bring him up to be wise, sensible, courageous, liberal-minded, good and pure. He was never to lack courage. But the atrophied arm hung down at Wilhelm's side blue and cold and lifeless, for all the warm oil that was rubbed into it, despite all the massage and flannel wrappings, and the pricks of electric needles. Otherwise he was growing into a fine, fat, 'pretty' boy, and Queen Victoria found him "such a little dear".

Historians remain deadlocked on the question of whether the Princess Royal subconsciously deplored—'hated' seems too strong for such a loving creature—her son because of his affliction. There is something typically Prussian about this notion, as there is about the treatment to which the boy was subjected by the Calvinistic Dr. Hinzpeter, who forced him to ride horseback without stirrups in the hope that he would miraculously throw out the devitalised arm to save himself from falling, as he did again and again, but without reaping anything except purple bruises. The possibility is that the Crown Princess neglected some of her children most of the time, or all of them some of the time, but never all of them all the time, to pursue her political, artistic and public activities. The eldest son certainly worried her all the time, and she was heartbroken to see how his " wretched unhappy arm " deformed his character. Willy's defect remained throughout her life " an inexpressible source of sorrow ". He was " a dear boy ", she wrote when he was 13. He had then seen his great-uncle proclaimed Emperor of Germany at Versailles, and she hoped and trusted he would grow up " a useful man ".

Over the years Willy built a reputation for what Mr. Edmond Taylor catalogued as " militaristic belligerence, boasting and verbal intemperance ". It is no secret now that members of the Royal Family believed him to be mad. The first to discern this was the future Queen Alexandra, herself almost insanely anti-German. But the real villain of the immortal tragedy of the Hohenzollerns was Otto von Bismarck-Schönhausen. When Willy was born he was ambassador at St. Petersburg. Soon Bismarck stepped from the shadows. The fanatic who fired his pistol at Wilhelm I at Baden Baden on 4th July 1861 bore possibly a greater responsibility for the ' terrible ' twentieth century than the assassin of Archduke Franz-Ferdinand of Austria-Hungary at Sarajevo, for the subsequent shock-wave throughout Prussia created just the kind of atmosphere the monarch needed to force army reforms on the Diet. His instrument was at hand. Bismarck, a great, burly squarehead with a zest for food, drink and power, was on leave in Berlin at the time of the assassination attempt. Now, with immaculate timing, he offered the shaken ruler that Assyrian programme of ' iron and blood ' which was to make him a dictator, his country a major military power bent on aggressive war, his master an emperor. The puppet strings which he surely and deftly manipulated turned out to be fuse-wires leading to the destruction of a dynasty and an age. To achieve these remarkable results over a period of twenty-eight years Bismarck had first to neutralise or demolish his enemies at home.

The Princess Royal and her husband were his primary targets. For a young woman the Crown Princess was undeniably astute about Bismarck. She distrusted him from the outset—one of those first impressions which proved to be justified—and for once found Queen Augusta, her mother-in-law, in agreement with her. For his part Bismarck convinced himself that Crown Princess Frederick did not like him. This Anglo-German ' marriage of true minds' irked him because it was pro-British in spirit, thanks largely to the Prince Consort, and contrary to Bismarck's plans for Greater Germany. The man who came to muzzle and feed poisoned titbits to the controlled Prussian press, to hobble the Reichstag and organise the Prussian army behind him found little difficulty in trumping up falsehoods about a marriage which was such an unyielding obstacle to his malevolent foreign policy. Conservatives at court unscrupulously magnified gossip about the ' young Fredericks' into scandal. When Vicky sprained an ankle they spread the myth that the Crown Prince had thrown her downstairs and that Queen Victoria had hurried secretly to Potsdam, where they were now living in Frederick the Great's Neues Palais, to prevent a divorce. " They have a pretty opinion of us," said the Crown Princess wryly. Bernhardi, the Potsdam ' Greville' complained in his diary that the Princess Royal " thinks everything here must be the same as in England; the government must ever be by majority, the ministry always chosen by the majority ". Her frequent visits to England vexed him, poor man. It was during one such absence that Germany lurched into the parliamentary crisis which brought Bismarck to power.

The Princess Royal was already describing the future Iron Chancellor as " my *bête noire* ". To her husband she burst out " For heaven's sake *not that* man as Premier!" But ' that man ' after a trip to London which stamped unfavourably on his mind the diverse personalities of Prime Minister Palmerston and his Foreign Secretary, Lord John Russell, returned to Berlin determined not to foist the ' Westminster system' upon Prussia. If there were to be any ministers they would not be drawn from the parliamentary majority in the Diet but appointed by him. The

Crown Princess deplored his 'dishonesty'. He was wicked, too—so wicked that he did not care "how many fibs he tells". The thought of his governing Germany "makes my hair stand on end!" Bismarck's elevation split the Prussian Royal Family, and King William was so irked by it all that he threatened to abdicate. He also warned his son and his daughter-in-law to be careful in the choice of their intellectual acquaintances. Frederick William was too obedient a son to seize the levers of power. Bismarck at 47 was ambassador in Paris when he stepped into the limelight, settled the crisis and persuaded the King to tear up his abdication instrument.

During the early years of his dictatorship the Princess Royal, according to Bismarck, "took pleasure in provoking my patriotic susceptibilities". Attempts to unite Germany through orthodox diplomacy had failed in 1848. The alternative was force coupled with an aggressive foreign policy. The new Chancellor regarded the marriage of the Prince of Wales and Princess Alexandra as a slap in the face, a deliberate frustration of his plan to annex the Schleswig-Holstein duchies to Prussia. The painful misunderstandings between the Neues Palais and the Chancellery sprang from Crown Princess Frederick's miscalculation of Bismarck's political skill and his deep Junkers conviction that women should keep their place and not meddle in politics and other man's work. Frederick William warned Bismarck that a repressive policy would stimulate anarchical movements inimical to the monarchy and the constitution; people who led his father into such courses were 'dangerous' But when Bismarck took over the press and the young heir to the throne complained about it in a speech at Danzig the King turned furiously on his son.

"Be kind to the boy Absalom," Bismarck advised him.

At the same time the Chancellor forced Ernest von Stockmar's resignation and set spies to watch the movements of Vicky and her husband, whom the King was treating "quite like a little child", she complained. She would, she told her mother, stand by Fritz "in the face of all the Kings and Emperors of the whole world", and she added fervently: "Thank God I was born in England, where people are not slaves!"

The seriousness of the crisis within the Royal Family was revealed by Sir Robert Morier, a counsellor at the British embassy, who reported that the Crown Prince had narrowly escaped banishment to a fortress after the Danzig speech. Fritz, like his father a professional soldier by choice, also came close to being stripped of military rank and offices, but he was reprieved in time to be of service when Prussian troops at Bismarck's behest stood by on the eastern frontier while the Russians crushed a Polish uprising—an act of 'iron and blood' diplomacy which was designed to ensure Russia's lasting gratitude: Poland's lasting hatred was of little moment to Bismarck. And when Prussia and Austria moved against Denmark later in 1863 the Crown Prince rode at the head of his troops and was present at the controversial bombardment of Sønderborg which his wife approved. But she lamented: "What shall I feel like this evening when I have to go to bed without my angel?" And her mother, without *her* angel to stand by her, was "wretched, almost frantic" as the war over Schleswig-Holstein divided the Queen's family, Edward and Alexandra supporting Denmark and the other members, notably the Princess Royal, justifying Prussia's aggression. Indeed, Vicky regretted "not being a young man and not able to take the field against the Danes". Yet her enemies at the Prussian Court spread the calumny that she was unhappy at Prussia's success.

In the following year, after Denmark had been forced to surrender her claims to the duchies, Bertie met his sister and her husband at Cologne and found it "not pleasant to see him and his A.D.C. always in Prussian uniform, flaunting before our eyes the most objectionable ribbon which he had received for his deeds of valour??? against the unhappy Danes."

The upsets, the spying, the feeling of being by-passed and neutralised, could not disturb Fritz's blissful home life and he thanked God "for having given me a wife like mine" as she sat at her spinning wheel singing little ballads, or recited Göethe and Heine. According to her chamberlain Pürlitz, who wrote plays (like Hervey), she could debate as ably as any historian, and her manners were impeccable. But always in the shadows, lurking, shuffling, vigilant and baleful, crept "that wicked man" who, after tasting Danish blood, now turned in 1866 against his former ally, unlucky Austria, with her proverbial capacity for embracing large causes only to invite even larger disasters. The Austrian troops were smashed at Sadowa. This victory made the Crown Princess "every bit as proud of being a Prussian as of being an Englishwoman ", and, echoing Napoleon III, she assured her mother: " I must say the Prussians are a superior race."

Harsh terms were imposed upon the Habsburgs, whose Hanoverian and other German allies now passed under Bismarck's hegemony. The next step was to found a North German Confederation, since the southern states were suspicious of Prussian ambitions and refused to join. Twenty-one German states adhered to the embryo empire which was beginning to feed on the various kingdoms and duchies of Germany and Denmark; and when the four south German states of Hesse-Darmstadt, Baden, Württemberg and Bavaria held out against incorporation Bismarck's diplomacy came to full flower. The only way to unite northern and southern states was to find a common external enemy. Who better than France, that ' age-old aggressor '? With a cunning worthy of the greatest practitioners of the art of political skulduggery, Bismarck accordingly contrived to trick Napoleon III into declaring war on Germany with a staggering speed which outpaced European diplomacy in any effort to avert a catastrophe, although it was commonly believed then that Imperial France would sweep all before her.

This opinion was scarcely modified even when, by a remarkable feat of logistics, the Germans mobilised 1,183,000 men in eighteen days. Here was a sinister forerunner of that élite military machine which was to change the world forty-four years later.

III

THIRTEEN YEARS of residence in Berlin had wrought changes in the Princess Royal, not all for the better. Her husband's compatriots still regarded her as a foreigner. But when war came —" a dreadful trial "— she was almost as anti-French as they were. She had approved the shelling of Sønderborg: now she condoned the bombardment of Paris. Yet when the French struck Saarbrück with their heavy artillery she denounced the operation as " barbarous ". Bertie did not help, of course. A widely reported ' private ' expression of hope by him that Prussia would be cut to pieces was seized on by his sister's critics to condemn her as a potential enemy capable of spying for England. The charge was the harder to bear because Fritz was away at war, commanding the Third German Army, consisting mainly of those Bavarians and Swabians who had resisted Prussian domination in the past but now at the time of common danger, as Bismarck had calculated, rallied against the foreign invader. Fritz briefly returned to Potsdam for the christening of his penultimate daughter and fifth surviving child, but considerately left without saying good-bye because he wished to avoid upsetting his wife.

" The thought was *so* kind," she wrote, " and yet I feel as if my heart would break."

Now she was left alone to face the rising hostility of the anglophobes. Yet even they could have no valid reason to doubt her basic loyalty to Prussia. Every German victory struck a chord of patriotic satisfaction in her breast. Her enthusiasm was unbridled when Napoleon, suffering agonies from stones in the bladder, surrendered with 120,000 Frenchmen at Sedan, the birthplace of Turenne. " How they have been punished! " she exulted. The curious fact is that, whilst disbelieving nearly every-thing Bismarck said, she apparently was convinced that he was the innocent victim of French conniving. Truly, the French generals were not geniuses, as Napoleon found to his cost, but they had not entirely lost their sense of proportion or of grim humour.

"*Nous sommes dans un pot de chambre et nous y serons emmerdés!*" exclaimed Ducrot, a corps commander.

French discomfiture was by no means assuaged by the spec-tacle of Bismarck, in *pickelhaube** and spurs, sitting bolt upright and immense, astride his horse alongside William I and his generals as the humiliating disaster unfolded before their eyes. Now the shouts of "*Nach* Paris!" from the throats of the triumphant Germans deadened the fading echoes of the defiant Frenchmen's "*À Berlin!*"

War fever seized Germany. The Princess Royal was caught up in the fervour. Her eldest brother had, as usual, been talking ' twaddle ' off his royal cuff, so Gladstone thought, about ways of restoring peace, and he seems to have criticised the liberal warm-hearted Fritz for having taken up arms against the French. ' Pussy ' spat back at him that she would prefer her husband to serve his country than to " sit by my side ". It was a scarcely veiled insult: the ambition of the Prince of Wales since his youth to play some active part in the British Army had been thwarted by his parents and their advisers. With memories of Florence Nightingale thick upon her, the Crown Princess began pestering the Government to allow her to organise hospital services for war wounded. But the ' Englishwoman ' was not needed and her offers were tossed back in her face, partly because of her odd notions about the therapeutic virtues of fresh air. She tended to throw open windows which German doctors, of whom she had gained a poor opinion since the birth of Willy and the death of Sigismund, decreed should be kept tightly closed. Consequently, as in the Crimea, more victims died from germs than from wounds. But her fighting spirit was aroused and she did not rest until she had set up a hospital at Homburg, defying the King's command to return to her neglected family at Potsdam.

*Pickelhaube: the great eagled superstructure which adorned the brazen helmets of the Prussian warlords.

As the German armies clanked towards the French capital, and Herr Krupp sent up his big guns for the siege, the Bismarck-inspired campaign of slander against the King's daughter-in-law reached a new level of spite. The French, with their new secret weapon, the mitrailleuse, a development of the American Gatling gun and the parent of the machine-gun, suddenly recovered their martial ardour and slowed down the pace of the German advance. For this Bismarck and his friends incredibly blamed the Crown Princess, who was alleged by Bismarck's wife to have insisted that the German bombardment of Paris should not start until ammunition supplies were ensured. If she ever expressed this view it seems to have been a sensible one. But she was engulfed in Bismarck's general anglophobia. British newspapers, unlike the majority of the British Royal Family, were pouring out vituperation on the Germans and encouraging the French, whose Emperor and Empress with their children were soon to seek refuge in England, to which Eugénie escaped with the aid of her American dentist, posing as " a poor woman on her way to a lunatic asylum ".

Bismarck's exasperation with the Crown Princess welled up when the British demanded to send gunboats up the Seine to carry besieged Britons to safety.

" *What swine!*" he exploded.

From that time he kept Fritz ignorant of political developments, fearing that he would pass on vital information to his babbling wife, who ' thought British' and could not bear to believe that " shabby little Prussia should prosper so "—a fair example of the Chancellor's self-delusion or of his downright lying. With Paris at last surrounded but defiant, the super-heavy German guns opened fire. Fritz desperately tried to deter Bismarck and the generals from their policy of reducing the city to rubble and starving out the citizens, and it is unquestionable that his wife became as anxious as he to limit the suffering—especially she, who under great difficulties was battling to reorganise the German hospital system. Frederick William poured out his heart to Russell of *The Times*.

" I pass sleepless hours," he said, " when I think of the women and children."

Prussian shells tore into a church while the congregation were celebrating Mass.

" Such a piece of news wrings my heart," he groaned.

The unsuspecting French, of course, knew nothing of the kindlier side of the Prussian nature and, when the Crown Prince was (falsely) reported to have been captured by Marshal Mac-Mahon, the joyful Parisians seized a famous opera tenor in the street and made him sing the " Marseillaise " from the top of a horse-drawn omnibus. At home Pussy risked further displeasure by visiting French prisoner-of-war camps. She was told of five ' unlucky wretches ' whose feet had been frozen on the railway and would have to lose them.

" All these horrors make me too miserable."

She did not then know that nothing would be more horrible than the spectacle of Frenchmen inflicting even greater butcheries upon Frenchmen as the establishment of the Commune was followed by civil war together with some of the most senseless and wanton slaughter and carnage Europe had ever witnessed.

Meanwhile the German Empire had been created, not without some assistance from Frederick William, although Bismarck claimed the sole credit for it. On 18th January 1871 the four kingdoms, five grand duchies, thirteen lesser duchies or princi-palities, and the three free cities of Greater Germany, together with the newly-annexed French provinces of Alsace and Lorraine, confederated under the sovereignty of Prussia, with William I assuming the Imperial hereditary crown as Kaiser in Louis XIV's Hall of Mirrors at Versailles. The ceremony much affected Fritz, who wept in his field-marshal's uniform. Now he and the Princess Royal had become Imperial Highnesses or, to be exact, Kaiserliche und Königliche Hoheit Kronprinz des deutschen Reiches und von Preussen. Vicky was " proud to bear this title ". Presumably she did not reflect that it was the product of ' iron and blood '; but whenever the German newspapers criticised her native land she rushed to its defence.

" I cannot hear a word said against England—and I give it back (I fear not always gently) when I hear sharp words."

However, for reasons of prudence she stayed at the German embassy when she visited London with Fritz and the two eldest sons, Willy and Henry, in the summer of 1871. A useful by-product of their stay was a reconciliation with Bertie and Alix, thanks to the intercession of Queen Victoria. To his mother-in-law Fritz expressed " the intensest horror " of Bismarck, who had

L

become all-powerful. The new Kaiserliche felt that he was sitting on an unexploded mine.

A Bismarck cult grew up during the next decade. He became a prince. Beer mugs were kilned in his likeness. Bismarck seats were dedicated in parks in the shade of Bismarck oaks; and, of course, the humble herring was called after him. The more the Chancellor's influence grew, the more the Bundesrat (representing the Imperial states) degenerated into a shadow parliament, the more the frustration deepened in the bosom of her Imperial Highness. Through Bismarck she had become "the object of universal distrust and suspicion". Even hitherto loyal friends of the Princess Royal went over to Bismarck, who berated the "British petticoat government" of Queen Victoria, her daughter and the Empress Augusta. The very mention of the names of these three made him bridle. Little wonder that Queen Victoria, herself about to become an empress, drew the conclusion that in his malice and insolence Bismarck was merely a synonym for the first Napoleon.

With the recrudescence of the Eastern Question in 1877 the German dictator moved even more mischievously into the arena of international power politics. Russia's designs on Turkey irked Austria and, anxious to nourish his friendship with both the Romanovs and the Habsburgs, the German Chancellor passed through the Princess Royal to the British Government a proposal that Britain should seize Egypt, formerly a part of the Ottoman Empire but then ruled by an independent Khedive under French influence. Clearly such a *coup* would thrust Britain into conflict with France, as Bismarck knew, though a few years later when Britain took exactly the course he had plotted he threatened France, and the French abandoned Egypt to the British. For the present Disraeli suspected that the Princess Royal's letter had been dictated by Bismarck, and he replied coldly: "Her Majesty does not require the suggestion, or permission, of Prince B" to take Egypt. Yet Vicky, who was hurt when her mother added her own admonition, seems in her gullibility to have had Britain's rather than Germany's interests at heart, for when Russia menaced Constantinople she wrote to the Queen: "*How* I do long for *one* good roar of the British Lion from the housetops and for the *thunder* of a British broadside!"

She advised that the Royal Navy should occupy Gallipoli and in explanation of her own policy of 'iron and blood' confessed that she was " perpetually in a pugilistic frame of mind ". Whatever her part in this affair, it was in Berlin that the Eastern Question was temporarily resolved, and the man who presided over the Congress of 1878 was, of course, Bismarck—' the honest broker '—who according to Disraeli could say " awful " things with a sweet and gentle voice. Russia was checked, Turkey saved, Disraeli achieved ' peace with honour '. Thirty-six years later the Balkans blew up directly, if belatedly, as a result of Bismarck's effort to please Austria, which in 1878 had been made a present of Bosnia.

In that fateful year Fritz and his wife were visiting Queen Victoria when two further attempts—the third since 1861— were made on the Kaiser's life. The second attempt seriously impaired William's physique. He was nearly 82. Bismarck sent for the Crown Prince, who became Regent, but the Chancellor kept all the threads of government in his own grasp. Fritz found himself on the verge of his fiftieth year a mere figurehead with few responsibilities and less power to influence Germany's inexorable surge towards autocracy. The one action of which he would have wished to be excused concerned Hoedel, who was sentenced to death for the first of the two later attempts on the Emperor's life. The Regent had a conscientious objection to capital punishment, but Bismarck forced him to sign Hoedel's death warrant. The decision was particularly hard for him because he believed the assassin to be insane. Had William I died then the probability is that the next ten years would have given his son and daughter-in-law, together with the liberal elements who would have come to power with them, time to steer Germany away from the disaster course which ' the pilot ' had charted. But the Emperor's animal constitution defied the assassin's bullet.

Apart from the political turmoil of 1878 the Princess Royal had to endure yet another personal loss: her sister Alice, married to Louis IV, Grand Duke of Hesse, died in December from diphtheria. She took solace from the company of her infant grand-daughter: earlier that year her eldest daughter Charlotte had made Vicky a grandmother at the age of 39 and Queen Victoria a great-grandmother at 60.

The Princess Royal's change of attitude towards her growing family had been noted when ' dear little Sigi ' died at the time of the Austrian war. From then on the education of Willy and Henry was left more and more to others while she pursued her political and other activities, although she was still to bear another son and two more daughters. Before the sadistic Dr. Hinzpeter was appointed in 1865 the two princes had suffered under Fräulein Doberneck, a governess who believed that a sound thrashing stimulated academic curiosity and a zest for learning. Hinzpeter, working zealously upon the foundations thus sedulously laid, contrived to reduce them from a mood of morbid sullenness to a state of torpid resignation. The mother, if not the father, might have foreseen that once the stifling Calvinistic restraints of Hinzpeter were removed, especially from a boy with a built-in sense of inferiority, the product of his physical affliction, Willy would plunge into social and military life with the wildness of a mountain goat. He emerged from this spartan regime with a forbidding charm designed to impress and intimidate all who fawned upon him. The young princes spent three years together at a boarding school—" I feel giving them up very much ", their mother sighed—and then Willy's career followed the pattern of his father's, a period at Bonn University and then an officer's life in the army.

Willy began to indulge his self-importance when he came of age at 18 and went to the university. The estrangement from his mother dates from that time, although he was grateful to her when he expressed a wish to get the Order of the Garter from his grandmother Victoria and she affectionately, but unsuccessfully, interceded for him. Army training brought out Willy's worst traits. Anything ' strong ' appealed to him: he was old enough to understand Bismarck's ' strength ' in reducing the Prussian Diet to sycophancy and the Bundesrat to impotence. These examples of ' controlled ' parliamentary democracy were not lost upon the future Kaiser. He regarded his parents as old-fashioned, out of touch, and from then on treated his mother with ever-diminishing chivalry and consideration. She certainly had need of sympathy from everyone around her, including her eldest son, for in 1879 a few months after her sister Alice's death her youngest son Waldemar died. He was 10 years old.

The mother's grief at losing a second son in a dozen years was intolerably exacerbated by an Orthodox Protestant minister who defiled his cloth by declaring that Waldemar had died because the Lord wanted to humiliate her hardened heart. As Dr. Barkeley comments in his brilliant biography of the Princess Royal, it is " difficult to understand hatred when it goes as far as that."

In a sense family history was repeating itself, for the Princess Royal was now making complaints about her eldest son similar to those of Queen Victoria against Bertie at the same age. Young Wilhelm " does not care to look at anything ", and he took no delight in works of art. Even a guide book failed to interest the youth who oddly was to win a reputation as " the travelling Emperor ". But when Willy became engaged in 1880 to Princess Augusta Victoria and prepared to leave his parents' hearth and rooftree for the last time, his mother noted sentimentally: " It is the last time we have Willy unmarried in the same house, in his old rooms with me."

When they married on 27th February 1881 she hoped ' Dona ', the family name for the bride, would never suffer from *Heimwech* (home-sickness)—" as I do to this day ". Dona was the daughter of the Duke of Augustenberg, a claimant to the Duchy of Schleswig when such claims were considered important. Bismarck hoped that " the cow from Holstein " would stimulate the sluggish Hohenzollern blood of that " very nice young gentleman ", as he called Willy. The Chancellor had every reason for self-satisfaction and could afford to dispense compliments: he had snuffed out liberalism in the German Empire once and for all.

Six years later Wilhelm, himself the father of an expanding family, had acquired all the ritualistic polish of the autocratic prig. He had earache on one occasion, and when his mother saw him he enquired neither after her health, his father's nor his brothers' nor, most callous of all, his younger sisters', although he knew they were laid up with measles. A curious creature, she thought him. No kindness or civility from Willy. She found it painful to " a soft-hearted Mama " that her own child did not care " whether he sees her or no, whether she is ill or well, etc.". But Willy was playing a subtle game. Not uniquely for a grandson, he loved his august German grandfather—as in his manner he loved his even more august grandmother Victoria—better than his own parents. The old Emperor, never quite the same after the assassination attempts of 1878, and alarmed by a threat by Bismarck—his first—to resign in 1879, in his declining years fell more and more beneath the spell of his grandson. Among other mischiefs Willy managed to have his parents excluded from a meeting at Gastein between the German and Austrian emperors, convincing his grandfather that the Princess Royal would use the occasion to harass Franz-Josef about the Battenberg affair.

Prince Alexander of Hesse-Darmstadt was the first of the ambitious and manly Battenbergs to rise above the disadvantage of morganatic blood and to achieve the monarchical status when in 1879, under the benign influence of the Berlin Congress, the oppressed Bulgars were liberated from the Turks and elected him their king. ' Sandro ' was twenty-two and of independent mind. Bulgaria might lie within Russia's sphere of influence, but he was determined to reign for the greater good of the Bulgars. At the start he won the goodwill of the serf-freeing Alexander II, who believed the Battenbergs had saved his life by arriving too late—not their fault—for a St. Petersburg banquet at which a bomb was timed to explode; but when the Czar was finally murdered in 1881 his son Alexander III clamped down on all liberal ideas and called all lackeys to heel, including the unfortunate Bulgarians and their monarch. Two Russian generals were appointed to run Bulgaria while Sandro was in St. Petersburg for the Czar's coronation. On his return he expelled the generals and rescinded their orders, which had deepened the gloom in which political activities in the Balkans so often seem to be shrouded. Relations with Russia thereafter deteriorated.

Sandro did nothing to restore confidence at St. Petersburg when in 1883 he became secretly engaged to Victoria, second daughter of the Crown Prince and Crown Princess of Prussia. Her parents blessed the proposed union, especially the Princess Royal, who found her prospective son-in-law as irresistible as Queen Victoria had found Fritz; but when Bismarck heard of it he flew into a passion, chiefly because the marriage would have cut right across his scheme of European alliances, to say nothing of his friendly policy toward Russia. To give Bulgaria a Prussian Queen would be " like throwing a marshal's baton over the walls of a besieged fortress ", no less. He swore that Queen Victoria was doing her best to force Prussia and Russia apart.

" In family matters," he complained, " she is not accustomed to contradiction, and would immediately bring the parson with her in her travelling bag and the bridegroom in her trunk and the marriage would come off at once."

The marriage did not come off. On Bismarck's insistence the Emperor vetoed it, although the lovers kept in touch. For reasons which need not detain us here the King of Bulgaria and his youngest brother Franz-Josef were captured in 1886 after a Russian *coup d'état* in Sofia, but were freed. After a family re-union in Austria the question arose: should Sandro return to Bulgaria? Both Queen Victoria and his prospective mother-in-law urged him to resume the crown. The Bulgars greeted his return with tears of joy. But soon they were wringing their hands. The Czar formally announced that Russians could never coexist with Bulgars so long as Alexander remained King. To avoid a fatal confrontation with Czarist troops the pride and joy of the Battenbergs abdicated. The Princess Royal now looked forward to preparing her daughter's nuptials, for there would seem to be no objection to the marriage now. But Bismarck's opposition stiffened, possibly to thwart the Princess Royal; and Willy, who seems to have had some insane notion about an affront to his sister's honour, hopped into a rage whenever the subject was mentioned. In his memoirs, however, he made light of his contri-bution to his family's unhappiness. He was, of course, deeply grieved to have caused his mother such pain, but he added in a truly touching passage: " As the wellbeing of the fatherland was at stake, all personal desires had to be silenced ".

In 1889 Sandro renounced his styles and titles and morganat-ically married Johanna Loisinger, *prima donna* of the Darmstadt Court Theatre. " When my mother hears of this," chortled Willy, " she will enjoy her lunch." At that time his mother was almost consumed with grief over the tragedy of her husband's death.

IV

THE BATTENBERG affair has been described at some length because it coincided with the overriding calamity of the Princess Royal's life. Her sister, the melancholy Princess Alice, had died from diphtheria caught from her children; the two Prussian princesses who contracted measles, as noted earlier, unfortunately passed on the contagion to their father and unwittingly brought about his early death. Fritz developed a severe cold after the measles attack, and from January 1887 a slight and persistent hoarseness afflicted his throat and gradually worsened. The gruffness made itself apparent in a speech made by the Kaiserliche on his father's ninetieth birthday.

Various German specialists were called in. Professor Bergmann proposed to slit the larynx. The Princess Royal almost collapsed with horror and distress—" the idea of a knife touching his dear throat is terrible to me ". Bismarck stopped the operation, although not exactly from motives of kindness towards his royal master's daughter-in-law, and a German laryngologist was consulted. He boldly diagnosed cancer. Such a verdict was unthinkable. It was in these circumstances that Britain's leading throat specialist, the Scottish Dr. Morell Mackenzie of London, was sent to Berlin at the behest of Queen Victoria.

Medical case histories of the exalted often throw a lurid light not so much on the patient as on the conduct of doctors, diarists, court meddlers, politicians, professional biographers and undertakers; in some instances the penultimate have managed to get their foot in the door of the death-chamber simultaneously with the morticians and the most grisly details of fatal illness have come to light almost before the corpse is cold in the grave.

The medical history of Frederick William from the onset of his fatal illness in the autumn of 1886 to his death in the summer of 1888 is so harrowing that the detail of it as cautery followed tracheotomy, as doctors diagnosed and rediagnosed and applied the crude instruments of their day, German against German but German always united against British for reasons of politics and vulgar personal spite against the Princess Royal, must take second place in this narrative to the intrigues which beset the distracted wife as she approached the end of her hopes.

The campaign of vilification against the unhappy woman which followed the retention of Mackenzie, in whom she reposed touching faith, has few parallels in modern history. Emil Ludwig, although he was not in possession of essential facts, blamed the employment of Mackenzie on the Princess Royal's " nonsensical idea " that German doctors had been responsible for Willy's withered arm, and further blamed the Scottish doctor's " erroneous treatment " for Frederick William's premature death. A later biographer, von Kurenberg, distorted the evidence to proclaim: " Triumphantly the Crown Princess decided that it only needed an English doctor to come and show the German nitwits what ought to be done."

To operate or not to operate became the crucial issue on which the fate of a dynasty was to hang. Mackenzie was opposed to surgery in the early stages and seems to have done his best to quieten the Princess Royal's fears that her husband was actually suffering from cancer. In this process he was assisted when Fritz visited him in Harley Street after the celebrations of Queen Victoria's Golden Jubilee, for when he removed a small portion of the growth on the vocal chords and sent it to the German professor Virchow the subsequent pathological examination proved it to be benign. At his patient's request the Queen knighted Mackenzie at Balmoral.

Willy had vainly exerted himself to exclude his father from the Jubilee festivities, having hoped to hog the show himself. Frederick William in his white uniform, the Garter Star upon his breast and field-marshal's baton in his hand, looked like the hero of a Wagner opera as he rode his horse in the centre of a group of thirty-two kings and princes, all related to the great Queen. The Princess Royal rode with her mother and the Princess of Wales in a gilded landau drawn by six of the Windsor

Creams. Outwardly the Crown Prince appeared hale, but those nearest to him winced to hear the thin reedy whisper whistling from the excoriated windpipe of this handsome blond giant.

Summer cooled into autumn, and as the air of Berlin was unsuitable for the impaired throat the Princess Royal took her husband from England to the Tyrol, thence by way of Venice and Lake Maggiore to the Italian-owned Villa Zirio in San Remo on the Mediterranean coast near the French frontier. Now in the Prussian capital, as the old Emperor slid into senility and his son was clearly succumbing to mortal disease. Willy virtually took over the Foreign Office, with the assiduous aid of Count Herbert von Bismarck, who was a rather more unpleasant version of his illustrious parent. Friends of the Bismarcks divided their time between fawning on Willy and spreading the legend that an Emperor suffering from an incurable disease could not reign, and that the Princess Royal had opposed an operation because if her husband lost his voice he could not succeed his aged father on the throne. In casting around for scapegoats they blamed Frederick William's plight not only on Mackenzie and the Princess Royal but also on liberals, Jews, Freemasons, *The Times*, Queen Victoria and the hated British people in general. Doctors were encouraged by Bismarck to hint publicly that the Crown Prince had cancer, and newspapers under the Chancellor's control used the word for the first time. Bismarck aimed not so much to tell the truth as to annoy the patient and wear him down. The Princess Royal realised that because of her liberal and artistic tastes she was an abomination to the Bismarcks.

" I keep as quiet and make myself as small as I can," she told her close friend Lady Ponsonby, " but I cannot change my skin to please them, nor shall they tread me underfoot."

Blow fell upon blow. " My darling has got a fate before him which I hardly dare think of! How I shall have the strength to bear it I do not know!" Mackenzie had at last broken the news that the poor throat had " a distinctly malignant look ". In comforting her he proffered grains of hope. Eventually his compassion was used against him by such as Dr. Schroetter— the rising star in the constellation of seven German doctors assembled at San Remo—who was " rough, uncouth and arrogant ". As the Prince of Wales observed, the doctors did not agree among themselves—" all very sad ". Worse was to befall:

Willy descended upon the Villa Zirio on the panoply and flush of youth. The sight of his careworn mother brought out the Hun in him: he stormed at her. The quarrel, the more violent because of the Princess Royal's jangled nerves, was unfortunately witnessed by the Crown Prince, who by now was " dying pitifully ". On his return to Berlin the dutiful son told his toady von Eulenberg that his mother had treated him " like a dog ". As for his father, it was a " question whether a man who cannot speak will be Emperor at all ". Willy was in imagination already fitting on the Imperial crown. At the famous San Remo interview he had nauseously tried to persuade his father to surrender his position as Kaiserliche in his favour. There remained one further trial to complete the morbid charade of the Villa Zirio: the Berlin set accused the Princess Royal of taking a lover, her Court Chamberlain, Count Seckendorff. Of all the slanders scattered about the sorrowing wife this was perhaps the most vicious and grotesque. Seckendorff, who was not without those canine virtues of unquestioning loyalty which royal ladies throughout history have inspired in favoured courtiers, offered to resign. Fritz told him not to be silly; he had unbounded faith in him and in his devoted wife.

Soon Frederick William's laboured breathing could be heard half a dozen rooms away. But he was well enough to walk in the garden, and there on 9th March 1888 an equerry handed him a telegram addressed to " His Majesty Emperor Frederick William ". He was led weeping back to the villa. Power had come to him too late to save Germany. But he wept more for his country than for himself. The tears dried on the wasted cheeks as he donned the uniform of his regiment, adjusted the ribbon and star of the Hohenzollerns' highest order, the Black Eagle, and silently wrote out the proclamation of his accession. Then he took the star from his tunic and pinned it to his wife's dress. The pent-up grief, admiration and devotion gushed forth and she fell sobbing into his arms.

" I thank you," he wrote to Mackenzie, " for having made me live long enough to recompense the valiant courage of my wife."

At this heart-rending hour the voice of a faithful minority was heard. The Jewish deputy Bamberger declared, " The story of the national baseness and stupidity against Morell Mackenzie and Victoria [the Princess Royal] is one of the most peculiar chapters in the psychology of vileness." Jews saw in the new Emperor Frederick III a protector from the anti-semitism which had begun to sweep through the fledgling fascist empire. For this he was denounced as ' Judenkaiser '—Emperor of the Jews— and accession posters addressed " To my People " appealing for religious toleration were mutilated, or painted through with the word " Israel ".

For the sake of his health the Emperor stayed at Charlotten-burg Palace outside Berlin, but he and the Empress considered themselves mere " passing shadows " who would soon be swept away by Willy together with all the hopes of a new and liberalised Germany. The redoubtable Queen Victoria announced her intention to visit Berlin, mainly to see Fritz before he died. Bismarck expostulated, but as the Queen's will-power was superior even to his she arrived with bag, baggage and retinue on 24th April 1888. Probably for the first time during his reign of power Bismarck quailed. But the old lady, now approach-ing her sixtieth year, was kinder to him than he expected, asked him to stand by her daughter at that black hour, and quite dis-armed him by inviting him and his wife to tea at the British embassy. The Queen was distressed to find her favourite son-in-law in bed and languishing in the final stages of the disease. When she left Berlin she could hardly tear herself from her daughter's embrace. Pussy gazed forlornly through her tears as the train bore her mother away.

" I feel so like a wreck, a sinking ship, so wounded and struck down, so sore of heart, as if I were bleeding from a thousand wounds," she wrote as the Emperor perceptibly faded; and the King of Sweden, coming in to see him, burst into tears and hurriedly left.

Release came to Fritz at the age of 57 on 15th June 1888, a lovely day with the noon sun streaming through the open win-dows. The Empress, gaunt with strain and exhausted by the racking vigil, collapsed on his bed, as her mother had done when the Beloved One died. But to some degree Queen Victoria had suffered less than her daughter, for Frederick's agony had been prolonged and painful and the malice of enemies quite unbeliev-ably savage. " Why does such pain not kill immediately?" the Empress asked her diary during the last days of anguish. A post-mortem was carried out against her wishes. She cried out, " I was mad with sorrow, anger and agitation that they dared to touch his dear, sacred mortal remains." To her mother she wrote of her loneliness—" I am his widow, no more his wife! How am I to bear it?" Now she must stumble along, alone and unprotected. The reign of ninety-nine days had achieved nothing; Bismarck had seen to that. For the future she was at the mercy of her extraordinary son, the 'little darling' and 'little pet' of all those years ago when her seraphic father had ruminated fondly on whether Willy would go down to posterity as William the Great.

Scarcely had Frederick III drawn his last breath than the new Emperor, aged 29, ordered troops to surround Charlottenburg so that no documents, especially his mother's letters, should be carried off. He was too late. Most of the private papers of both parents lay securely in the archives at Windsor, together with Fritz's war diary. Extracts from this diary were later published: they put into perspective Frederick William's part in securing the unification of Gemany in 1871. As Bismarck had claimed the whole credit for this he was mortified by the disclosures and visited his wrath upon Professor Geffker, who for the crime of editing the excerpts was accused of treason. Soon Wilhelm II was comporting himself like a megalomaniac. Even in private he demanded to be addressed as ' Imperial Majesty '. The Dowager Empress gazed sorrowfully on her two sons—Henry had also dutifully turned against his mother—and reflected that now she understood what Julius Caesar felt when Brutus stabbed him, for they as well as their sister Charlotte joined those conservative elements in German society who rejoiced over the fallen liberal Kaiser.

The new Emperor poured out his " rage and distrust " against his mother when the war diary was followed by the revelations of Mackenzie defending his treatment of the dead Emperor and accusing Bergmann of hastening his death. Wilhelm supposed his mother had influenced the decisions to publish these works. Mackenzie's book was banned in Germany, but the repercussions of overseas publication swept the country and in the deafening din, which almost drove her to despair, the Dowager Empress fled to Windsor. Had her eldest son dared he would have prevented her, since he suspected her every move, but he feared to antagonise his grandmother, who had advised him to " help and do all you can for your poor, dear Mother and try to follow in your best, noblest and kindest of father's footsteps." Almost at the same time the Prince of Wales was writing to his son George: " Try, my dear Georgy, never to forget Uncle Fritz. . . . He was one of the finest and noblest characters ever known. If he had a fault, he was *too* good for this world." And Edward wrote to his mother describing the late Emperor as the noblest and best man he had even known, except his own dear father Albert.

During the Dowager Empress's absence the Bismarcks continued their vendetta against the British. This time their target was Sir Robert Morier, the former counsellor at Berlin who was now British ambassador to Russia. During the Franco-Prussian war he had represented Britain in Hesse, where, the Bismarcks alleged, he had betrayed Prussian military secrets to the French. The story was false, but by the time the truth came out Britain and Germany had advanced far along the road to Armageddon.

The royal widow, in the sable weeds which, like her mother, she was to wear to the end of her days, spent three months in Britain. On her return to Berlin her grief burst out afresh when her husband's precise instructions for his funeral were found in a sealed envelope. No one had known of their existence. Some of his dying wishes had not been carried out. The discovery dealt his widow a blow to the heart, and she could not sleep at night thinking about it. But by the summer of 1889 she was busy planning the conversion of a large country house near Krönberg into an English mansion. The task took two years. Friedrichshof, or Frederick's Court, was dedicated to her husband's memory. Located among the firs which richly garnish the smiling Taunus hills, this became the retreat of her last years on earth. But she was to have no real peace of mind. The ineffable Duke Ernest of Coburg—the Prince Consort's interfering brother —again caused mischief. During the Emperor Frederick's ephemeral reign Ernest had written a pamphlet anonymously attacking his niece. Now he came out with another one, *The 99 Days*, criticising both the Emperor and the Empress Frederick. With impeccable chivalry a Gustav Freytag then published a polemic accusing the Dowager Empress and her dead sister Alice of having betrayed Prussian military intelligence to the French during the war. Wilhelm II and the Bismarcks did nothing to refute these malicious inventions.

Yet the Dowager Empress bore no lasting ill-will towards Chancellor von Bismarck. When the Kaiser dismissed him in 1890 she feared " nothing good will come of it," and was graciousness itself to the fallen dictator, who had wrecked her ambitions for the liberalisation of Germany, when on parting he said to her, " Perhaps your Majesty will be pleased to know me, should you see me at a social gathering." With the eclipse of Bismarck's influence she suffered more not less. One snub followed another as the new Kaiser and Kaiserin settled themselves on the Imperial throne. Dona—" on her high horse ", in Bertie's phrase—pushed her mother-in-law aside, taking over the leadership of the German Red Cross when the family mausoleum closed over the old Empress Augusta. A Berlin citizens' movement to erect a monument to Fritz—' the last Berliner '—was snuffed out by Willy. He and his precious wife elbowed the Dowager Empress more and more into the background and let favour-seekers know that their prospects of advancement would be hindered if not extinguished if they visited Friedrichshof. This ban extended even to the Kaiser's children: they were rarely allowed to visit their grandmother, still pilloried at court as ' the Englanderin '. She often felt that she had been " buried alive ".

Once during her widowhood she was called upon to play a diplomatic role, and then with unfortunate results. Her last unmarried daughter Margaret had quarrelled with Willy and was living in France. The Kaiser asked his mother to try to bring about a reconciliation. When she reached France memories of that brave time during the war of 1870-71 poured in upon her. Like self-centred people anywhere, she found it impossible to put herself in the place of others. She could not assess the lingering bitterness of the French people, especially Parisians, towards the war; and she made the fatal mistake of driving to Versailles, where her father-in-law had been proclaimed German Emperor. An unworthy feeling that she had come to ' gloat ' oppressed the sensitive French, so many of whom remembered the horrors and privations of the siege and bombardment of Paris, and the royal visitor deemed it prudent to withdraw with a swiftness barely compatible with dignity, especially as the staff at Louis XIV's palace, some of whom acted as though the Sun King still lived there, loudly condemned her failure to gratify their highest expectations of foreign travellers, the provision of largess. But, of course, had she lavished tips she would no doubt have been accused of bribery. However that may be, her tactless mission served no purpose but to delight her enemies in Berlin.

That was her last venture into politics. After that she became an onlooker of events, no longer a participator in them. From the sidelines, as Willy contrived to alarm and antagonise one by one of the nations with whom Germany was nominally in amity, she was " a silent and much-distressed spectator ". The Diamond Jubilee came and went and with it, at last, the rumour that she had secretly married her 'lover' Count Seckendorff. Those who had maligned the Kaiser's mother had not long to wait before it could be said of them that they pursued her to the tomb. In the autumn of 1898 she fell on her head from her horse, which trod on her right hand. 'Lumbago' set in, but by the following spring she told her friend Fraulein Bunsen that the constant pain was caused by cancer. Dr. Barkeley says: " She almost gave the impression that she derived a certain secret satisfaction in suffering from the same disease as had her husband."

Professor Renvers from Berlin gave her two more years of life. She calmly prepared herself for death. Even Willy expressed filial concern, but the secret was withheld from Queen Victoria then approaching 80.

In her forty years in Germany, the Dowager Empress Frederick had tried hard to become wholly German, but she never succeeded. Various reasons, notably her mother's growing frailty and her own illness, prompted her to visit the land of her birth in February 1900. She felt it would be for the last time. Jingoism raged as the Boer War shook the foundations of the British Empire and the relief of Kimberley was followed by the relief of Ladysmith. Ill though she was, she found it hard not to 'flare up' when the German newspapers censured Britain. It was, she said, " enough to make a saint swear ". Eight months later, after having vainly sought escape from pain in Italy, she wrote her last letter to her mother. Morphia was now bringing her relief for only fifteen minutes at a time, and she could not concentrate long enough to force quill over paper. Her mother died on 22nd January 1901. " I wish I were dead, too," her daughter wept. But her last days were cheered by the new King Edward VII, who in his good nature was deceived by Willy's apparent docility into believing that he had changed his spots, and he wrote to tell the Kaiser's mother so. " William's touching and simple de-meanour . . . will never be forgotten by me or anyone." But the King privately described his nephew as " William the Great ", an ironical echo of the Prince Consort. He conferred the long-withheld Garter on Willy—whose favourate affectionate descrip-tion of his uncle was " that old Peacock "—and also on the Kaiser's namesake and heir, who because of his height went down to history as " Little Willy '. Both were struck off the Garter roll by the King's successor in 1915.

Edward's solicitous hope that God might mitigate his sister's sufferings were not borne out, but he showed himself a kind and dutiful brother when, soon after his mother's burial, he sailed to Germany aboard the new royal yacht *Victoria and Albert* to see the Dowager Empress at Friedrichshof. Even on her deathbed she was not spared the kind of unpleasantness from which she had suffered early in her married life and again during her husband's fatal illness. Her sufferings horrified and distressed the King, who asked the medical adviser attached to his suite, Sir Francis Laking, to suggest to the German doctors attending the Dowager Empress that morphia should be in-jected in larger and more frequent doses; but they recoiled from what they probably regarded as an invitation to apply euthanasia and the request was not renewed. The King, whose brother Alfred, Duke of Edinburgh, had died from cancer the same year, felt a shiver of apprehension when he discovered that for three nights the royal party had been sitting thirteen at table. He threw off his depression only when one of his fellow guests, Princess Charles of Hesse, pointed out that she was with child; but Edward was glad to return to London and dine alone with Mrs. Keppel in Portman Square.

One remaining good office was performed for the dying Dowager Empress as a result of her brother's compassionate visit. His private secretary, Sir Frederick Ponsonby, had accompanied him to Germany. He was her godson and the son of her mother's

M

former private secretary, Sir Henry; and she begged him to remove her later correspondence and other papers out of Friedrichshof and take them secretly to England so that her son should not get his hands on them. Ponsonby was astonished to find that these papers filled two heavy chests, which it took four stablemen to carry. As the mansion was heavily guarded by the Kaiser's secret police Ponsonby arranged to have the boxes smuggled out at night. The successful completion of this mission relieved the Dowager Empress's mind. But her nephew, King George V, expressed his displeasure in unmistakable terms when Ponsonby on his own responsibility caused extracts to be published; the King's Aunt Vicky had been dead twenty-seven years then.

The end came on 5th August 1901 in the presence of the Kaiser as the sun was westering and the scent of the firs wafted down from the Taunus hills and, with it, a butterfly which flew fitfully around the room and, finding the window again after a few minutes, fluttered into the beyond. Her troubles were over. As the funeral train from Krönberg steamed into Potsdam with the coffin—she was to be buried beside Fritz and Waldemar— her bodyguard announced to Edward VII and other assembled princes, " Her Majesty the Empress-Queen Frederick."

Louise, Duchess of Fife

I

In a sheltered youth Princess Louise of Saxe-Coburg and Gotha secretly read the poems of Byron with longing, if not passion. They evoked in her pale and delicate person pleasant visions of some handsome knight-errant who would one day sweep her off her feet and ride her to some romantic nest in the Highlands of Scotland. She had one reservation, however. No foreigners need apply. Not that the future Edward VII's eldest girl was a xenophobe. Rather she was a home-keeping body, happy in the bosom of her possessive and rather over-powering, ethereally beautiful Danish mother Alexandra, herself the embodiment of Continental charisma; in the breezy patronage of her two elder brothers, Eddy (fated to die young) and Georgy (the future George V); and in the shared confidences of her two sisters, Victoria, who was forced to remain a spinster, and Maud, the future Queen of Norway. And, of course, there was great big Papa whose frequent absences from home—he had to mingle much with foreigners and men of affairs—were worth enduring for the gladness he shed on his return, his dear voice echoing in the corridors of Marlborough House as he explained to darling Motherdear the intricacies of some point of private diplomacy which hitherto had baffled her unsuspicious mind.

Then, at sudden last, the incredible happened. Her Don Juan declared himself. He had all the advantages of youth save one: he was 40. Otherwise he was unexceptionable. Moreover, he was British. Better still, he was a Scot. He was Alexander William George Duff, sixth Earl of Fife. Above all, he was a friend of Papa's. From the moment she set eyes on him Louise loved him madly. The merit and misfortune of the fourth and fifth

Princesses Royal was to love their husbands to distraction. Both marriages ended tragically and prematurely, but where it had been the fate of the Empress Frederick to see her lord dying by inches over an agonisingly long period, her niece Louise suffered widowhood with an abruptness that almost deprived her of reason when " poor dear Macduff "—the future Queen Mary's poignant phrase—died after gallant exertions in the wreck of the liner *Delhi* in 1912. Like her grandmother, Queen Victoria, the unlucky princess retired into her shell. To the end of her days she emerged little into the blaze of state affairs: she shaded her sad blue eyes from the light which beat upon the throne successively of her grandmother, her father and her brother, the three Sovereigns of her day.

Pathetically she tried to communicate with her lost one, from whom it was claimed that she received spirit messages. Louise in her later years derived much comfort from the companionship of Miss Elizabeth Gordon, a Scotswoman whose clairvoyance had disconcerted her family when they first discovered it: her mother gave her a dose of castor oil and put her to bed. Years later Miss Gordon forecast that her mother would die in child-bed but that the baby would survive. All this happened as she had predicted, and it was then, around 1925, that Miss Gordon decided to settle in London, where she entered the service of the still grieving princess, whose reluctance to assuage her spiritual loneliness in any kind of regular or permanent public work had gained her the unsympathetic style of ' Her Royal Shyness '. Her only consolation, apart from family pleasures, was the conviction that she could penetrate the unknown to send messages to and receive replies from her husband. Miss Gordon loyally kept her confidence for years after Louise had sent her last message, but from what she said then it appeared that the Princess Royal had drawn comfort from this reassurance of the existence of life beyond the deathbed. There is some evidence that Queen Alexandra, equally lonely in old age, was not unimpressed by super-natural manifestations, but it would be pure conjecture to suggest that she influenced her daughter along this path, especially as most of the Queen's correspondence was formally destroyed at her death in 1925.

Alexandra in her strong maternalism enjoyed a separate relationship with each individual child as well as with them all collectively, and a special flavour was imparted to her love for Louise by the anxious circumstances of her birth. The Princess of Wales was deprived by a difficult pregnancy of a visit to Russia with her husband in November 1866 for the marriage of her favourite sister Dagmar to the future Czar Alexander III. Shortly before Louise was born on 20th February 1867 panic seized Alexandra's doctor when she complained of violent pain and stiffness in the right leg. Rheumatic fever was developing. In those days fatal blood poisoning sometimes ensued. The patient's condition was complicated by the pregnancy, and for a time her life seemed threatened. Queen Victoria came out of her seclusion at Windsor to command her daughter-in-law to live, and the princess's parents, King Christian and Queen Louise, thoroughly agitated the country by hurrying from Denmark to their daughter's bedside, while the doctors, not for the first time in royal history, acted their way through a pantomime which told the waiting public nothing and added to their alarm.

Out of this anxious period came an infant daughter tinged with sadness (as well as the ' Alexandra limp ' the painful legacy of the streptococcus rheumatism which had fortunately lodged in the knee joint and not in the heart.) Alexandra despite her usually abnormal pregnancies was the soul of maternalism, and when she recovered she bewailed that her baby had been deprived of a mother's intimate care during the formative early months of her life. Louise led an unsettled existence until after her mother's return from Wiesbaden, where she had pursued the vain hope that the spa waters would effect a complete cure. Alexandra, spoilt from childhood, was not an easy patient and Edward not always a tolerant, compassionate or discreet husband. Life at Marlborough House was subject to strains sufficient for those who throve in royal chit-chat to accuse the Prince of neglecting his wife. Indeed, while Edward, always a dutiful father, was superintending plans to celebrate his eldest daughter's third birthday in 1870 thunderclouds gathered: three days after the birthday party he was in the witness box denying on oath that he had committed adultery with the young wife of Sir Charles Mordaunt, and he and Alexandra were thereafter hissed and booed in the London streets. Never since the early days of Queen Victoria's reign had the monarchy been so unpopular. Providence, however, worked the miracle of Edward's recovery from almost fatal typhoid fever in 1871 and the rising tide of republicanism and the threat to monarchy subsided.

The family was by that time complete, for Alexandra's third son and sixth child, Alexander John Charles Albert, had died soon after birth in April 1871 and she bore no more children. The five Wales children who survived had been born over a period of five years and ten months. Victoria and Maud arrived in the two successive years after the birth of Louise, who shyly tried to mother them. The clannishness of the Wales establishment was equalled if not surpassed by the arcane family rites of the Christians, whose gatherings most autumns were a joy to little Louise; to the end of her days she treasured recollections of happy times in Copenhagen and biennial visits to Rumpenheim. As the first girl in the family Louise was petted by her bustling and domineering grandmother Queen Louise, but the child was named not so much after the Queen of Denmark as for her godmother, her father's sister Louise, Duchess of Argyll, the sculptress who among other activities adorned Kensington Gardens with the statue of Queen Victoria which is admired to this day. Louise was also named after the Queen, her mother Alexandra and her aunt Dagmar.

The child's upbringing was conditioned by her mother's enthusiasm for hospitals, dating from the period of her recovery from rheumatic fever. Louise was whisked from one great London institution to another, or when in the country to cottage hospitals and nursing homes and other places of healing. A favourite staging post was the children's hospital in Great Ormond Street. In common with the young of the Victorian middle and upper classes Louise and her brothers and sisters were encouraged in the virtues of Christian piety and charity. Canon Teignmouth Shore supervised Louise's religious education and she regularly attended the flower services with the canon inaugurated at the Berkeley Chapel for the benefit of the children's hospitals. Charlotte Knollys, the maiden lady who as secretary-companion supervised Alexandra's affairs to the end of her days, was given the oversight of the girls' education, which ran more or less along lines laid down years earlier by Queen Louise for her own children—good plain living, plenty of fresh-air exercise coupled with hard work and strenuous play, the pursuit of perfection in languages, music and art. They were the first royal generation to explore the joys and mysteries of 'dear old Sandringham' with its numerous pets, ponies and dogs, its summer picnics and winter skating, its tennis and shooting parties.

Louise gradually acquired some virtuosity as a pianist—she sometimes also played the organ at Sandringham church—and a taste for grand opera. Monsieur Bertrand taught her fencing, so good for the figure, and in the dairies at Sandringham she learned to make butter and cheese. She could cook little things and never tired of picking up recipes for homely dishes from the local countryfolk. Alexandra's own childhood had been spent in comparative penury as one of the six children of an army officer. The Christian family were homespun and cheese-paring as a consequence, and although Alexandra was the reverse of parsimonious after she had married into the wealthy Saxe-Coburg dynasty she ensured that her daughters were tutored in kitchen economics, for in those uncertain times when people were clamouring for still more reform one never knew what rough tasks royal hands might sooner or later have to undertake. At Sandringham and in London, and also at Abergeldie, where summer holidays were enlivened by contact with young Scottish lairds, Louise appeared timidly in the wake of her exotic mother.

"The public appearances entailed by her rank were few, and this accorded well with her own inclination," as a contemporary chronicler put it.

Out of this quiet life Louise was plucked by the irresistible Macduff. The eighteen years between them evaporated in the warmth of mutual affection which, nourished by the kindness and understanding of the perceptive male, blossomed into love. The Prince of Wales bellowed with astonishment. The Earl of Fife was a man of the world, a founder of the British South Africa Company—an important factor in thwarting the African expansionist ambitions of fat little King Carlos of Portugal—and an associate of Horace Farquhar, who had started life as a junior clerk in a Society bank and from that modest beginning had become financial adviser to the Royal Family. Moreover, the future bridegroom had been of the greatest value to the Prince of Wales by introducing him to Sir Charles Dilke, then Under-Secretary for Foreign Affairs, who fed him those choice scraps of political and diplomatic information which on no account would the Queen share with her son. There was a certain piquancy in the fact that Dilke was a radical and a republican and consequently detested by the Queen, who was not surprised, and indeed felt some gratification at the sureness of her instinct, when the divorce scandal burst over his head.

The echoes of that *cause célèbre* were still reverberating in Mayfair salons when the thoughts of Princess Louise turned to romance. She had previously rejected offers of marriage in ' the Royal Caste ', but so long as she demurred at living abroad, at being cut off from the beloved relations by seas and frontiers and foreigners, the choice was circumscribed. Her mind was influenced by the experience of the older Louise, her godmother, who had married a Campbell; he became the ninth Duke of Agyll. The territorial titles held by the Campbells read like an ordnance survey of the better parts of Scotland, but the Duffs were not far behind.

" He is a good fellow and a man of business," wrote the Prince of Wales, " and he and his family own half the County."

Above all, he had been a Member of Parliament, and what could be better than that? Next to royalty the landed gentry of Scotland had few rivals in those days when, as Sir George Arthur so exquisitely expressed it, the Queen clung to Balmoral and " the whiff of white heather was so sweet in her nostrils ". News of the engagement depressed a number of solid citizens. The heir to the heir apparent was the weedy Duke of Clarence (Eddy), of whom it was already being said that he would never live to be King, a prognostication of tragic accuracy; and of course Prince George might be drowned in the Navy (in fact he almost died from typhoid, like his father). The Cassandras of the court, flicking back the pages of the *Almanac de Gotha*, proved from inescapable fact that the first three sons of George III had expired without legitimate issue. From this they argued that Princess Louise was too close to the throne to marry importunately. Whatever they might think in Scotland, the Earl of Fife was hardly to be considered a suitable successor of the dear Prince Consort should Louise become Queen—indeed, it was not until 1885 that plain Earl Fife had been transmuted into Earl *of* Fife. Such considerations might become of paramount importance to the future of Crown and Empire, and one must weigh above all the feelings of the children of the union when they realised they were not quite one hundred per cent royal.

No worry on this score had the Princess of Wales, especially as her own father had become King of Denmark only because her mother had become Queen, and she was soon on her way to Windsor to obtain the Queen's permission: Louise was only 24 and conceivably incapable of seeking her grandmother's consent in person. The Queen, whose respect for the earl's father as a fine type of Scot had been transferred to his successor, expressed delight and surprise. Her understanding of the situation—and little escaped that bright blue eye—was that Louise had hitherto regarded her lover as an elder brother, but that he was now rather more so. On constitutional grounds she raised no objection: an annual rent roll of £80,000 and other large revenues powerfully reinforced the Prince of Wales's argument that he should be made a duke. Immediately after the Queen had approved she recorded her reactions in her diary: " That my beloved grandchild should have her home in dear Scotland and in the dear Highlands is an additional satisfaction to me."

She also wrote congratulating " My dear Fife " and signed herself " Your very affectionate future Grandmamma ". However, she quibbled about the dukedom. The Queen could never understand this odd passion for dukes, especially on the part of people who, as in her own family, so often held the much worthier rank of prince. But she supposed there was a cause for creating a Duke of Fife and Marquess of Macduff: it had not been necessary in the case of her daughter Louise's husband because the Marquess of Lorne, as he was on marriage, had inherited the dukedom of Argyll. The dear Conqueror himself, to whom they were all so indebted, had introduced dukes into Britain with a lot of other unpleasant or useful innovations, and one had to take the rough with the smooth. Accordingly when her granddaughter married Macduff in the private chapel at Buckingham Palace on 27th July 1889 the Queen at the wedding breakfast announced her resolve to confer a dukedom, by patent dated two days later, although she thought it all unnecessary and even slightly ridiculous. The marriage ceremony was also historic in that Barnby's now-familiar " O Perfect Love " was sung for the first time. No doubt these two factors, the dukedom and the hymn, sweetened the Prince of Wales, for whom life had recently been made unwholesome by the importunities of what he called " uninteresting and tiresome people ", among them the Shah of

Persia. For some obscure reason the Shah found it difficult to stay away from Britain, where his presence was a costly and intolerable inconvenience. Princess Alexandra, busy superintending every last detail of her daughter's trousseau ("darling Mother-dear always knows best") almost shrieked when the occupant of the Peacock Throne offered his palace at Teheran for the honeymoon. He had already upset her ladies-in-waiting by suggesting that because of their modest looks they should be executed; in his oriental simplicity he thought they were the Prince of Wales's concubines. The Princess gently corrected this pardonable error and rejected the offer, having some absurd notion that if it were accepted her son-in-law might find himself headless and her daughter a reluctant member of the Shah's harem.

The new duke was not exactly homeless, and he and his bride settled in one of the more modest and charming of his residences, Sheen Lodge, a white, ivy-covered mansion near Richmond Park in Surrey. Here they were not far from Town or from the Teck family, then eking out a precarious existence on a few thousand a year at the White Lodge in the park itself. Sheen Lodge remained their favourite home, and there Louise's two daughters were born. If the Fifes needed change they had the choice of the family seat, Duff House, or Mar Lodge in Aberdeenshire, a town house in Portman Square, and a seaside place in Chichester Terrace, Brighton, with a superb view of the unchanging sea.

It was to Mar Lodge that the Prince of Wales fled from the "uninteresting and tiresome people" while the duke and his bride were visiting the Scottish estates soon after the marriage; here the prince in the quiet of the Scottish moors refreshed his spirit before the inevitable trip to Denmark in the wake of his wife and the two unwed daughters. But the glittering gaiety of the Marlborough House Set was not for Louise and her husband. They kept much to themselves. Simplicity was the watchword. There was no need to maintain the royal style. Ladies-in-waiting were offered but not taken up: the Princess shrank from publicity and one never knew what sort of things a lady-in-waiting might write in her *diary*. But guests of the Fifes were left in no doubt about the royal status of their hostess: Louise when she entertained always preceded them into dinner. Nor was she gregarious. She preferred the simple countryside to the town with

all its false values. In rural Scotland she and her husband could
jog along on their bicycles—they were pioneers of the Victorian
cycling craze—and of course there were the great rivers to be
fished. Louise showed surprising skill as an angler. In September
1893 she played and landed seven large salmon, a feat which was
at that time a record for a lady's rod on Deeside. It later years
she golfed. She had time and means to pursue her hobbies. Her
mother had become one of the most persistent amateur photo-
graphers of the day, and Louise, too, was ever busy ' snapping '
the nearest and dearest. In London she was an ardent and
selective theatre-goer, but it was always to brush and easel that
she returned: in some respects she was the most talented of the
Princesses Royal. Fire destroyed the old Mar Lodge and the new
one was designed and built largely on the basis of sketches made
by Princess Louise, who also designed the interior of her home
at Brighton.

Life was always very full, but if time dragged the Duchess
of Fife had her possessive and loving family to visit or write to.
Her sentimental heart responded to every chord of romance, and
she developed her talent for match-making. The exception was
her second sister Victoria, who loved a commoner, the fifth Earl
of Rosebery no less; but with capricious unkindness the Princess
of Wales disapproved, although she had condoned the morganatic link in the affairs of Louise herself. As the future Prime
Minister decided not to pursue the lady poor Toria went through
life unmarried, the invaluable and valued confidante and adviser
of her brother George to the end of her life in 1935, and before
that the unpaid companion of her demanding but still darling
Motherdear.

In two other historic romances the Duchess of Fife had mixed
success. Eddy became desperately enamoured of Princess Hélène
d'Orléans, the lovely daughter of the exiled French Pretender,
the Comte de Paris. The Prince of Wales, then stealthily working towards the ideal of the Entente Cordiale, welcomed his son's
choice and even Princess Alexandra steeled herself for the great
sacrifice she would be called upon to make when her eldest
child left her for another woman. One insuperable obstacle remained: the princess had the misfortune to be a Roman Catholic,
although inexplicably she seemed not to worry about it. Indeed,
she was prepared to apostatise to marry the man she loved;

the joyful prospect of accompanying the Prince of Wales and his family to church on Sunday mornings also profoundly influenced her mind. When her decision was made known there was great rejoicing, for it was not every day that an heretic is won over to the Established Church, and arrangements were made for the engagement to be announced. The Prince of Wales was too occupied to interrupt his devotions in Homburg, where the natural waters and other treatments were doing him good, and as Princess Alexandra was at Mar Lodge with her son and the French princess the young couple became there and then betrothed.

Princess Louise, having to some extent liberated herself from her mother, was anxious to see her brothers and sisters settled, especially the Duke of Clarence, who seemed to be running to seed. The young lovers also had an ally, powerful in more ways than one, in Hélène's mother. The Comtesse drank, smoked and spat like a man and was a tireless huntress of the stag; she, too, was keen to see her daughter on the throne, any throne, and had little doubt that she would turn out to be as good a Protestant as the Prince of Wales himself. But the Comte was adamant: his daughter was a Roman Catholic and a Roman Catholic she must remain. Hélène journeyed to Rome to consult Pope Leo XIII. But he was a Roman Catholic, too, and his advice was the same as her father's. The engagement was broken off, but Eddy never ceased to love Hélène, even after he had become engaged to Princess Mary of Teck, and in the delirium which preceded his death in the winter influenza epidemic of 1891-2 he cried out her name again and again.

Some years before this tragedy Princess Mary (May) had attracted the attention of Queen Victoria, and as one of the poor relations of the Royal Family she was patronised by the ' whispering Wales sisters ', who felt free to criticise " poor May's " appearance behind her back. When Mary became engaged to Eddy his eldest sister, having played no small part in the affair of Princess Hélène, was under no illusion: they were not in love. She sensed May's preference for her surviving brother George, and although the Princess of Wales vowed that no woman should ever take her " darling Georgie boy " from her, the Duchess of Fife ensured otherwise. The Duke of York, as George had now become, only slowly grew aware of his manly attractions and of his grandmother's " terrible fuss " about his marrying: the Queen was most anxious for him to wed Princess Mary. Alexandra, who wept at the thought of poor Eddy, at last realised that she could not keep her younger son wrapped up in cotton wool for ever. When Louise, intervening for the second time in an historic affair of the heart, added sisterly pressure to all other influences which good family women can bring to bear in such circumstances, George had no option, even had he sought one. On 2nd May 1893, after a Mediterranean cruise with his mother, which she realised would be her last time alone with her " Georgie boy " and where she finally shed the delusion that none of her children had any inclination for marriage because they wished to remain with her, he went to stay with the Duke and Duchess of Fife at Sheen. On the following day Princess May was invited along " to see the baby "—her second daughter Maud, called after George's youngest sister, the future Queen of Norway. The pond in the grounds was well stocked with frogs that spring, and Louise thought it would be a good idea if George took May to see them.

" You'll enjoy them," she said eccentrically.

Her brother, whose interest in frogs had never been pronounced, thought this a singularly odd remark and often recalled it in later years.

" Do you remember Lulu asking me to show you the frogs that time?" he would say. " She didn't know I was going to ask you to marry me."

He also remembered it as " a lovely day, as hot as summer ". They were married on 6th July, thanks in no small measure to the shyest of George's sisters, and in the Chapel Royal at St. James's, too. The latest addition to the Royal Family was, through her mother, a great-grand-daughter of George III, but on her father's side there was an unfortunate mixture of blood, the result of an imprudent earlier marriage in the Teck family, and Louise, although hers was by no means an unkindly nature, could not forbear to remark upon May's " poor Württemberg hands ".

Nine months before her death Queen Victoria granted Macduff a fresh patent creating him Duke of Fife and Earl of Macduff, this time with the important provision that in default of male heirs these titles should pass to his daughters and their male issue. The duchess's health was then so indifferent that clearly she would bear no more children. The Fife succession must be secured. Her elder daughter, Princess Alexandra Victoria Alberta Edwina Louise, in time therefore became Duchess of Fife by inheritance, though this charming lady was better known in her day as Princess Arthur of Connaught, and the dukedom passed on her death to her nephew, the son of the second daughter Maud, Lady Carnegie. The Queen was quietly dying, and yet within a few months of the grave she showed inflexible purpose and constancy in one matter which is of no small importance. She was genuiunely fond of the first Duke of Fife and, although she felt that dukes were apt to think too highly of themselves, she wished to see his line and the dukedom endure. But one thing she would not do: she would not make the daughters *royal* merely because their father had had the good fortune to marry her grand-daughter.

No one regretted her resolution more than the Prince of Wales, and he made amends. When Louise was married he had ensured that all his children should be adequately provided for by Parliament, and each daughter received £3,000 a year and a £10,000 dowry; the annuity was doubled when he became King. Then, with that rare intuition for pleasing the ladies, he brought off a brilliant domestic ' double ' on his sixtieth birthday on 9th November 1905: he created his eldest daughter Princess Royal (she was then 38) and at the same time conferred the title and style of ' Princess ' and ' Her Royal Highness ' on both Louise's daughters. Later that month, when Norway withdrew from the ninety-year-old union under the Swedish Crown, the Prince of Wales used his considerable diplomatic wiles to elevate his youngest daughter still higher, and he was gratified when after a referendum his Danish son-in-law Charles was elected King Haakon VII of Norway and Maud entered Oslo in triumph as Queen at his side. For the second daughter Victoria he could do nothing comparable and, as though he divined the sadness with which her life had been tinged by the shattering of her romance, he startled Lord Salisbury one day earlier in his reign by suggesting that Lord Rosebery should be tempted back to public life and assume the leadership of the Liberal Opposition.

The new Princess Royal was destined never to be very active. At her creation—her ' declaration ', as it was called in those days—she was in declining health. The shock of the *Delhi* disaster took out of her what little heart she had left for public appearances. She resembled Queen Victoria and the Empress Frederick in the depth of her grief for one whom she had so passionately loved and whom she was to mourn for the remaining nineteen years of her life.

II

POSSIBLY LOUISE blamed herself for 'poor dear Macduff's' death. In 1911, while the new King George V and Queen Mary were at the Durbar in India, the fatal decision was taken to visit Egypt. One reason was the necessity to winter abroad for the sake of her health, for Louise never enjoyed travel for its own sake. Another was that since childhood she had heard from her parents such wonderful stories of Egypt, where Alexandra in 1869 had left a deep and lasting impression on the inhabitants, from the Khedive Ismael down, that she felt bound just to take a peep at a place which darling Motherdear rated so highly. And it would give her a chance to meet Lord Kitchener once more, such a dear man, even though his stare was so very disconcerting. There were also official duties to be carried out.

On Tuesday 12th December 1911 the shareholders of the Peninsular and Orient Steamship Company met to hear their chairman, Sir Thomas Sutherland, render his annual report and declare a dividend. They were gratified to learn that the company had a large fleet standing at between £3 and £4 a ton—" all the vessels being in the best possible order, of the highest possibly quality, and all capable of performing efficiently the services for which they were intended ". One of the ships was the *Delhi*, of 8,090 tons gross weight. She was six years old, sound in every respect and from the beginning of 1911 until 4th November she had been plying between India and China. Then Captain Bradshaw brought her home from Bombay, and Captain William Hayward, who had returned from the East in the *Persia*, took over command of the *Delhi*. Hayward was a first-class seaman in the highest P and O tradition, 52 years old, and during the last

Louise Princess Royal with her husband the first Duke of Fife

Queen Alexandra with her children: Princess Louise is on the right

The daughters of Edward VII in 1883; Princesses Louise, Victoria and Maud

thirty-five of those years he had become as familiar with the coasts of North Africa as any man afloat. Before he transferred to the *Delhi* he had commanded various vessels of the P & O line such as the *Arcadia*, the *Oceana* and the *Caledonia* over a period of thirteen years.

A few hours after Sir Thomas had spoken the *Delhi* was fighting for her life against the incessant pounding of black Atlantic waves on a sandbank 5 miles from Cape Spartel on the Moroccan coast.

All had seemed well when the Princess Royal and her family joined the *Delhi* at Tilbury that winter's day. The other eighty-five passengers included Mr. Gilbert McCaul Bell, a young Glasgow civil engineer; Mr. George R. Halkett, the celebrated cartoonist of the *Pall Mall Gazette*; a Dr. Essery; and a Miss Byng from Ryde, the daughter of a naval captain. Another hundred or more passengers were to join the vessel at Marseilles or Port Said. The *Delhi*'s cargo included gold specie valued at £500,000 for Bombay, a quantity of silver bars, and some of Britain's first exports of motor-cars, about £3,000 worth.

The liner had hardly left the Thames estuary than south-westerly gales began to blow. The rest of the passage was a nightmare. Most passengers remained below decks. The royal party discreetly withdrew.

" Sunday in the Bay was appalling," Miss Byng recalled. " People groaning, waves banging against the side, babies squalling!"

The *Delhi* lagged half a day behind schedule as she approached Cape Trafalgar at half speed, nosing forward cautiously in driving remorseless rain. But by some trick of current and wind she was beaten past the opening to the Straits and when, with engines silenced, she eventually buried her bows in the sandbank, some passengers thought they had berthed at Gibraltar, so slight was the shock. They were soon to discover that they were some 50 miles away to the south-west, stuck fast 5 miles from the rocky cliffs of Cape Spartel rearing up 1,000 feet out of the sea. The liner had come to rest broadside to the shore, facing south, easy prey for the breakers which like famished wolves leaped with ravening shrieks out of the Stygian night as though they would devour her whole.

N

Aboard the listing liner, only 80 yards out from the beach, the British went calmly about their business as though shipwreck had been a daily occurrence. They felt secure in the new-fangled wireless telegraphy. Only the previous year Dr. Crippen had been apprehended by the intrepid Inspector Drew and Sergeant Mitchell of Scotland Yard aboard the *Montrose*, the first criminal to be called to account through the medium of the radio. Anxiety began to mount at Gibraltar when the *Delhi* failed to appear on time in the afternoon of 12th December. The Atlantic Fleet was alerted, and when the first faint Morse distress signals were heard French warships in the vicinity moved towards the *Delhi*. Within an hour or two a formidable force was racing to the rescue, at its head the battleships *London* and *Venerable* with the cruisers *Duke of Edinburgh*, *Weymouth* and *Queen*, a torpedo boat and the dockyard tug *Energetic*, towing the Gibraltar lifeboat. The owners sent the fast steamer *Rocket* to Ceuta to order two more salvage vessels, *Hermes* and *Valkyries*, to make full speed for Cape Spartel, but by lucky chance the salvage ship *Gebel Yedid* had left the Rock the previous night for Larache and, coming across the *Delhi* in distress, stood in as close as she could. Later she was joined by another salvage vessel, the *Gebel Musa*. Operations were directed by Admiral Sir Christopher Cradock from *London*.

A detachment of Royal Artillery with rocket apparatus was landed by *Weymouth* at Tangier: from there they marched through the raging night overland to the cape where they could provide an alternative rescue force if the surf should block any approach to the doomed liner from seawards. But the French cruiser *Friant*, closely followed by the *Duchlaya*, reached the scene first. The Frenchmen found the liner wallowing helplessly in the strong under-current which—one of the mysteries of the sea—had swept her away from the Pillars of Hercules, the western frontier of ancient man's little flat earth. Coming to rest just below the Caves of Hercules, she had begun to tilt dangerously: in those tumultuous seas breakers occasionally dashed over her bridge, by which time—around half-past ten on the Wednesday morning—the *Delhi* had been stranded for more than twelve hours. The story of those hours was told by Miss Byng.

" The day before I had one of my funny presentiments, and I had wondered what were the most important things if we had to take to the boats. So I hurriedly got my keys, my money and my tickets, put on my warm clothes and a small bottle of brandy in my pocket, taking a small nip so as not to feel faint."

There spoke the sailor's true daughter! After the first shock the passengers had been assembled in the first-class saloon, where Miss Byng found some of the women in the oddest attire—hair in large curlers and tied around with veils. "But I clung to my little green hat and veil." Presently she found herself in a corner where she was joined by the Fifes.

The duchess might have been dressed for an ordinary journey, and she clung to an umbrella, but Princess Maud only had her night-gown on and a big coat over it, as far as I could see. They were all quite calm and the duke was very kind and considerate, insisting that all the ladies must sit, and talking to anyone he found himself near. Then the lascars came running up the companion way with the lifebelts and we were each buckled into one. A man began to play the piano. It was very kind of him but somehow it seemed out of place. The scene of the lascars running about under the electric lights made me think of nothing else but a cinematograph, and I sat and tried to think that I was looking at one. All this time it was pitch dark outside, rockets were banging off, and the Marconi wireless working hard. There was nothing to be done with us until daylight came except get the boats—some of them had been banged to pieces—ready for use.

Terrific squalls of wind and rain blew up at intervals—" in one of which the Duke of Fife ventured forth and was blown over and hauled in. The duchess rushed at him saying, ' Do come in. If we are to be drowned we will drown together ' ".

Louise then sat down and, tapping her lifebelt, declared: " Fancy me a sandwichman! I never thought I should be a sandwichman!" Miss Byng went on:

The captain, poor man, kept coming up and reassuring them. At one moment we heard we were 25 miles from land, and another something else was said. The first moment of relief was when we were told a French cruiser had answered our signals and then a British. After about four hours of waiting in the saloon the dawn came. We found we were almost on the African shore with the worst sea and surf between I have ever seen in my life. We were then allowed to go and have some breakfast which, all sea-sickness having vanished, we ate with a fair appetite. The lascars with great trouble got a lifeline ashore and we got our hand bags packed with the help of the stewards, but after all we were not allowed to take them, except those who had all their valuables in them. As I had only necessaries in mine I could not say anything, so most reluctantly was parted from combs and hairpins and toothbrush and all the little things that make life so comfortable.

The subsequent rescue operation was to rank with the most hazardous in maritime history. The French warships pushed the limits of safety in an effort to get as close to the stricken vessel as possible and, believing her to be in imminent peril, immediately lowered steam-driven pinnaces to take off the passengers. One pinnace struggled alongside the *Delhi* with the greatest difficulty.

One of the sailors called out, " We come save." Then our order came. The women with children were put in the steam pinnace and we other women were all put in a huge boat with four lascars which the pinnace was to tow through this terrible surf. Then my heart sank. The Duke and Duchess refused to leave with us, and we started packed like herrings and going over waves and surf like mountains. One moment came in which we were in the greatest danger. The Frenchman's rope towing us broke and we were at the mercy of the surf and even with lifebelts there would have been small chance for any of us.

But by a remarkable manoeuvre the pinnace swung across the bows of the overladen boat and got another rope aboard.

The French are very high in our estimation at present [Miss Byng conceded]. They did splendidly. As we passed their cruiser on the way to the *Duke of Edinburgh* where they were taking us they waved to us and we waved back. At last we got alongside our cruiser and the sight of our own sailors was the most comforting moment, though we had another trying ordeal as the sea would not let us get very close. A sailor made a springing leap into our boat, and one by one we had a rope thrown over our heads and under our arms and we were told to jump at the right moment and we were pushed and hauled on board, where our troubles finished. The officers petted us and gave up their cabins.

Miss Byng soon recovered her *esprit* and after completing her toilet with the aid of three hairpins she again donned the little green hat, which she had clutched to her bosom through the whole perilous adventure, and was again most comfortable.

Fears were now entertained for the royal party who had refused to leave the *Delhi* until the other passengers had been rescued. After Miss Byng and her fellow-passengers had been deposited aboard the *Duke of Edinburgh* the weather worsened and Admiral Cradock decided to get the Fifes and the remaining men off the *Delhi* to the shore, and not through the deeper and more turbulent water between the liner and the warships. By this time the admiral had boarded the *Delhi* and himself took the tiller of the ship's boat in which the landing was to be made. The Princess Royal ' invited ' Mr. Halkett and Mr. Bell to accompany her, the Duke and the princesses, just as serenely as though she was going for a sail in the royal barge on the Thames. A rope was attached to the boat so that it could afterwards be drawn back to the liner. As the boat approached the beach the admiral ordered the bluejackets to leap overboard when the keel touched sand, but the weight of the rope suddenly jerked the bobbing craft away from the land. Cradock left the tiller, threw off his jacket and seized an oar to steady the boat. A sailor sprang forward and chopped through the rope with an axe, but he was almost too late.

Wave after wave smashed down on the boat. The first of these swept over the stern the distinguished cartoonist of the *Pall Mall Gazette,* who floundered ashore after a desperate struggle for life. The same wave tore the Princess Royal's jewel case from her hand. Then Princess Maud was washed into the sea, fortunately on the shoreward side. Her mother managed to grasp one hand and her father the other, and all three waded ashore with Cradock's help. Princess Alexandra owed her life to the young Glasgow civil engineer. Just before the boat was swamped the princess noted that Mr. Bell had no lifebelt. She fished about in the water at the bottom of the boat and, having found one, tied it around him. This action saved her life. A second or two later Alexandra disappeared over the side.

Mr. Bell grasped her as she fell to leeward into deep water [it was reported]. The young Scotsman did not lose his presence of mind. He held the princess firmly with one hand and, buffeted by the heavy waves, at last reached out towards a floating barrel-buoy, to which Dr. Essery was clinging. At this moment, perhaps fortunately for her, the princess lost consciousness. Partly drifting and partly swimming, Bell reached shallow water at last, terribly knocked about, as all the party were, by the breakers, and he and the princess were assisted ashore. The princess recovered after a few moments, to the joy of her parents, who stood on the sand beside her.

Bell and Halkett spoke highly of the bravery of the royal ladies. " When all seemed lost they seized buckets, cheerfully and eagerly lent a hand in baling out the boat, and the Princess Royal again and again urged on the sailors with firm commands."

Their troubles were not over. Now they faced a 5-mile walk in blinding rain through another black night across trackless rocks and soft sand to Cape Spartel. The Duke was still in his nightshirt and Louise and her daughters were hampered at every stage by the weight of their wet night-clothes; they had lost all their baggage, including the jewels. Now they all set out doggedly, led by Moorish guides and escorted by four British sailors. After 4 cheerless and fatiguing miles they were met by the German Resident from Tangier, who lent the party his horse, which the Princess Royal and her daughters used in turn, and by 2.30 the next morning, more than twenty-four hours after the wreck, they sighted the lights of Cape Spartel. Princess Maud walked uncomplainingly for a long time with only one shoe. The lighthouse keeper at the cape supplemented supplies of clothing and food brought by the British Resident, Sir Reginald Lister, who placed the legation at Tangier at the Duke's disposal, and from there Macduff cabled: " The Princess Royal and the young princesses are suffering from the effects of fatigue and shock, but so far no serious consequences have supervened."

Not for them—but for him. By 29th January 1912 he was dead at Assuan from pleurisy contracted after the ordeal of Cape Spartel. He was 63.

For Captain Hayward the loss of the *Delhi* was a " great misfortune "—in Admiral Cradock's compassionate phrase—but although he was held to blame at the Board of Trade inquiry his fine personal qualities and unblemished character and his able command of the situation after the casualty impressed the court and his master's certificate was not ' dealt with '. For the families of three sailors of the French cruiser *Friant* who (alone of all the passengers and crews involved in the rescue operation) lost their lives when a pinnace capsized the wreck of the *Delhi* was an even greater misfortune, especially for the widow and children of Engineer Carel, whose body arrived at Brest from Tangier on Christmas Night. Only the family had been told, and so at four o'clock next morning a pauper's hearse went to Brest railway station and took away the corpse. Naval and military veterans who had intended to honour the young hero with a *marche funèbre* learned too late of his homecoming, and the flowerless funeral on Boxing Day was attended by the widow and orphans, a few sailors in a private capacity, and the British Vice-Consul who, complained *Le Petit Journal*, represented his country's gratitude while "official France stayed away". The widow complained of this indifference. The authorities explained that military honours had been provided at Tangier and could not be repeated. Moreover, as no orders had been received from the Ministry of Marine, the widow was told that she would have to pay the cost of her husband's interment. The paper condemned this appalling parsimony as "deplorable and odious". The British naval men fared better. Admiral Cradock, whose prompt decision to direct the rescue boat ashore saved the lives of the King's relations, received the Medal for Gallantry in Saving Life at Sea. More than sixty officers and ratings received silver or bronze medals.

"My heart is very full of gratitude," wrote the Dowager Queen Alexandra, "to the gallant sailors who took so great a part in rescuing my dear daughter and her family in their great peril."

For Princess Louise the death of Macduff struck a devastating blow from which she never recovered. Widowed at 45, she was never really well again. Towards the end of her life she lingered for months at a time in Scotland where her husband's spirit breathed to her out of the heather. There at Mar Lodge in the autumn of 1929 she suffered a heart attack. An ambulance train took her to London. For the next fifteen months she languished at the Portman Square house, and on 4th January 1931 she died there while the Royal Family were at Sandringham. "A bad beginning for a New Year," wrote the King, who felt "very depressed". The bells of St. Paul's Cathedral tolled for an hour. It was left to Lord Parmoor on behalf of Mr. Ramsay

MacDonald's Labour Government to extol in Parliament her homely virtues before her temporary burial on 10th January at St. George's Chapel, Windsor, from whence the remains were transferred four months later to lie beside the Duke of Fife in the mausoleum at Mar Lodge. But it was the *Daily Mail* which sounded the apt note: " She stood in all men's minds for an ancient and noble tradition of womanhood—the wife and mother who sought no applause, who mixed in none of the traffic and business of state, but who was yet a shining influence on many lives by the sheer force of that example to which Ruskin attributed a power ' purer than the air of heaven and stronger than the seas of earth '."

Mary, Countess of Harewood

∝≺≼≼≼≼≼≼≽≽≽≽≽≽∝

I

Two or three months before Lord Kitchener disappeared in the wreck of HMS *Hampshire* in 1916 a Grenadier Guards officer, having lunched at one of the five exclusive clubs to which he could afford to belong, turned into Bond Street. He was old-looking for his 35 years, an impression heightened by the 'mudguard' moustache and weathered face, but so imposing in faultlessly tailored regimentals that young women tittered as they passed and hoped he would notice them. But Harry Lascelles had no eye for young flappers, even while he was on leave from 'the trenches'; and he was spending the last day or two of furlough shopping for old porcelain, in the collection of which he was served by considerable expertise and an even more considerable purse. The landed nobility in search of the rare and the precious have ever appealed to the romantic instincts of the antique dealers, and Captain Lascelles was ushered into an establishment famous for superb bric-à-brac embracing examples drawn from the artistic output of several centuries and many climes. Lascelles was about to train his monocle on the well-known Fitzwilliam griffin which distinguishes the better Rockingham pieces when he was distracted by a quite extraordinary sight.

At the rear of the shop a tramp in a greasy and ragged coachman's cloak and a battered stovepipe hat was actually fingering a valuable Delft plate of that cobalt-blue brilliance which proclaimed its native Dutch origin. Lascelles observed with horror a fish-head protruding from the frayed rush frail dangling from the old man's other hand. Under his arm was a decrepit umbrella rusty with age and neglect. The monocle slid from the well-bred eye. Gad! Drawing aside the woman assistant, Harry offered to keep an eye on the tramp if she wished to seek help to have him removed. The woman blushed with embarrassment and asked him to lower his voice. He was no tramp, she explained: he was Lord Clanricarde, and despite his appearance he was one of the shrewdest collectors in London.

If anyone should have heard of the Marquess of Clanricarde it was Harry Lascelles, for the eccentric and unsavoury Irish peer was his great-uncle, his grandmother's brother. A modest point in Clanricarde's favour was that he was a multi-millionaire. The legend, and there is no reason to dispute its factual basis, is that the old man and his grand-nephew had not met for ten years until that day in the Bond Street shop, and Lascelles was so appalled at the change in his noble relative that he failed to recognise him. Clanricarde, so mean that he wore his valet's cast-off clothing, rarely appeared in dealers' shops, so Lascelles might never have seen him again. Indeed, it turned out to be the first of two major pieces of good fortune so bizarre as to challenge the inventive powers of a Whig historian: the old marquess left the grand-nephew most of his fortune and Harry a few years later married King George V's only daughter, the last Princess Royal of this series.

Clearly the mutual interest of Clanricarde and Lascelles in antiques led to this happy dispensation. We are told that Harry chatted kindly with the old gentleman and invited him to dine that night at one of his numerous clubs, but this is doubtful. At his own club the Marquess was an unwelcome if not an embarrassing adornment, for he sometimes arrived there with a bag of unfresh meats and sent them to the kitchen to be cooked for his luncheon. As he was in receipt of some £80,000 a year from the rents of 56,000 acres in County Galway alone, and was renowned as an astute investor and connoisseur, the club committee seemed within their rights to impose a small extra charge, especially as the quality of the produce which he brought in from the outside sometimes challenged the credulity and tested the ingenuity of the chef. Clanricarde ridiculed this trivial objection, until at last the committee rebelled and altered the rules to forbid any member from bringing victuals of any description whatever into the club premises.

Records of the meeting of Clanricarde and Lascelles, heir

to his father's earldom of Harewood in Yorkshire, are inevitably sparse, as the chronicles of the time were monopolised by other events, and little reliability can be placed on the unkind suggestion that the Viscount sought out his elderly relation of set purpose, for the Marquess was clearly not the type of person whom anyone in Society would be anxious to cultivate. The old man was said to have embarked in his youth on a promising diplomatic career, but some disappointment clouded his spirits and turned him into a miser, almost a recluse. Money-making and the collection of *objets d'art* became the ruling passions of a life which he preferred to spend cut off from the human race. except for his servants. His meeting with Harry Lascelles was a chance in a million, so to speak. Clanricarde was more likely to be found in auction rooms than in shops. At Christie's and other sale-rooms he could be found shuffling around in search of pictures and pieces, as many still do, more for their future realisable profit than for their intrinsic merit or historic associations; he also liked to score over other collectors. But even the Marquess must have wondered for whom he was amassing his remarkable hoard. Certainly the thought crossed his mind after he had met Harry Lascelles and they had begun to exchange artistic opinions among the shelves of the Bond Street dealer's.

The outcome of this reunion, whether it was arranged or accidental, was a cordial invitation from Clanricarde to his grandnephew to accompany him to his apartments in Hanover Square, whither he had moved from his Albany rooms for reasons of economy. In Hanover Square he ate frugally from cheap plates, although his cupboards were stuffed with rare Sèvres and Wedgwood dishes and with jewel-encrusted gold and silver plate. One of the cheap plates fell to pieces one day; he spent hours hunting his apartment for a tube of adhesive gum rather than spend two pennies on a new tube. When Lascelles arrived at this strange establishment his great-uncle was allowing his housekeeper 6d. a day for fuel, and since his rebuff by his club she also had orders to cook for him, but only dishes which she could produce on a small fire.

" I want to show you some of my little things, Harry," he said, as the housekeeper opened the door. " You'll like 'em."

Among other items he produced the unique Canning Jewel,

attributed to Benvenuto Cellini and then valued at a mere £10,000—" one of my trifles," said Clanricarde, who usually employed the word ' trifles ' when he meant ' bargains '. One priceless possession after another was pulled out to be shown and admired. The two men warmed towards each other. Their Irish blood was a common denominator, coming down through the eldest daughter of the first Marquess of Clanricarde who had married Harry's grandfather, and it was probably because Lascelles reminded him of himself as a young man that Clanricarde broached family matters and even drew Harry out on his life on the Western Front.

Next day Lascelles returned to Flanders, after promising his great-uncle to call during his next leave, if he lived to get one. Clanricarde was strangely moved. He was 83. He had deliberately kept his relations at arm's length. But Harry had struck some tender note. He had actually made the old man laugh, especially at a story culled from his experiences as aide to Earl Grey, the Governor-General of Canada. Once when he was moose hunting in the backwoods Lascelles was caught by a forest fire which deprived him of all his possessions except the clothes he wore. He was in such a sorry state—and this was the part of the story which old Clanricarde most enjoyed—that he had to apply for government relief. The notion of getting money out of any government was most gratifying, and Clanricarde capped it with the story of how he had once received a tip from a stranger in Oxford Street who mistook him for a beggar. Clanricarde had never made a will. When Harry had left he took a pen from his desk. Forcing a rusty nib into service, he scratched two hundred words on a piece of cheap writing paper leaving £20,000 to a nephew, £1,000 to a niece and the residue to " Harry Lascelles by courtesy called Viscount Lascelles, son of my nephew Henry Earl of Harewood ". Then he called his housekeeper, Louise Cole, and his valet, Morgan.

" Sign here," he commanded. " You're witnesses, you understand?"

That was in February 1916. By April he was dead. The chief beneficiary learned in the trenches that he had become a multimillionaire overnight virtually by the stroke of a pen. The ' residue ' of Clanricarde's estate totalled nearly £3,000,000. Harry might, of course, not have lived to inherit his fortune. But he led a charmed existence on the battlefield, had several miraculous escapes, won the Distinguished Service Order and bar, and the Croix de Guerre, and ended the war as a colonel leading his regiment into Cologne after the Armistice.

Harry earned the nickname of ' Lucky ' Lascelles. Apart from having amassed no small contribution to the enjoyment of the good life without the exertion of working for it, he had an uncanny gift for buying and backing victorious bloodstock. He once gave a racing tip which made a whole Yorkshire village £5,000 richer; it cost him nothing and made a lot of people happy. With part of his Clanricarde money he bought Chesterfield House in Mayfair—where in the library Lord Chesterfield had launched his series of effusions to his son. He filled the mansion with Clanricarde's and his own art treasures, started a racing stable, and in one way and another cut a dash in Society. He was nearly 40 when his thoughts turned to marriage.

No doubt the flower of the British aristocracy was open to him, but his choice fell on Princess Mary, who was 24 and living quietly with her parents. By this time Lascelles was in high favour with the King: their relationship resembled the association between Edward VII and the Duke of Fife. George V was a generation older than Lascelles, and he probably regarded ' young Harry ' as being about the right age for his daughter. Harry was more the model of what a modern ' young man ' should be, and the King contrasted his sober parts favourably with the relatively unconventional behaviour of his own sons in that age of flappers and fast night clubs. The Prince of Wales, known in the family by his last name of David, was Mary's favourite brother, and although the Abdication was to cause her deep pain she kept in touch with him to the end of her days.

David was touring India when Mary married Viscount Lascelles. He was 27, protective towards ' little ' Mary, as he always called her, and his brotherly reaction to the match was not noticeably warm. After the marriage there were stories that he and his brother-in-law did not quite agree on many matters, not the least of which appears to have been the future Edward VIII's attitude towards what he called ' the Royal show '. Lascelles traced his lineage back to one of the barons of Edward I. But the family riches were founded by two Lascelles brothers whose father had supported Oliver Cromwell; they had prudently sought fresh pastures in the West Indies at the Restoration. Plantation wealth created the Harewood estate near Leeds, and at that great house Harry's forebears had more than compensated for their family lapse into republicanism by entertaining numerous later monarchs, to say nothing of Queen Victoria. But after some little spat David is reported to have observed, " Every day I get commoner and commoner and Lascelles gets royaller and royaller."

The relationship seems not to have improved after Lascelles became sixth Earl of Harewood in 1929. Much speculation was caused by a remark of the Prince of Wales after his sister had undergone an operation for appendicitis. That same night at a public dinner he said, " The best information I can give you of my sister is that I spoke to Lord Harewood about half an hour before I left my house, and he told me he was going to fulfil a dinner engagement."

The exact meaning of the last few words exercised the dowagers in their salons, the bishops at their clubs and the typists in their teashops for the usual nine days. But, naturally, nearly everything the Prince of Wales said was news.

One of Princess Mary's biographers claimed that she showed a " lifelong preference for people older than herself ", but this was written with hindsight some years after her marriage. Like her Aunt Louise, she had no wish to marry or live abroad— " I couldn't bear to go away from England." But any assumption that the marriage was a great love match has often been discounted by armchair judges of such matters. Lascelles was said to be a man of sharp tongue and uncertain moods, not always kind or tolerant, especially towards fools, although there are plenty of stories of his rough good nature and his generosity, or what passes for generosity in a certain type of Yorkshireman. By contrast his wife was kind, considerate and reserved and of equable temperament. She was born at York Cottage, Sandringham, on 25th April 1897 while her parents were yet Duke and Duchess of York. The old Queen telegraphed her grandson and and his wife: " All happiness to you and my little Diamond Jubilee baby." And Mr. Gladstone solemnly declared: " This event is of no direct political significance, but it is gratifying because it makes the direct line of succession to the throne still more secure. The Duke and Duchess of York have already borne two sons, and perhaps for that reason this little daughter will be doubly welcome."

The British public were undoubtedly relieved to hear of any conceivable event which bore no direct political significance for Mr. Gladstone, and this ranked as one of his last public pronouncements before he died the following year. The Queen wished Mary to be called Diamond, but her son the Prince of Wales observed that no girl would thank her parents for a name which so positively indicated her age, and so she was christened Victoria Alexandra Alice Mary at Sandringham church by the Archbishop of York, Dr. Maclagan. Her six godparents included the reigning Princess Royal, the Dowager Empress Frederick.

In childhood the princess, called after her mother and her maternal grandmother, the Duchess of Teck, was known as ' Goldilocks '. The biographer who recalled this also praised " the tremendous efficiency and skill with which Queen Mary brought up her children ". Five out of ten marks may be given for that assessment. Had Queen Alexandra's wish prevailed, Princess Mary would have been sent to a boarding-school, but her daughter-in-law resolved to keep her ' chicks '—as her mother had kept *her* chicks—under her own eye at home. The family divided their time between Sandringham, Abergeldie, Frogmore and, when the Duke of York became the Prince of Wales in 1901, Marlborough House, although Mary preferred Buckingham Palace, where she and her brothers were atrociously spoilt by the King and Queen.

At the coronation of 1911 Mary wore state robes for the first time, with a coronet uncertainly balanced on her golden curls. She and her four brothers—the future Dukes of Windsor, York, Gloucester and Kent—occupied one coach. Freed from all restraint, the brothers interspersed the monotony of waving to the crowds with some horseplay; the youngest, George, was pushed to the floor and used as a footstool on the return journey from the Abbey. Mary, we are told, had constantly to call them to order, but her dignity was sadly shaken when she bowed so low to the crowd that her coronet rolled into the carriage to the joy of her brothers. Mary and David accompanied their parents on their post-coronation state visits to Ireland, Wales, and Scotland. culminating in the Prince of Wales's investiture at Caernarvon Castle.

Mary grew up very like her mother, whose rather low-pitched voice she inherited: Dame Nellie Melba thought the princess might have developed as a concert mezzo-soprano but for the restraints imposed by the blood royal. Edward and Albert had different views on the subject, and when Mary took singing lessons from a Mr. Hutchinson they lurked beneath the music-room window at Frogmore giving " quite a passable imitation of the midnight serenades of a tom-cat ". Under the outwardly stiff, shy public image bubbled a high-spirited personality with " a lively sense of fun ", as it was called. Mary named some of her dolls after court officials. She seemed to be less intimidated than her brothers by their father, whose disciplinary methods were well-meant but sometimes misunderstood, especially by David. Yet the awe in which all the children held George V was sensed by Mr. Asquith, who said of Mary: " She has that shy, girlish charm which leaves one with an impression of nervous pleasure and fatherly respect."

Queen Alexandra's Comptroller, Sir Dighton Probyn, pene-tratingly noted that in repose the princess looked " so regal yet so sad ". Her tastes were simple, but she also inherited her mother's flair for antiques and had learned a lot about old china before she met her husband. The art galleries at the royal resid-ences were an unfailing source of joy and inspiration to her. Out of doors her interest in gardening had blossomed while she was young—she had green fingers—and a passion for riding and hunting played some part in bringing about her marriage to a member of the Jockey Club and Master of Foxhounds. At Bal-moral, in sensible shoes and tweeds, she tramped the moors with her brothers or watched them shoot or play golf. Sometimes she tooled a four-in-hand along the Highland roads. Cookery fell rather low in the scale of her accomplishments. Once she baked some cakes for a Balmoral picnic. Her brothers fell silent when they were asked how they tasted, but at last Henry said: " I've always understood that it was high treason to speak dis-respectfully of the daughter of the King."

Mary's life was overshadowed by the two world wars—in the second of which she knew real fear for the safety of her two sons—and by the Abdication, but it was, on the whole, happier than the lives of any of her predecessors. Before war broke out in 1914 the King's daughter had little chance and less inclination

Mary, Princess Royal

1922: The homecoming of the Prince of Wales: left to right, Queen
Mary, Prince Henry, the Prince of Wales, the Duke of York, King
George V, Lord Lascelles and Princess Mary

The sixth Earl and Countess of Harewood at their home

to travel abroad, but in 1912 her father, who had not inherited his father's dislike of the German Emperor and wished to improve relations, thought Mary might further his aims and at the same time broaden her mind with a visit to his German family connections. The Duchess of Teck's sister, Queen Mary's devoted Aunt Augusta, the fabulous old Grand Duchess of Mecklenburg-Strelitz, was most anxious to meet her grand-niece, but Mary found the stiff formality of the German courts depressing. A German princess asked her, " In England do they allow you to forget you are royal?" To which Mary replied. " No, but they allow us to remember that we are human." A Berlin newspaper described her as " that delightful English rose ", and Wilhelm II wrote to his Empress: " The visit of the little English Princess is a delightful gesture on the part of George. They tell me that she has found Germany a treasure-house of interest." At the end of 1912 an ambassadorial conference of the powers met in London to resolve the Balkans war and the *Morning Post* trusted that it might " terminate an old era of unrest in Eastern Europe and be the means of establishing a long period of peace and prosperity in the Balkan Peninsula ". But the Sarajevo assassinations dashed all these hopes. Germany and the Allies went to war in 1914, and Mary moped when she had to bow to the prevailing Germanophobia and part with her German maid Else, who had served her loyally. Hostilities ended Mary's formal education and opened up that life of service which distinguished her from all previous Princesses Royal.

Within a few months a vast correspondence was flooding into the palace. Mary acted as her mother's secretary and also packed ' comforts ' for the troops. In 1915 she publicly appealed for £100,000 to provide each man serving with a brass box of tobacco or cigarettes, a pipe and a tinder lighter; for Indian troops there were boxes of sweets. Her portrait appeared on each box with the inscription *Imperium Britannicum*. Inside was a Christmas card: " From Princess Mary and Friends at Home, with best wishes for a Happy Christmas and a Victorious New Year." A Private Brabston of the Irish Guards owed his life to his box: a bullet struck it instead of his heart. One day Lord Kitchener and General Haig stood watching Mary as she smiled and chatted with a draft of troops about to leave for Flanders.

" There's a little soldier," remarked the war lord to the

o

general, "whose example has done more than anything to rally the women of England to the Colours."

For a teenager Mary applied herself with unusual diligence to an amazing variety of activities—Girl Guides, Women's Land Army, Needlework Guild, Red Cross. She also worked in a canteen at a munitions factory in Hayes, Middlesex. One day the canteen was inspected by the Queen. An old woman who had worked for a court *modiste* brought along a mysterious bag full of scraps of material from trains worn by Queen Mary at court functions, intending to show her strange horde to the visitor. The Princess asked if she had shown them.

"Lor', no, miss," she said. "The Queen came so sudden-like that she took me at the *non plus*."

From that time "I was taken at the *non plus*" became Princess Mary's favourite phrase. But her basic war work was nursing. She joined the Voluntary Aid Detachment and at Great Ormond Street children's hospital earned the respect of the medical and nursing staffs for the skill and tenderness with which she mothered ailing babies. She stayed on at the hospital until 1920.

Repeated pleas to be allowed to tour allied hospitals behind the battle lines during the war fell on dead official ears. No concession was made even for her twenty-first birthday in April 1918 after the last great German push had failed. As a consolation she was made Colonel-in-Chief of the Royal Scots in August that year. It was formerly the First of Foot, the British Army's senior regiment: one of its colonels a century earlier had been the Duke of Kent, Queen Victoria's father, a distinction for which those under his command were not conspicuously grateful. An 8-year-old boy wrote confidently to Mary: "Daddy has joined your regiment but we don't feel afraid because we know you will look after him." Then came the Armistice and Mary was at last free to travel. Her tour of the silent battle-fields, from Rouen to Ypres as far as Bruges, was exhaustive and triumphant. She was the first member of the Royal Family to cross the Channel after the war.

"Only an English princess," commented Marshal Foch, "would have braved the discomforts of the war area to share with the armies and the various women's corps the happy hour of the cessation of hostilities."

II

As a small child Mary was said to have wanted to marry a man like Edward VII. In almost every respect Lord Lascelles differed from his bride's grandfather. The betrothal was announced on 23rd November 1921 after a large house party at the Duke of Devonshire's place at Chatsworth in Derbyshire, where they hunted together, and after a joint visit to Balmoral, which during and since Queen Victoria's day had inspired many a royal romance. Mary cabled the news of her engagement to the Prince of Wales in India. In after years the Duke of Windsor wrote: "While I was in India my sister Mary had married an older man, Lord Lascelles, and with easy grace had become the chatelaine of his country home in Yorkshire."

The phrase "an older man" conveys a good deal. Lascelles might have made a career in politics, although he was more the diplomat than the politician, but after one or two unsuccessful attempts to enter Parliament, deciding that the Commons of his day, all so very 'hard faced', was no place for a gentleman, he settled to the role of a country squire, sharing in some of 'the Royal show' which his brother-in-law was coming to despise. On reflection it was probably found inappropriate for the King's son-in-law to become involved in the broils of party politics. Once more Mr. Asquith felt bound to say something and he said it: "Princess Mary, in accepting an Englishman and a soldier for her husband, has proved once again the real democracy of the British Royal Family."

So Mary, who had been four times a bridesmaid at royal weddings, was now the bride. She was married at Westminster Abbey on the last day of February 1922. Her wedding veil of

Honiton lace had been worn by her mother and her grand-mother, the Duchess of Teck; some of the lace had belonged to Catherine of Aragon. On her marriage she received the magnificent Clanricarde diamonds, which had lain unused in the strong rooms of a London bank for more than a century. There was a prophecy that these superb gems would be worn by a king's daughter, and they were re-set for Mary. The King, in a scarlet uniform gleaming with orders, gave his daughter away with a heavy heart. That evening before she departed he went to her room to take leave of her and " quite broke down ". But he expressed confi-dence in Harry's ability to make her happy: before the ceremony he conferred on him not only the Garter but also a knighthood in the Royal Victorian Order.

The Queen accepted the parting more philosophically. When a relation of the bridegroom offered him her Villa Medici at Fiesole outside Florence for the honeymoon the Queen, who as a girl had spent a useful ' exile ' in Italy with her bankrupt family, drew up a honeymoon itinerary. After a week at Weston Park, the Shropshire seat of the Earl and Countess of Bradford, the bride and bridegroom made their way to Florence, whom whence Mary wrote her mother long descriptions of art galleries and historic beauty spots. The presence of a member of the Royal Family in their midst stimulated the hospitable instincts of the British colony in Florence. But there was one lady of the *nouveau riche* at Fiesole who had not yet been quite accepted into local Society and resolved to make up for this deplorable deficiency.

Although this lady was not on visiting terms with many of the British residents she invited them all to dine at her villa " to have the honour of meeting Her Royal Highness the Princess Mary, Viscount Lascelles ". Many of those invited, although puzzled that their hostess should be on such easy terms with the King's daughter and her bridegroom, arrived at the villa in all their finery, only to learn after they had imbibed their first cock-tails that ' an official engagement ' had at the last minute pre-vented the princess from attending. Nothing was left but for the hungry company to take their seats at the table—from which two unwanted chairs were ceremoniously removed—and avail themselves of a good meal. Except that the food was not poisoned, the scene was worthy of the Borgias. Only later was the whole

affair discovered to be a hoax. Meanwhile the hostess had ex-
acted her trivial revenge at the expense of the local snobs.

On their return home the squire and the princess made the
West Riding at once their empire and their parish, with the
eighteenth-century Harewood House as the focus. Mary needed
no introduction to the countryside, and she soon settled into the
ways of the bluff, homely Yorkshire folk.

" She's aw reet," one villager summed up after she had been
seen at race meetings and agricultural shows. " If Ah hadna
known she's no' so lucky, Ah'd 'a thowt she was fra Yorkshire
herself."

Throughout the winter of 1922 Mary prepared for the birth
of her first child, George, named for his grandfather, was born on
7th February 1923 at Goldsborough Hall, on the Harewood
estate, which her husband's father had given them as a wedding
present. Parliament sent a special message to the King and the
parents on this ' historic ' and happy event. George was sixth in
the succession and grew to eminence in the sphere of classical
music, by which time he was more than twenty lives from the
throne. The Prince of Wales, his godfather, was so unused to
babies that he is said to have held George upside down at the
font. The next family event of importance was the marriage
of the Duke of York and Lady Elizabeth Bowes-Lyon later in
1923, and when on 21st August 1924 a second son, Gerald, was
born Mary's family was complete. Music was also Gerald's passion,
with the emphasis on modern jazz. Eventually he was to live at
Fort Belvedere, the last British residence of his Uncle David,
whose name he also bore. The King thoroughly spoilt both
these grandsons, his first, and their early memories were of tea
parties at Windsor, especially when their cousin Lilibet, the
future Queen Elizabeth II, was present.

Little disturbed the tranquillity of Mary's first five years at
Harewood. Her public work was limited to the region, but she
carried it out with the single-mindedness which had character-
ised her war work. Human suffering of any kind immediately
engaged her sympathy, especially the lot of the unemployed in
the inter-war years, and a good deal of her mother's interest in
social problems brushed off on her. Wherever she went, even in
summer, she carried an umbrella—' Mary's twin ', her brothers
called it. She did not set foot outside the country until 1928 when

she and her husband in March travelled to Egypt, a land which had fascinated royal ladies since Queen Victoria's accession, and where she tried to make polite conversation with the ladies of King Fuad's harem. They returned through the Holy Land.

In October they were in Ireland, which Mary had not visited since 1911 and Lascelles since 1919, when he tried to placate his tenants for years of neglect under the Clanricarde regime. Old Clanricarde, as his beneficiary was soon to confirm, was hated and despised by the Irish tenantry. He was one of the worst types of absentee landlord who, as Lord Egremont, a great British landowner, was to say of that breed many years later, rather " let the side down ".

" I've got a nice place in Ireland—Portumna Castle in Galway—but I daren't go near the place; they'd kill me. I'm the most hated man in Ireland, don't you know?"

Clanricarde accepted his unpopularity as irrevocable, and a year before he died the Congested Areas Board relieved him of some of his land to save his tenants from utter misery. For this privilege they had to pay £238,000 to the landlord who was known throughout Galway as ' the Marquess of Clanrackrent '. Much of the damage was repaired by his successor after the war. Viscount Lascelles redressed the more glaring grievances, repaired broken-down cottages, pensioned many tenants, and subscribed liberally to charities which his great-uncle refused to patronise. But bitternes rankled yet. Two days before the 1928 visit an attempt was made to burn down Portumna Castle. The flames were checked, but feeling against the British in general ran so high that the visitors were advised to travel to the castle in a bullet-proof motor-car. Mary was received kindly by the tenants as she toured the huge estate, and when she went to church she found in her pew a sheet of paper with the words which had been read to Queen Victoria when she visited Dublin—

> Blessed for ever is she who relied
> On Erin's honour and Erin's pride.

In 1929, on the death of his father, her husband became the sixth Earl of Harewood and inherited another cool £300,000. But the demands of the Exchequer after the Second World War were to fall so heavily on the great estates that the Irish lands were sold off. The sixth Earl left assets of only £1,500,000 on which his

heir had to find £800,000 in estate duty. As time went on the
seventh Earl had to sell family jewels and other treasures,
including Titian's *The Death of Actaeon*, which in 1971 fetched
£1,680,000 at auction.

When Princess Louise died in 1931 Mary was 34. She succeeded
her aunt as Princess Royal on 1st January 1932, but it is doubtful whether this gave her as much pleasure as the unofficial title
of ' Queen of the North ' which Yorkshire people had already conferred on her. Involved as she appeared to be in the broad acres
of her West Riding estate, she was nevertheless acutely aware of
events in the wider world. Stories of her brother David's 'restless-
ness' caused her much anxiety. The Prince of Wales had told her
of his plans for the restoration of Fort Beldevere, near Windsor,
which he rescued from decay and neglect to create a comfortable
bachelor's establishment, and she knew more about the place than
did her parents. It took its name from the Belvedere Gallery at
the Vatican where an ancient statue of Apollo stands.

In January 1935 the Princess Royal was at Sandringham watching her father slowly die: the King's last words to her were a
question—had she been skating? From then on she was to know
little peace of mind for her brother proceeded on his headstrong
course towards abdication and exile. She knew his impulsive
nature better than did any of their blood relations because she was
closest to him; and it was with consternation and foreboding that
she read Bishop Blunt's mild and misconstrued strictures on
Edward VIII's shortcomings as head of the Established Church.
The unfortunte bishop had no idea what forces he was unleashing;
and he probably gave no thought to the impact it would make on
the King's sister, sitting there at Harewood not far from Bradford where this formidable sermon originated. At any rate, his
motives were less sophisticated than those of Lord Beaverbrook,
who supported the King " to bugger Baldwin ", according to
Mr. Randolph Churchill. As the Duke of Windsor afterwards explained, convincing the Prime Minister that he was determined
to marry Mrs. Simpson at all costs was easy compared to breaking
the news to his mother. He was therefore grateful to find that
this unbearable ordeal would be softened by the presence of the
faithful sister who had been his confidante in many a scrape of
his boyhood and youth. He had arranged to dine with the widowed

Queen at Marlborough House, to which she had now transferred all her possessions from Buckingham Palace.

" My mother had leaned more and more on Mary since my father's death ", wrote the Duke in his memoirs, " and had therefore asked her to be present, realising that the meeting might be painful."

In fact the Queen Mother had not realised how painful it was going to be. She had not bargained for his obstinacy at this supreme crisis of his life. " To give up all that for this! " she exclaimed when the Abdication Instrument was shown to her. Neither she nor her daughter could do anything. Mary perceived perhaps more quickly than her mother that David's mind was double-locked against reason.

" Do you really think that I would be crowned without Wallis at my side?" he asked the grass widower Ernest Simpson.

On his last night in England the Princess Royal and her mother and three brothers dined with the Duke of Windsor at Royal Lodge, the Windsor home of the Duke and Duchess of York, now King and Queen. Together they listened to the departing monarch's last broadcast from Windsor Castle. There was nothing more to be said. But Mary seems to have been the first member of of the Royal Family to propose a whip-round for her exiled brother. The Duchess was not only *persona non grata* but exiled as well. Her name was never mentioned at the homely court of George VI, who refused her the style of Royal Highness, and she was no more eager to meet the Royal Family than any of its members was to receive her.

Yet by chance the ice was broken—though only temporarily— by the Princess Royal. In March 1953 the Queen Mother was dying at Marlborough House. The Princess Royal was in New York. Arrangements were made for her and the Duke of Windsor to fly home together for the funeral. The Duchess came to express her sympathy. At first Mary was highly embarrassed, but her sister-in-law's natural charm melted her reserve, and they parted friends. They did not meet again. By the time the Duchess of Windsor met the Royal Family in London in June 1967 at the unveiling of a Marlborough House memorial to Queen Mary she had been dead more than two years.

At the outbreak of the Second World War the Princess Royal

was 42 and in her prime. As in the 1914-18 War, she threw herself into the national effort with exemplary zest, supplementing the work of the Royal Family without stint. Work prevented her from thinking too deeply about the risks her sons were running overseas. Both served in the Grenadier Guards, and in June 1944 the elder was captured during the Italian campaign and, with other officers, all members of noted British families, became one of Hitler's hostages. There was a real fear, happily not realised, that the hostages might be executed before the Allies could liberate them. They escaped thanks to the fluent German and quick thinking of a captured British agent.

After her husband's death in 1947 the Princess Royal lived a simple life in a wing of Harewood House, but continued her public service in Yorkshire without a break. Indeed, she seemed to take on a new lease of life. In 1955 she visited Canada, where the crowds in Quebec mistook her for Queen Mary, greeting her as ' Reine Marie ', so remarkable was her facial resemblance to her mother. In 1964, the year before her death, the Royal Family found itself in a dilemma when Queen Elizabeth the Queen Mother underwent an operation and the Queen, her sister Princess Margaret, the Duchess of Kent and Princess Alexandra increased the number of George V's descendants by one each. A massive programme of engagements fell to the Princess Royal, but she came cheerfully out of retirement to lend a hand and, among other activities, at the age of 67 flew to Africa to represent the Queen at the independence celebrations of Zambia, the former colony of Northern Rhodesia.

" The Princess has never been afraid of hard work," said her equerry.

And so it continued to the end, when a heart attack at Harewood removed the hardest-working of the Princesses Royal on 28th March 1965. Her greatest quality was reliability. In the words of an obituary notice: " *When she was needed she was always there.*" It could be the epitaph of a gracious lady whose self-effacing personal service to throne, family, nation and Commonwealth distinguished her from all her predecessors.

Works Consulted

Arthur, Sir George, *Queen Alexandra*, Chapman and Hall, 1934.

Barkeley, Dr. Richard, *The Empress Frederick*, Macmillan, 1956.

Battiscombe, Georgina, *Queen Alexandra*, Constable, 1969.

Birkenhead, Lord, *The Life of Viscount Monckton of Brenchley*, Weidenfeld and Nicolson, 1969.

Blake, Robert, *Disraeli*, Eyre and Spottiswood, 1966.

Bolitho, Hector, *George VI*, Eyre and Spottiswoode, 1937.

Brice, Raoul, *The Riddle of Napoleon*, Putnam, 1937.

Bryant, Arthur, *King Charles II*, Longmans, Green, 1934.

Carey, M. C., *Princess Mary*, Nisbet and Co, 1922.

Churchill, Sir Winston, *The Second World War*, Cassell 1948-54.

Churchill, Sir Winston, *A History of the English-Speaking Peoples*, Cassell, 1956-58.

Corti, Egon Caesar Conte, *The English Empress*, Cassell, 1957.

Cowan, Samuel, *The Royal House of Stuart*, Vol. II, Greening and Co., 1908.

Egremont, Lord, *Wyndham and Children First*, Macmillan, 1968.

Feiling, Keith, *The Life of Neville Chamberlain*, Macmillan, 1946.

Fulford, Roger, *Royal Dukes*, Gerald Duckworth and Co, 1933.

Gooch, G. P., *History of Modern Europe 1818-1919*, Cassell, 1923.

Graham, Evelyn, *Princess Mary, Viscount Lascelles*, Hutchinson, 1929.

Greenwood, Alice Drayton, *Lives of the Hanoverian Queens of England*, G. Bell and Sons Ltd., 1911.

Hall, Mrs. Matthew, *The Royal Princesses of England*, George Routledge and Sons, 1871.

Hatch, Alden, *The Mountbattens*, W. H. Allen, 1966.

Hervey, Lord, *Memoirs of the Reign of George II*, 3 vols., Bickers and Son, 1884.

Hibbert, Christopher, *The Court at Windsor*, Longmans, 1964.

Horne, Alistair, *The Fall of Paris*, Macmillan, 1965.

Keppel, Alice, *Edwardian Daughter*, Hamish Hamilton Ltd., 1958.

Lucas, Reginald, *George II and His Ministers*, Arthur L. Humphreys, 1910.

Madol, Hans Roger, *The Private Life of Queen Alexandra*, Hutchinson, 1940.

Magnus, Philip, *King Edward the Seventh*, John Murray, 1964.

Marie Louise, Princess, *My Memoirs of Six Reigns (1872-1956)*, Evans Brothers, 1956.

Nicolson, Harold, *King George V: His Life and Reign*, Constable, 1952.

Nicolson, Harold, *Diaries and Letters*, 3 vols., 1930-39, 1939-45, and 1945-62, Collins, 1966-8.

Pope-Hennessey, James, *Queen Mary 1867-1953*, George Allen and Unwin, 1959.

Robb, Dr. Nesca A., *William of Orange*, Vol I, Heinemann, 1962.

Senior, Dorothy, *Charles II, His Court and Times*, Stanley Paul and Co., 1909.

Strachey, Lytton, *Queen Victoria*, Chatto and Windus, 1921.

Stuart, Dorothy Margaret, *The Daughters of George III*, Macmillan, 1939.

Taylor, A. J. P., *Bismarck: The Man and the Statesman*, Hamish Hamilton Ltd., 1955.

Taylor, Edmond, *The Fossil Monarchies*, Weidenfeld and Nicolson, 1963.

Tisdall, E. E. P., *Unpredictable Queen*, Stanley Paul and Co., Ltd., 1953.

Wheeler-Bennett, John W., *King George VI: His Life and Reign*, Macmillan, 1958.

White, T. H., *The Age of Scandal*, Jonathan Cape, 1950.

Windsor, H.R.H. The Duke of, K.G., *A King's Story: Memoirs*, Cassell, 1951.

Woodward, Kathleen, *Queen Mary*, Hutchinson, 1927.

Index